Michael W. Klein
Paul J. J. Welfens (Eds.)

Multinationals in the New Europe and Global Trade

With 24 Figures and 75 Tables

Springer-Verlag

Berlin Heidelberg New York
London Paris Tokyo
Hong Kong Barcelona
Budapest

Ass. Professor MICHAEL W. KLEIN
Fletcher School of Law and Diplomacy
Tufts University
Medford, MA 02155-0000, USA

PD Dr. PAUL J. J. WELFENS
American Institute for Contemporary German Studies
The Johns Hopkins University
Suite 350
11 Dupont Circle, N.W.
Washington, D.C. 20036-1207, USA

Correspondence address:
Universität Münster
Fakultät für Wirtschaftswissenschaften
Am Stadtgraben 9
D-4400 Münster, FRG

ISBN 3-540-54634-0 Springer-Verlag Berlin Heidelberg New York Tokyo
ISBN 0-387-54634-0 Springer-Verlag New York Berlin Heidelberg Tokyo

2143/7130-543210 - Printed on acid-free paper

Preface

After a decade of Eurosclerosis the EC is moving with renewed economic growth and increasing multinational investment toward a single European market under the heading "Project 1992". The creation of a single EC market creates dynamic adjustment needs and opens up new opportunities for international business in a period of intensified global competition and dramatic politico-economic changes.

Since the mid-1980s Eastern Europe is undergoing a radical shift towards market-based economic systems - a difficult and fragile development so far which is further complicated by economic and political unification of Germany in central Europe.

After the era of British and, later, U.S. leadership in multinational investment German and Japanese multinational companies are becoming more influential players worldwide. Firms from Germany play a special role because German unification of 1990 implies a bigger home market, but also the diversion of total investment activities towards the greater German home market.

While the political divide of Europe has ceased to exist, the economic division is becoming more apparent, and it could indeed transitorily increase because the EC 1992 project primarily generates growth impulses in Western Europe, while systemic transformations in Eastern Europe reduce output growth in the short term. East European economies are opening up towards the world market (with Poland and Hungary taking the lead role) which requires changes in monetary policy, price setting patterns and exchange rate regimes if the desired growth of trade and investment flows is to take place; privatization schemes envisaged and macroeconomic adjustment policies taken are opening up new opportunities for multinational companies' investment. Whether and under which conditions actual investment flows will increase and be conducive to greater intra-European and rising global trade remains to be seen.

Europe is facing a period in which a bigger integrated European market with larger firms is emerging. This process is taking place in a period of global capital shortage and accelerated modernization needs in Eastern Europe and other regions of the world. With trade barriers changing and investment barriers falling in the reforming countries of Eastern Europe, investment by multinational companies could be as much an engine of growth as trade has been for more than four decades in the world economy.

The multinationals were subject to much criticism in the 1970s and were rarely directly promoted by host governments, but now the multinational companies are back on the stage again - this time with a very important role in both Western and Eastern Europe. International investments can entail significant technology transfer and stimulate the growth of trade and employment, but it can also confront the host countries with new side-constraints for economic policies. Nation states, supranational institutions and international organizations all face the challenge of MNEs and have to adapt their policies accordingly. In the field of trade policies the Uruguay GATT round testifies to the problems in achieving consensus in a rapidly changing world economy.

With the New Europe emerging it becomes very interesting to analyze the changing role, scope, behavior and impact of multinational companies - most of which emphasize (often for fear of Fortress Europe) EC markets and production facilities, while there is still an uncertain perspective in Eastern Europe. This book aims to focus on selected topics in the broader realm of multinational companies' activities in the whole of Europe - the main focus still being the EC.

We are very grateful to the Director of the American Institute for Contemporary German Studies (AICGS), Robert Gerald Livingston, and Jackson Janes, Deputy Director, who generously supported the idea of a conference on Multinationals in the New Europe and Global Trade in the 1990s in a period in which German multinational companies are becoming more influential and in which the unified Germany is increasingly important as both a source country of and a host country for international investment. The conference - organized under the auspices of the AICGS while Paul Welfens was the McCloy Distinguished Research Fellow at the Institute - is part of a series of seminars, conferences and research activities in German and European economics, political science and the humanities upon which the AICGS has a continuous focus. Tim Yarling provided valuable research support and assistance in the editing process of this volume; Lynn van Norstrand's continuous support in the organization of the conference is also appreciated. We wish to express our gratitude to American Airlines, The Multinational Companies Inc., and - above all - the German Marshall Fund for a generous grant which provided the financial basis for the conference.

From a modern historical perspective multinational companies have provided not only important transatlantic links but have helped to keep the international system open for trade - except for the inter-war period when cartelized firms in Europe and protectionist tariff policies in both the U.S. and Europe reduced economic growth, curtailed trade and finally output as well as employment. Since 1945 multinational companies have played a major role in the North-South context on the one hand, and, on the other hand, in the development of transpacific trade and investment links. The 1990s could become the beginning of an era in which the global economy is shaped by international investment and multinational business. The dynamic changes in the Old World offer some interesting developments, theoretical topics and policy issues that point to new and more complex challenges in the global economy. Whether a relatively free flow of trade and investment can contribute to prosperity and stability in a growing world market economy is still an open question.

Washington, D.C., February 1991

Paul J.J. Welfens   *Michael W. Klein*

Table of Contents

II. MULTINATIONALS IN ACTION

List of Tables

Chapter G:

List of Participants and Contributors

Claude Barfield, American Enterprise Institute

Manfred Borchert (session chairman), Universität Münster, visiting fellow at the Board of Governors of the Federal Reserve Bank, Washington, D.C.

John Cantwell, University of Reading

John H. Dunning, Rutgers and Reading Universities

Claudio Frischtak, The World Bank

Michelle Gittelman, UN Centre on Transnational Corporations

Edward Graham, Duke University and Institute for International Economics

Werner Hasenberg, Department of Commerce (retired)

Günter Heiduk, Universität Duisburg

Ulrike W. Hodges, Universität Duisburg

Andras Inotai, The World Bank

Michael Klein, Tufts University

Henning Klodt, The Kiel Institute of World Economics

Michael M. Knetter, Dartmouth College

Robert Lawrence, The Brookings Institution

Robert Gerald Livingston, Director, American Institute for Contemporary German Studies/The Johns Hopkins University

Peter Murrell, University of Maryland

Terutomo Ozawa, Colorado State University

Eric Rosengren, Federal Reserve Bank of Boston, Research Department

Jim Tozzi (session chairman), The Multinational Companies, Washington, D.C.

Anthony Wallace, Westinghouse Electrics and George Mason University

Paul J.J. Welfens, American Institute for Contemporary German Studies/The Johns Hopkins University and Universität Münster

MULTINATIONALS IN THE NEW EUROPE AND GLOBAL TRADE

Introduction

The economic and political map of Europe will be dramatically altered by events recently witnessed and by projects soon to be completed. Economic boundaries on the map of the "new" Europe will be more faint as the removal of barriers to trade and factor movements approaches its scheduled completion in 1992. The economic map of the "new" Europe must also include many new countries in the wake of the political events of 1989. The challenge to economic researchers and policymakers is to help draw and understand this new economic and political landscape as well as to study its effects on the rest of the world.

This volume addresses some timely issues as the "new" Europe emerges. The focus is the role of the multinational corporation and foreign direct investment, especially across industrial countries and in the "new" Europe. The eight papers collected here were prepared for and presented at a conference organized under the auspices of the American Institute for Contemporary German Studies of The Johns Hopkins University in Washington, D.C. in September 1990.

While recent events have highlighted the importance of multinational corporations, foreign direct investment and access to global markets, these issues have been a recurring and important theme of the development of the world economy in the past forty years. There has been a striking increase in the economic integration of the industrial countries since World War II. The growth in international trade, which increased thirteen-fold between 1950 and 1990, dramatically outpaced the growth of the world economy. Recently, economic integration has also been marked by a rapid growth in international factor movements. For example, between 1983 and 1988 foreign direct investment worldwide grew by more than twenty percent annually, four times the pace of the growth of international trade. The papers in this book both draw lessons from recent experience and study likely outcomes of projected developments.

The first paper in this volume, by Paul J.J. Welfens, provides a wide-ranging overview of many issues related to multinational corporations and global trade. The discussion in this chapter covers the interplay between trade and technology and also the political and policy aspects of multinationals. Some of these issues, such as macroeconomic aspects of foreign direct investment, exchange rate pass through, and the potential role for foreign direct investment in reforming the economies of the formerly socialist CMEA countries, are taken up in more detail in later chapters.

A focus of Welfens' paper is the interrelationship between technological advance and multinationals. He points out that the creation of multinationals are both driven by innovation and technological advance and serve as an important conduit for the worldwide dissemination of technological progress. It is not surprising, then, that the source countries for foreign direct investment are those advanced countries which have a strong technology base and, often, a government policy that promotes technological progress and innovation. Welfens also mentions, as motivations for foreign direct investment, the desire to maintain control over sourcing and, for flows to Europe, the potential profits of a unified market, the fear of a fortress Europe, and the potential of the Eastern European market.

In the next chapter of the volume, Michael Knetter studies the pricing behavior of United States, Japanese and German automobile exporters over the 1980s. This paper begins with the observation that, during the wide swings of the dollar in the last decade, the prices of foreign goods, especially manufactured goods, changed proportionately less than the exchange rate. Knetter's tests lead to his conclusion that the pricing behavior of these exporters reflects "pricing-to-market." For example, the price of German autos sold in the United States rose in price only eight percent when the dollar depreciated by twenty percent. There is also evidence of substantial differences between the pricing behavior of firms in the United States, on the one hand, and Germany and Japan, on the other. Japan auto exporters selling in the United States almost completely offset movements in the yen keeping dollar prices mostly unchanged. In contrast, United States exporters exhibited almost no offset in response to dollar movements.

Why would firms in the same industry behave so differently when exporting to foreign markets? Knetter proposes an interesting explanation that is based upon the locational patterns of production. Diversification in location of production by American producers serves the same purpose as pricing to market by Japanese producers. For a variety of historical reasons, United States firms tended to produce in markets where their automobiles were sold while, at least until recently, German and Japanese automobile producers relied almost exclusively on domestic production. Pricing to market behavior thus arose because of the importance of maintaining persistent links with dealerships and service networks due to the fixed costs of exit from or re-entry into a market. We may expect to witness a change in this behavior in the future, however, as Japanese firms set up production facilities in the United States.

The third chapter of the volume is also motivated by behavior correlated with the dramatic dollar swings of the 1980s. Michael W. Klein and Eric Rosengren note that the theory of the determinants of foreign direct investment has typically focused on firm-specific factors. Recent evidence demonstrates a strong correlation between the United States real exchange rate and foreign direct investment, suggesting a more general channel of causation. There are two candidates for the channel through which the real exchange rate affects FDI. A change in the real exchange rate affects relative labor costs, with a depreciation making labor cheaper. An increase in FDI may then represent an attempt to combine capital with relatively inexpensive labor. Alternatively, FDI represents a purchase of a domestic asset that requires a down-payment. The cost of capital for a foreign firm falls with a depreciation of the domestic currency, allowing the foreign firm to win the auction for the asset. Klein and Rosengren distinguish between these two channels by constructing indices of relative wealth and relative labor costs in order to study the determinants of outward United States FDI to seven other industrial countries from 1979 to 1988. They find that, when controlling for differences in outflows to Japan, FDI is significantly affected by the relative wealth term but not by the relative wage term.

The final chapter of the first section of this volume again takes up the issue of the interrelationship between technology and multinationals. Henning Klodt begins his paper with the observation that the share of world exports of high-tech goods by industrial countries has been shrinking as the newly-industrialized countries of South-East Asia have gained larger market shares. A traditional product-cycle analysis, in which there is a fixed hierarchy of products with respect to their technological intensity and a corresponding hierarchy of countries, may fail to capture aspects of the newly-industrialized countries which export high-tech products.

An important contributing factor to the shift in high-tech production to the newly-industrializing countries is the transfer of technology through multinational corporations. The profitability of technology transfer depends upon its cost, which may differ across industries. Klodt presents a model that illustrates the main features of shifting comparative advantage in high-tech industries. In this model, decreasing costs of information transmission lead to the possibility that developing countries specialize in high-tech goods. An empirical investigation across industries supports the model's predictions. The author closes with some discussion of the potential competition from emerging CMEA countries facing industrialized countries in those industries with mobile technologies.

The second section of this book, titled "Multinationals in Action," begins with an overview of foreign direct investment in CMEA countries by Andras Inotai. Inotai documents the dramatic growth in the number of joint ventures in the European CMEA countries and Yugoslavia in the last years of the 1980s, with particular emphasis on the experience of Hungary and Poland. Joint ventures in these two countries were on a small scale during this period. Foreign direct investment, which began in the service sector, is still concentrated in services and retail firms, but there is an increasing presence in manufacturing activities. Inotai suggests that major changes in the economic environment are required to promote further FDI into reforming Central and Eastern European economies. Of foremost importance is the continued reform of the legal and institutional framework to allow for foreign ownership, to liberalize the economic environment and to clarify issues of property ownership.

Günter Heiduk and Ulrike W. Hodges discuss the pattern of German FDI. Foreign direct investment by Germany increased by more that 150 percent in the 1980s, but compared to other industrial countries the stock of German FDI is relatively modest. The primary avenue for German internationalization remains exporting. FDI by German firms may be serving this end. The close correlation between those countries to which Germany exports and host countries for German multinationals suggests the use of FDI for marketing of exports. The globalization strategies of Daimler Benz and BASF are used as case studies by Heiduk and Hodges as representative of the general trend of German FDI.

John Cantwell studies the effect of integration of the European market on multinational activity in the European Community. The "American Challenge," representing the surge in U.S. multinational activity in response to the institution of the EC after 1957 is now being repeated with a new "Japanese Challenge." This new inflow of FDI is a response to the increased economic integration of EC-1992 and the fears of a fortress Europe. Cantwell also explores the recent behavior of US foreign affiliates in Europe. He discusses characteristics that encourage the integration of multinationals including economies of scale, economies of experience, research-intensive production, distribution channel concentration with limited local servicing requirements, and differences in tax treatment and financial arrangements across countries.

The volume ends with a paper by John Dunning and Michelle Gittelman that compares and contrasts the behavior of Japanese multinationals in Europe and in the United States. They identify three different types of advantages arising from foreign direct investment. One set of advantages arise from the privileged possession of assets such as patents or access to markets, or from an ability to coordinate separate but related activities. Locational advantages represent the extent to which firms wish to create or acquire advantages due to transport or production costs. Firms may also wish to internalize markets in response to certain market failures. Japanese FDI in the early 1980s had, as its main goal, securing access to export markets in which Japanese firms had organizational advantages. A second function was to absorb technologies developed in the West. Greater direct investment in the United States during this period reflected locational advantages. The strength of the yen after 1985 and the prospect for a unified European market altered FDI strategy in the latter part of the decade. A case study of the auto industry provides some insight.

The U.S. is still a very open country for foreign investors, and this is due both to traditionally low barriers for capital flows and to very competitive, often oligopolistic markets. In recession periods sharp competition among American competitors reduces profit margins and raises liquidity needs which then give EC (or Japanese) investors a welcome opportunity for acquisitions; in the presence of foreign investors competition processes in the U.S. are thus changing. By contrast, the EC markets are - despite the EC 1992 project - less competitive and government interventions to save struggling companies are more likely in the traditionally interventionist style of economic policymaking in Western Europe. Moreover, restrictions to foreign ownership are still common in many European countries. This is significant for the direction of international trade flows because a change of the parent company country will partly entail a rerouting of trade via the impact on affiliated trade. However, the EC countries are becoming more open in many areas, and U.S. companies are well positioned to benefit from this. In the trilateral and very uneven investment flows between the U.S., the EC and Japan the latter enjoys the option of directly investing in the EC to obtain a greater share of industrial assets in Europe, or, more indirectly to target U.S. companies with major subsidiaries in the EC. High economic growth in the second half of the 1980s has increased the attractiveness of the EC markets in which the prospects for intensified competition in a single market contributed to the demand for capital equipment: U.S. manufacturing exports to the EC almost doubled between 1985 and 1990 - the other big winner being Germany as Europe's major producer and exporter of manufacturing capital goods. The cheaper U.S. dollar supported the strong growth of U.S. exports to Western Europe and in this sense the international exchange rate regimes are effective. However, within the EC the exchange rate adjustment mechanism has been used less since most EC countries (in 1990 also the U.K.) have joined the European Monetary System and the Exchange Rate Mechanism. Whether macroeconomic adjustment in the EC and high economic growth can be maintained in this changing environment is unclear. With the U.K. and Spain being reluctant to accept a depreciation of their respective currencies and others unwilling to accept a nominal appreciation, a stabilization crisis could reduce economic growth in the EC. Whether adjustment on the supply-side, necessary for sustaining growth, will be strengthened by a greater role of multinational companies is an open question. Under favorable circumstances a united Germany could generate additional growth in Western Europe, but the net effect of trade creating demand-pull effects from East Germany and Eastern Europe on the one hand, and, on the other hand, higher real interest rates worldwide are uncertain.

Eastern Europe offers new opportunities for foreign investment as the former socialist economies with their pent-up demand for modern capital equipment open up to the world market. The privatization issue in Eastern Europe poses complex economic and, even more so, political problems for foreign investment. There is not only a need for opening up East European economies for international trade but also for a liberalization of the capital account in the medium term. Foreign ownership of industrial assets is a novelty for the former socialist countries in which private capital ownership was banned for systemic reasons. Only if a stable macroeconomic policy framework can be established in the course of broad institutional changes can foreign investment flows be expected to reach significant levels. EC firms and U.S. as well as Japanese affiliates in Western Europe are favorably positioned to benefit from new investment opportunities in Eastern Europe; however, the global quest for capital requires that the formerly socialist economies generate competitive profit expectations. Strong reinvestment incentives could be provided by host governments to defer the problems of profit transfers. In the long term multinationals' investment can promote economic growth and raise exports.

From a host country perspective the share of politically acceptable foreign ownership will not least depend upon a diversified regional pattern of investment inflows. German, British, French as well as U.S. and Japanese multinational corporations are not equally attracted by the same set of incentives, and, of course, they bring to the host country different impulses for industrial organization, supply-side adjustment and trade orientation. Whether individual countries can mobilize significant foreign investment inflows into a region where politico-economic uncertainties are high is an open question. The creation of a single EC market suggests for Eastern Europe that regional integration can be useful not only to create trade but to stimulate capital flows as well. If functional domestic capital markets can be created and rapid growth of income and savings be achieved domestic capital formation will accelerate which in turn could raise foreign investment inflows. Only if Eastern Europe decisively moves beyond the traditional joint venture approach in international investment can significant inflows be expected.

Given the multitude of economic rigidities, multinational corporations are likely to play the role of an important catalyst of institutional change. In this respect Japanese multinationals have played an important role in the U.S., the U.K. and other OECD countries where the behavior of domestic firms, trade unions and public authorities has often changed. Eastern Europe might well be another case of a region in which multinational corporations play a decisive role in the quest for structural adjustment, growth and employment. For policymakers in Eastern Europe - but in developing countries as well - a prime problem with respect to learning how to live and prosper with multinational companies is that low per capita income levels and high foreign indebtedness in combination with rising income aspirations of the population do not leave much room for policy mistakes. Confidence and credibility are both at a premium in Eastern Europe.

The world economy's requirement for growth in international trade and international factor movements will undoubtedly continue into the next century. The continuing liberalization of trade in goods and factors will be especially important to spur growth and development in Eastern Europe and in the developing countries.

The onset of the 1990s has put the multinational corporations in the focus of theoretical and political interest. The issues raised in this volume will probably continue to hold center stage for some time to come, and we hope that this book will stimulate further research.

Michael W. Klein   *Paul J.J. Welfens*

I. THEORETICAL AND EMPIRICAL ISSUES

INTERNATIONALIZATION OF PRODUCTION, INVESTMENT AND EUROPEAN INTEGRATION: FREE TRADE IN GOODS, TECHNOLOGY AND ASSETS?

Paul J.J. Welfens

1. Introduction

Since the second half of the 1980s European developments have generated prime impulses for changes in the world economy and the international economic system. Indeed with the EC 1992 program to create a single market and the unification of Germany on the one hand, and, on the other hand, the opening up of the former centrally planned economies (CPEs) in Eastern Europe a new Europe is emerging.

Economic developments in the 20th century have gone full circle in Europe: all European countries are once again market economies (or in the transition to it) linked by trade in goods, capital and technology. Free market approaches in Eastern Europe are still partial and contested. The switch to a market-based system is taking place in a dynamic period of global competition processes that hardly resemble the hegemonic Eurocentric structures of the world economy in the pre-World War I period and the US-dominated post-1945 Cold War period. The globalization of competition is shaped much by multinational companies and their networks of international production, where the internationalization of business presents a particular challenge to economic policy. In Western Europe the internationalization of production and trade which reduced policy autonomy at the national level has encouraged the internationalization of economic policy - most visible in the genuine EC policy area of trade policy and, more recently, competition policy and technology policy.

In a period of global competition free trade in goods and technology creates positive external effects, maiiiy by reinforcing competition via exports and production abroad. Import competition and competition effects from foreign subsidiaries are vital not only in small countries but increasingly so in big countries, too. Facing sharper global competition many companies have adopted a strategy of growing by mergers & acquisitions (M&As). Domestic concentration as a result of accelerating M&As in the home market has been observed not only in the U.S., but also in Germany, France, Italy and the U.K. U.S. firms have become prime targets of Japanese as well as European M&As. Cross-border M&As in Europe reached a new record of 749 in the first half of 1990, representing ECU 30 bill. (*Translink, 1990, appendix*).

In Western Europe the creation of a single EC market obviously has accelerated intra-EC mergers and contributed to the formation of "Euronationals" which will transform the industrial landscape in the EC. Continuing real and financial integration in the EC has encouraged the emergence of Euronationals with a mixed European capital ownership. Firms with an internationally diversified capital-ownership (dubbed "transnational firms", *Welfens, 1990*) are a relatively new phenomenon that goes beyond traditional multinational production activities and is mostly undertaken in order to compete in global markets. The internationalization of industrial property rights accelerated in the late 1980s in the EC. Unilever and the Royal Dutch Shell, being early transnational firms, were joined by many other transnationals and new forms of border-crossing joint ventures. More recent transnational formations comprising such firms as ABB or SGS-Thomson as well as a host of international joint ventures such as AT&T/Italtel, IBM Japan/Toshiba testify to the increasing role of international production and financing.

As the international network of trade in goods, services and technology is widely shaped by multinational companies, both directly and by their influence in politics, and since foreign direct investment (FDI) will be at a premium in a decade of global capital shortage, multinational corporate activities will play an increasingly important role in the 1990s - in the global quest for income, jobs, taxes and wealth on the one hand, and, on the other hand in economic adjustment. Highly mobile international capital could also contribute to an intensified international competition among political approaches and regulation regimes which is a particular characteristic of Western Europe in the context of the EC 1992 program. Systemic transformations in Eastern Europe will raise this issue for the former CMEA (Council of Mutual Economic Assistance) countries in the 1990s, too.

Foreign direct investment contributes to economic growth by eliminating regional differentials in the marginal product of capital and stimulating competition in host countries, promotes the international flow of technologies and broadens the know-how basis of the multinational firm. Moreover, multinational companies provide in the form of intra-company trade or trade among foreign subsidiaries a major route for international trade in goods and services. About 45 percent of U.S. trade is multinational trade; in Western Europe the corresponding figures are closer to 30 percent. 85 percent of all U.S. trade is accounted for by only 15 percent of U.S. firms (*Bergsten, 1991*) which makes it clear that in the political arena a limited number of influential players lobby for specific kinds of trade and investment policies.

FDI affects the transmission channel of endogenous and exogenous shocks and shifts: For example, depending on the degree of multinationality and the amount of sunk costs associated with FDI, exchange rate changes will have an impact on the pricing strategy of the firm and the effectiveness of exchange rate policies.

As the share of trade in goods, services and technology passing through multinational companies is growing, the development of the multinationals itself is important. If horizontal integration would dominate vertical international integration, monopolistic and protectionistic forces would gain in the world economy; increasing economic rents would then accrue to workers in the respective firms, their owners and the governments (via taxes).

In the 1980s there were many distortions in international trade flows. Some came from high exchange rate variability, others from economic policies in North America, Japan and Europe where policy approaches differ significantly in many areas - in particular in the regulation of service industries, the scope of state-owned industries, restrictions to foreign ownership and the role of R&D policies. Important policy fora to discuss diverging views were the G-7 meetings, multilateral organizations such as the Bank of International Settlements (for the banking industry), the IMF and the GATT - organizations in which European countries play an increasing role.

The 1990s will be a decisive transition period for the new Europe in which West and East no longer face a political divide but an economic divide that can only be overcome by successful outward-oriented policies. Fortunately the opening up of Eastern Europe is to be addressed after import-substitution strategies in developing countries were discredited by many experiences as well as by theoretical analyses (*Riedel, 1990*).

Integration-induced higher economic growth in the EC can be helpful for the difficult systemic transformation in the former CMEA countries, namely to the extent that a higher import demand in the EC raises exports from Eastern Europe and the USSR. However, at the same time the EC 1992 program and other changes in the OECD area could accelerate protectionist tendencies worldwide - in a period in which inherited institutional liberalization frameworks are covering a declining share of overall trade and cannot address substantial fields of national economic policy (e.g. technology policies which affect trade and are in effect trade policy substitutes).

In the following analysis we take a look at the links between trade and international competition from a Schumpeterian perspective which emphazises the interplay of trade, technology and asset market developments; government policies play a particular role for the long term dynamics of open economies and the global system itself, and the increasing mobility of multinational firms raises questions about the efficiency of common national economic policies (section 2). In section 3 we point out in which fields Europe - the EC and Eastern Europe - plays a particular role in the internationalization of industry and the growth of global trade. Finally we ask which global policy changes emerge from the shifts in the European economies (section 4). It is obvious that the subsequent analysis deals in many ways with problems raised in the Uruguay GATT round.

2. Trade and International Competition from a Dynamic Perspective

Multinational companies (MNCs) play a key role for the mobility of technologies - hence for incomes, tax payments and workplaces - and are decisive for innovation. This gives the MNCs a decisive role for economic growth. Moreover, multinational companies' international investment flows are important for the diffusion of technologies worldwide (*survey: Chesnais, 1988*), but given the link between firm-specific advantages and innovations, they also react in their investment policies to national R&D policies; certainly they also react to perceived future import barriers. About 1/3 of economic growth in OECD countries is attributable to the residual technology factor.

In Eastern Europe multinational or transnational firms and hence foreign direct investment are still an exception, but the systemic transformation - including opening up, privatization and reduced capital controls - will change this gradually. For systemic reasons the socialist countries did not accept private ownership of industrial assets, be it by domestic or by foreign individuals. Lack of multinational activities explains part of the East European stagnation (*Murrell, 1990*).

The CMEA countries have not only not accepted foreign direct investment inflows but have also largely foregone the opportunities of producing abroad and transferring foreign experiences and know-how back to the parent company and the home market, respectively. For the East European economies the envisaged opening up process will be comprised of not only the problem of trading goods, but of technology and real capital as well.

As is well-known, markets for technologies are very imperfect ones, and firms' internal transactions and hence multinational corporations play a special role for the international diffusion of technological progress. Advanced countries with a strong technology policy are often major source countries of FDI, but to the extent that firms operating in these countries particularly enjoy public funding of R&D activities and government support for R&D projects there is also a high attractiveness for foreign firms to acquire high-tech companies and to thereby buy into public R&D programs that could thus ultimately contribute to reinforcing foreign firms' technology basis. Trade in industrial assets and hence international capital flows are therefore important, and countries which impose restrictions on foreign capital ownership indirectly impede the international flow of technologies.

2.1 Links between Trade, Multinationality and Innovations

In the 1990s the bilateral U.S.-Japanese trade imbalances and conflicts will render U.S. leadership in trade policy more difficult than ever, and Europe with its opening up of new and bigger markets might be inclined to take advantage of this (vis-à-vis the EC, U.S. trade is likely to record a surplus in 1991). In a period in which Japan's FDI is employed to tap the technology pools in Europe and the U.S., there is a joint interest of the EC and North America to open up Japan to FDI and thus to establish truly free international capital flows among the OECD countries. To the extent that freeing capital flows implies increased cross-border M&As and rising average firm sizes, global innovativeness might reduce as a consequence of an observed inverse relationship between patenting per unit of R&D resources and firm size (*survey: Griliches, 1990*), where capital market inefficiencies in the form of short-termism may be part of the problem.[1]

While the EC is gradually getting used to hostile takeover bids, Japanese industry is reluctant to even accept friendly takeovers of company assets. For decades capital flow liberalization attempts, emphasizing the principle of national treatment, have focussed on non-equity investments and banking services - involving as principal actors the OECD (capital movement liberalization code of 1961, non-binding FDI/MNCs code of 1976) and, to a lesser degree, the IMF (Articles VII/XIV). The role of foreign investment and cross-border M&As needs to be addressed because ownership of firms matters for intra- and extra-firm trade in goods and services as well as for the access to technologies.

Governments are not free in their decision-making about trade policies. Domestic and foreign firms influence politics - by financing political campaigns and, more importantly for popularity and discretionary room to maneuvre, by providing jobs and generating tax revenues. Multinational companies are particularly important in an international context because the parent company can affect not only politics at home but politics abroad as well via the network of subsidiaries. Consequently, to simply postulate free international trade is analytically misleading; one has to analyze the political economy of protectionism (*Hillmann and Ursprung, 1989; Schuhknecht and Ursprung, 1989; Witzke and Hausner, 1989; Bhagwati, 1988; Giersch, 1987*) if one is to understand international impediments to global allocational efficiency. In this perspective trade protectionism, technology protectionism and capital market protectionism (capital controls) are three interrelated distortions of free international resource allocation.[2]

Technology Policy Matters

A common trait of government policies in major OECD countries in the 1980s has been the growing emphasis on innovation/technology policy. It not only is supposed to contribute to political power - as in the case of public sponsored military R&D -, but more generally to the international competitiveness of the domestic economy. OECD countries which spend between 2 and 3 percent of GNP on research and development expect to thereby support high value-adding production and profitable export positions such that positive employment and tax revenue effects are generated. However, for governments there are appropriation risks in the sense that tax payers' money spent on R&D programs might not be recovered by higher future taxes from profitable domestic firms and might also fail to pay off in terms of high-value-adding workplaces. The higher the share of profits from highly contested world markets and the shorter the innovation cycles worldwide, the greater is the risk that R&D projects cannot rapidly and succesfully be translated into commercially profitable products in world markets. In addition to this there is the problem that foreign multinationals benefit from public funded R&D programs in host countries such that considerable benefits accrue to the parent company and the source country of foreign direct investment, respectively.

High technology industries with strong militarily-oriented public R&D funding are often successful in keeping foreign capital outside because tax-financed R&D expenditures spur the interest of politicians to ensure a domestic pay-off by providing domestic jobs and reinforcing the technological competitiveness of industry whose international economic rents translate into higher profits and increasing tax revenues. Since R&D functions are dominantly located in the country of the parent company, changing international ownerships of R&D intensive firms will affect the allocation of a country's R&D budget and hence the structure of technologically-based comparative advantages and trade flows.

Foreign sourcing in the building-up of firm-specific advantages is an important avenue of economic growth as the example of successful OECD countries and NICs with their two-way foreign direct investment flows suggests. Via intra-company technology (back-)transfers high FDI outflows can reinforce long-term growth prospects of a source country, especially if a higher stock of outward FDI goes along with higher exports of goods and services; moreover, if the net effect of FDI outflows and FDI-generated exports raises the real exchange rate relatively cheaper imported intermediate products and inputs could raise economic growth via the supply-side.[3] The back-transfer of foreign acquired know-how and experience is often limited not only by firm-internal communication problems and a certain reluctance of the parent company's management to learn from subsidiaries, but more importantly it can be that the market environments as well as the policy framework abroad and at home differ significantly. As regards goods markets differences in per-capita-income and hence preferences for quality and variety can render a cross-border or even global application of know-how difficult. Short-term financial risks, such as interest rate or exchange rate volatility, can affect the choice of serving markets locally or via exports.

If there is a net effect in foreign exchange markets of FDI outflows and profit remittances of foreign subsidiaries, nominal and real exchange rate changes will result provided exchange rates are not fixed. Moreover, multinational firms affect exchange rates directly via currency substitution and, as shown by *Caves (1989)* for U.S. inflows after 1977, by adjusting the timing of long-run investments that take the short-run guise of stabilizing speculation.

Ownership Matters

It is well known that trade in technology as reflected in royalties and licences is dominantly an intra-firm phenomenon. The international diffusion of innovations is therefore closely connected with the regional pattern of the stock of FDI. Innovators rarely consider licensing as a feasible avenue to appropriate the returns of investing in technological progress. The information paradox that one has to reveal ex ante the content and hence the value of intangible assets whose price is still to be negotiated leads to market failure in the case of "purely" independent actors. In contrast to this is the case of establishing implicit know-how markets by a mutual commitment of resources from all major firms interested in and capable of using a new technology suitable for regional or global markets. Setting up a joint research project or a joint subsidiary in a specific field is a more success-promising approach to better appropriate dynamic rents. Joint R&D efforts which spread risks and pool complementary resources are thus likely to accelerate the diffusion of technologies because an ex ante commitment of resources on the side of would-be users of innovations reduces the free rider problem. Mutual trade in industrial goods, options for licensing swaps as well as cross-shareholdings - here the problem of capital controls enters - can reinforce the perception of interdependency and hence of the credibility of jointly exploring and exploiting new technologies financed by one's own or public funds. Finally, discriminatory public procurement policies which favor domestic (or domestically owned) firms affect trade flows as well as the asset prices of the firms concerned.

In a world economy in which non-tradable services play an increasing role in satisfying the need of manufacturing industry, consumers and government and in which the technology factor becomes more important for competitive production costs and product design, the adherence to free merchandise trade is not sufficient for allocative efficiency. With imperfect markets for know-how and taking into account that innovations are bred worldwide in firms eager to establish a competitive edge in world markets, the diffusion and exchange of technological know-how necessarily lead to the problem of international investment possibilities and the trade of industrial property rights. Explicit capital controls and the restriction of the M&A menu by way of organizing state-owned industries therefore impose not only barriers to entry, but generally restrain the opportunities to internationally organize the sourcing and diffusion of technologies and innovations. If governments provide capital to state-run industries which do not realize market rates of return on investments, the international competition process is biased because private firms face relatively higher capital costs and the hard budget constraint imposed by private capital markets whereas state industries enjoy the marvelous credit ratings of a public authority with immediate access to the taxpayers' pockets.

The international structure of industrial property rights and the type of multinationality prevailing is not irrelevant to protectionism. To the extent that EC (co-)ownership matters in antidumping cases, trade in goods - and assets - will be distorted. The mere threat of antidumping actions can be used to obtain voluntary export restraints, and an ownership stake in politically influential firms and industries can help foreign companies to influence trade politics abroad and at home. Keeping foreign investors out of the home turf - and this illustrates the role of capital controls - may facilitate concerted political lobbying and silent cartelization attempts in the home market.

Different national regulations hold for financial services and capital markets as well as for R&D activities. International competition as well as economies of scale and of firm-internal international transactions generate pressures for economic policy reforms across countries. Similarly, the presence of transplants (as in the case of Japanese firms in the U.K. or the U.S.) is not only conducive to industrial restructuring in the host country, but it can also induce adjustments in the politico-economic framework. This holds both for the host and the source country where governments are eager to preserve domestic investment despite potentially rising FDI outflows.

There is no simple trade-off between (higher) FDI outflows and (lower) economic growth at home. If, depending largely upon the profitability of FDI, domestic savings rise in proportion with FDI outflows domestic investment need not reduce. FDI inflows have ambiguous effects, too. Foreign competitors arriving with FDI inflows can not only provide jobs and income but also reinforce competition, dynamic efficiency and economic growth in the host country market. However, FDI inflows may also reinforce barriers to entry and impede competition, innovativeness and export growth as many developing countries experienced (the jointly owned and managed Ford-VW Autolatina firm in Latin America is an example). The size of the host country markets, government policies and the technological dynamics in "bordering" production areas - with would-be market entrants - determine together with the foreign investors whether more competition, improved efficiency and higher economic growth will characterize host countries having high FDI inflows. Exhibit 1 summarizes major aspects of this section.

Exhibit 1: Links between Trade, Multinationality and R&D

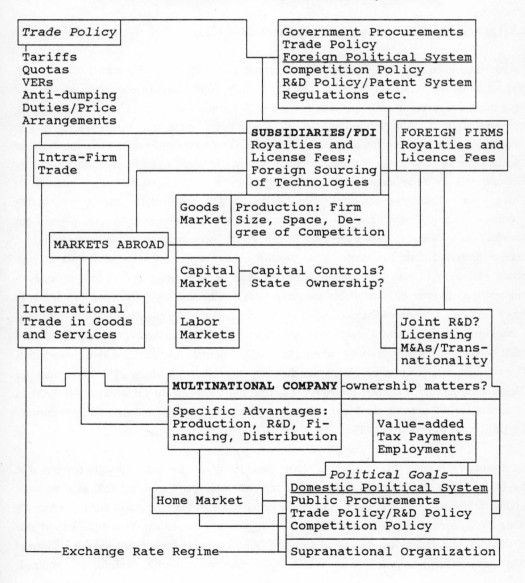

Firms that act under foreign jurisdiction at some point also become influential players in the politico-economic game of the host country. This ranges from lobbying for certain trade policies, favorable tax policies, and an increasing share in public procurements to obtaining a "fair" share in R&D programs. With technology becoming increasingly important in global competition, domestic firms that face more attractive R&D conditions abroad are induced to shift not only R&D activities to foreign locations, but - in some cases - also production facilities. This affects regional innovation cycles as well as trade flows.

2.2 Trade in Goods, Technology and Assets: Stylized Facts

International trade grew by 50 percent in real terms in the 1980s - having increased 13-fold in real terms between 1950 and 1990 - and significantly contributed to economic growth, but trade expansion is still mainly confined to the OECD countries and some Newly Industrializing Countries (NICs). Competition enhancing intra-industry trade dominates among OECD countries, where growing trade in technology-intensive goods testifies for the importance of "Schumpeterian" trade. In contrast to OECD trade, the Pacific Basin is characterized by Heckscher-Ohlin trade: countries export goods that use their abundant factors intensively. Trade among developing countries is still relatively low, particularly among neighboring countries in Latin America and Africa, where import-substitution strategies were pursued for decades; only recently, following most Asian NICs, liberalization and export promotion became preferred trade strategies. In the socialist countries of the CMEA per-capita trade in goods and services was low, where intra-CMEA trade dominated and largely reflected a monopolistic division of labor within the group. Besides the shift towards export promotion in many developing countries the opening up of the (former) CMEA countries in Eastern Europe - here including the USSR - strongly affects trade in the world economy. Global merchandise trade reached $ 3.1 bill. in 1989, where the OECD countries acounted for about two-thirds. The regional composition of global merchandise trade shows a share of 43.5 percent for Western Europe, 15.5 percent for North America and 23.5 percent for Asia. Latin America accounted for 4.5 percent, the Middle East plus Africa for 6 percent and Eastern Europe (incl. the USSR) for 7 percent in 1989.

As regards the leading traders the U.S., Japan and Germany - the latter strongly embedded in the EC - it is obvious from *Table 1* that regional trade plays a strong role as does trade among these leading market economies. In 1989 the share of the four Asian NICs ("4 tigers") Hong Kong, Singapore, Korea and Taiwan was higher on both the export and the import side of the U.S. and Japan than that of all former CMEA countries (*see shares for the USSR and other nonmember n.i.e plus that of the developing countries in Europe in Table 1*) combined.

With a share of some 18 percent in EC merchandise trade (excluding intra-EC trade) the U.S. is the EC's most important trading partner; Sweden, Switzerland and Austria are important as a group and currently account for a higher combined share of EC imports and exports than all former CMEA countries together. Poland, Hungary and the CSFR are likely to intensify trade not only with the EC but with the four Asian tigers as well, and this translates into reform pressure in both North Korea and the PR China. In the EC Germany accounted for 15.2 percent of total EC imports which makes it the most important market within the EC, whereas on the export side its share of some 11.5 percent is matched by France (unification will reinforce Germany's role).

Table 1: Exports(Ex) and Imports (Im) of Germany, the EC, the U.S. and Japan to and from the Countries Listed, 1989 (figures are shares in percent)

	(W.)Germany		EC-12		U.S.		Japan	
	Ex	Im	Ex	Im	Ex	Im	Ex	Im
Australia	0.7	0.4	0.8	0.5	2.3	1.0	2.8	5.5
Japan	2.4	6.3	2.0	4.5	12.2	19.7	-	-
Canada	0.8	0.9	1.0	0.9	21.5	18.2	2.5	4.1
U.S.	7.3	7.6	7.5	7.8	-	-	34.3	23.0
			18.5**	18.1**				
EC	55.0	55.1	59.8	57.2	23.8	18.0	17.5	13.4
Germany	-	-	11.7	15.2	4.6	5.2	5.8	4.3
U.K.	9.3	6.8	8.6	6.1	5.7	3.8	3.9	2.1
France	13.2	11.9	11.5	9.4	3.2	2.7	1.9	2.6
Italy	9.3	8.9	7.2	6.7	2.0	2.6	1.0	1.8
Netherl.	8.5	10.2	6.4	7.3	3.1	1.0	1.9	0.5
Switzerl.	6.0	4.2	3.8	3.0	1.3	1.0	1.0	1.8
Austria	5.5	4.1	2.5	1.8	0.2	0.2	0.5	0.2
Sweden	2.9	2.5	2.3	2.4	0.9	1.0	0.8	0.5
USSR and other nonmember Nie*	2.5	2.2	1.8	1.9	1.3	0.2	1.3	1.8
Developing Countries	14.6	17.8	15.5	16.7	35.4	39.8	38.3	48.2
Europe***	3.3	3.8	2.4	2.2	0.9	0.7	0.4	0.4
Africa	2.1	2.3	3.2	3.3	1.4	3.0	1.6	1.8
Asia	4.6	6.7	4.6	5.4	15.8	20.5	30.1	31.0
4 ANICs	2.3	3.4	2.1	2.5	10.6	13.3	19.2	12.9
China	0.7	1.1	0.6	0.8	1.6	2.6	3.1	5.3
Middle East	2.7	2.0	3.5	3.2	3.8	3.3	3.0	10.9
W.Hemisphere	1.8	3.0	1.9	2.6	13.5	12.2	3.2	4.1
Mexico	0.4	0.2	0.3	0.3	6.9	5.6	0.7	0.8

Note: 4 ANICs = Hongkong, Singapore, Republic of Korea and Taiwan
* USSR, Albania, Bulgaria, Cuba, CSFR, GDR, Mongolia and North Korea
** share for the U.S. if intra-EC trade is excluded from total EC trade.
*** includes Hungary, Poland, Romania, Yugoslavia, Turkey and other (Cyprus, Gibraltar, Malta, Faeroe Islands); n.i.e = not included elsewhere.
Source: Deutsche Bundesbank (1990), Beihefte zu den Monatsberichten der Deutschen Bundesbank, Reihe 3, Frankfurt/M.; IMF (1990), Direction of Trade Statistics, Washington D.C., own calculations.

The U.S. accounted for 34.3 percent of Japan's exports, whereas the U.S. accounted on the import side for only 23 percent in 1989. This reflected a considerable and sustaining bilateral trade balance deficit of the U.S. For the U.S. exports to the EC were the most important - the EC accounted for a share of 23.8 percent - but on the import side Japan's share of 19.7 % was nearly two points above the share accounted for by the EC.

Significant intra-regional trade characterized North-America with a rising share (compared to 1979) of 5.3% of world trade and Western Europe with a share of 31.1%, significantly up from 28.8 % in 1979. Low intra-Latin America trade shares, intra-Africa shares, intra-Middle East shares and intra-CMEA shares fell further between 1979 and 1989: from 1.1 to 0.5% , from 0.3 to 0.1%, from 0.4 to 0.3% and from 4.3 to 3.5 %, respectively.

Trade in commercial services which includes transportation, tourism, telecom, insurance, banking and other professional services, reached $680 bill. in 1989 which is nearly a fifth of the total value of global exports. Trade in services was also predominantly among OECD countries. In 1989 leading exporters of services were the U.S., France, the U.K. and Germany with a percentage share of 15.7, 10.3, 7.2 and 7 %, respectively, followed by Japan, Italy and Spain. Ranks 11 to 15 - with shares of 2.4 to 1.7 percent - include Switzerland, Canada, Hongkong, Sweden and the Republic of Korea (a leading NIC). The only socialist country among the top 25 exporters is Yugoslavia with a share of 0.8%. The leading importers of services were Japan, the U.S. and Germany with a share of 12, 11.7 and 10.5 percent, followed by France, the U.K. and Italy. Taiwan is a major importer of services with a share of 2.1 percent and shows a swing of 16 ranks up to position 11. Leading traders in commercial services are also leading traders in merchandise trade: in 1989 20 of the 25 leading exporters of merchandise were among the 25 top service exporters, and the same pattern holds for imports (*GATT, 1990*).[4]

In addition to trade in goods and services international flows in real capital have become a major engine of growth for many countries. Foreign direct investment reached a stock of $ 1500 bill. worldwide at the end of the 1980s in which the world stock of FDI doubled (world trade value increased by 3/4), and the share of services in FDI has grown in particular.[5] As with trade in goods and services one finds that FDI flows are heavily concentrated among major OECD countries. While Germany - the EC's leading industrial power -, Japan and the U.S. are comparable heavyweights in international trade, the stock value of foreign direct investments showed that the U.S. dominated with $ 327 bill. as compared to the U.K. with 184, Japan with 111, West Germany with 97, and the Netherlands and France with 70 and 58 bill. in 1988; adding Canada's figure of $ 51 bill. leads to $ 898 bill. and a share of 87 percent in the stock of global FDI for these seven countries (*JETRO, 1990, p. 3*). In the late 1980s FDI flows worldwide amounted to some $ 100 bill. annually.

Generally, the global role of multinational and transnational companies is expanding, where small and medium sized companies play a considerable role, although the 600 leading multinational companies which account for roughly 20 percent of global value-added in manufacturing and agriculture are primarily shaping international economic relations. Japanese companies have joined traditionally dominating U.K. and U.S. firms as powerful international investors in the 1980s and have caused considerable adjustment pressure with their transplants in the U.K. and other EC countries while contributing to modernizing the host economies.

According to FDI weights the Netherlands would replace Italy in the G-7 club of leading OECD countries; the fact that a hypothetical "I-7" club would not be a perfect overlap with the G-7 club might explain that the liberalization of FDI flows has not been as effectively addressed as problems in the area of merchandise trade (the seven leading OECD countries in terms of GNP are also the leading 7 exporters and importers).[6]

Outward FDI amounted to ECU 26 bill. in the EC, to 29 bill. in the U.S. and to 15 bill. in Japan in 1986, where the balance between outward and inward FDI amounted to ECU -16, -4 and -15 bill., respectively.[7] In the transatlantic setting FDI and trade represent a two-way street. As regards the triangle Japan-U.S.-EC, only trade represents a broad two-way flow (with a structural Japanese surplus position). Japan's inward FDI flows are extremely low because both U.S. firms and European companies find it extremely difficult to successfully launch viable investment projects in Japan. Its outward FDI has accelerated worldwide and in 1990 Japanese FDI flows in the U.S. exceeded the British inflows for the first time. Japan's FDI in the EC is rapidly growing, too.

As regards U.S.-European two-way investment links economic relations are relatively balanced as measured by the stock of EC investment in the U.S. relative to U.S. investment in the EC, where the U.K., Germany and the Netherlands are the three preferred host countries for U.S. investment (the U.K., the Netherlands and Germany are the EC's main source countries for FDI in the U.S., *see Table 2*). The relative balance of transatlantic FDI flows contrasts sharply with the transpacific case where Japan's unequal investment balance with the U.S. could reinforce the bilateral trade deficit and contribute directly and indirectly to transpacific politico-economic tensions; while the indicator d'/d reaches 3.52 for the case of the Netherlands (with Sweden being a more extreme case, the other extreme in Europe being Italy) and is nearly as high as in the Japanese case, bilateral U.S.-Dutch trade imbalances clearly do not cause conflicts.

Table 2: Direct Investment of the U.S. and Foreign Direct Investment in the U.S., 1989 (EC countries indicated in the order of US Investment Position in the EC)

Millions of U.S. Dollars							Millions of U.S. Dollars				ratio
(a) Reinvested Earnings	(b) Capital Income From Abroad	(c) Capital Outflows		(d) US Investment Position Abroad			(d') FDI Position in the U.S.	(c') Capital Inflows	(b') Capital Income	(a') Reinvested Earnings	d' d
22,416 (70.7% of c)	53,617 (14.4 % of d)	31,722	share in %	373,436	All Countries	share in %	400,817	72,244	14,004 (3.5 % of d')	-88** (0 % of c)	1.1
1,008	2,629	1,217	5.2	19,384	**Japan**	17.4	69,699	1ⁿ,269	1,277	-301	3.6
3,800	6,884	1,352	17.9	66,856	**Canada**	7.9	31,538	2,736	894	-150	0.5
10,619	27,082	15,315	47.3	176,736	**Europe**	65.4	262,011	47,368	11,788	895	1.5
9,132	22,327	14,503	40.2	149,975	**EC**	58.6	234,794	42,486	10,052	307	1.6
1,289	8,097	9,828	16.3	60,810	**U.K.** 29.7		119,137	20,235	6,778	-48	2.0
1,745	3,459	134	6.1	23,059	**Germany** 7.0		28,223	4,229	627	286	1.2
1,338	2,509	906	4.6	17,168	**Neth.** 15.1		60,483	9,826	2,464	378	3.5
1,361	2,235	635	3.9	14,747	**France** 4.1		16,375	5,299	-198	-493	1.1
637	1,495	660	2.8	10,634	**Italy** 0.4		1,586	987	-140	-91	0.2
541	1,281	674	2.2	8,290	**Belgium** 1.1		4,535	345	378	193	0.6
1,487	4,755	812	7.2	26,761	**Other Eu.** 6.8		27,217	4,882	1,736	588	1.0
170	266	-66	0.3	1,102	**Sweden** 1.2		4,925	-357	291	134	4.5
1,078	3,308	1,682	5.3	19,952	**Switz.** 4.8		19,329	3,586	1,470	546	1.0
1,257	2,081	1,459	3.9	14,495	**Australia** -		-	-	-	-	-
5,657	14,466	12,135	24.2	90,552	**Dev.Coun.** *7.7		31,036	4,032	234	-455	0.3

Note: In 1988 the U.S. accounted on the sources side (recipient side) for 30.5% (27%) of the FDI stock worldwide, Japan for 9.8% (0.9%), the U.K. for 16.2% (9.8%), Germany for 9.1% (6.8%) and other Europe for 24.3% (19.8%) and the developing countries for 2.8 % (21.3%), respectively.

* the FDI position of developing countries is biased and inflated by the FDI position of the Netherland Antilles which recorded a stock value of investment of $ 10,570 Mill. in the U.S. in 1989: for the developing countries the d'/d balance indicator reduces to 0.23 if investment in the U.S. is eliminated.

** this figure marks a dramatic swing against 1988 when reinvested earnings amounted to $6,560 million US dollars. With respect to FDI in the U.S. it is also remarkable that intercompany debt inflows in 1989 amounted to $ 25,649 million of which 64.7 percent was accounted for by EC firms. As regards US direct investment abroad intercompany debt outflow was 14,166 mill. in 1989 of which $ 7,072 mill. was accounted for by the EC.

Sources: US Department of Commerce (1990), Survey of Current Business, August 1990; Council of Economic Advisers (1991), Economic Report of the President, own calculations.

With ongoing strong Japanese investment in the U.S., the British pole position with a share of 29.7 % of the stock of foreign investment in the U.S. could be matched by Japan at the end of the 1990s. In 1989 it was also noteworthy that capital income from the U.S. was of minor importance for Japan (not exceptional for a "newly investing country"), which is in contrast to the EC, and Japan's reinvested earnings were negative. If Eastern Europe could attract 10 percent of U.S. investment outflows to the EC in 1989 and 10 percent of EC FDI in the U.S. this would amount to $ 1.5 bill. and 4.2 bill., respectively. This is not much in view of the tremendous restructuring needs in the former CMEA countries, although the qualitative impact could be very decisive and within two decades these countries should be able reach at least half the stock value of the developing country group. This country group which had a stock of $ 90 bill. of U.S. investment in 1989 demonstrates - given the experiences of the Latin American debt crises in the 1980s - that investment inflows are not a sufficient condition for successful development. Adequate economic policies on the one hand, and, on the other hand, creation plus diffusion of technologies as well as the capability of adapting technologies to local circumstances are of prime importance.

From a theoretical point of view FDI flows are strongly influenced by innovations and new technologies for which only very imperfect markets exist such that firm-internal transactions/transfers are preferred to arm's length transactions which impede the full appropriation of Schumpeterian rents. As Table 3 shows the major innovating countries are the big EC countries, Japan and the U.S. which accounted for about 85 percent of all patent applications - counting only those applying for a patent in more than one country - in the 1980s.

Table 3: Technology Trade Indicators for Selected Countries

Country of Origin	1982-88 (aver. p.a.) patent applications for > 1 country number	share (%)	1985 foreign asset share a)	b)	1985 patent pene- tration*	1985 patent ex-im ratio**
EC	27 184	39.1	-	-	.31***	-
Germany	13 368	19.2	17	78	.43	2.2
France	4 469	6.4	19	-	.22	0.9
U.K.	4 861	7.0	14	56	.29	0.8
Netherlands	-	-	-	48	-	
Japan	15 171	21.8	1	14	.90	2.4
U.S.	18 549	26.7	9	60	.55	2.8
other	8 641	12.4	-	-	-	-
Switzerland	-	-	-	-	.13	1.0
World	69 545	100.0	-	-	-	-

a) share of foreign-owned manufacturing companies in assets in percent (for France: foreign share in investment);
b) relative foreign asset share defined as stock of inward FDI relative to outward FDI stock (in percent).
* ratio of domestic patent applications to all patent applications in the respective country.
** ratio of patent applications abroad over foreign patents in the country concerned; this roughly corresponds to a patent export-import ratio.
*** average for the U.K., France and Germany.
Sources: Faust/Ifo-Institute, 1990, based on INPADOC data, Vienna. OECD (1988), Main Science and Technology Indicators Vol.1, Paris. Figures for a) are from EC Commission (1990), based on Julius and Thomsen; Tab. 1. Figures for b) are for 1983 and based on OECD (1987), International Investment and Multinational Enterprise, Paris; own calculations.

The Swiss role in innovation is akin to that of the Netherlands as a small economy among the leading FDI countries. Although of 100 patent applications in Switzerland 87 are from foreign applicants (suggesting a high patent penetration rate) Swiss patent applications abroad compare well with foreign patent applications in Switzerland - the "patent export-import ratio" is close to unity. Only big countries can normally be expected to reach a ratio close to unity or above. Germany, Japan and the U.S. reach patent export-import ratios above 2 which suggests that considerable resources have been devoted by these countries to generating innovations which in turn call for costly patent applications worldwide.

The fact that 90 percent of all patent applications filed in Japan come from Japanese companies suggests that the Japanese economy is the only major OECD country with a low patent penetration ratio. Japan, again, is a special case among OECD countries. Although cross-licensing is a common phenomenon among leading big business firms from industrialized market economies, Japanese companies seem to stand out in their emphasis on cross-licensing as a cheap strategy of technology imports from Europe and the U.S. Japan's patent system is very complicated for foreigners, and strategic "peripheral patenting" is used as leverage for obtaining a licence of a targeted core-technology.[8]

The foreign share of assets in manufacturing industry in the G-5 countries in Table 3 is between 9 and 19 percent, except for Japan where it is only 1 percent which partly explains the low patent import penetration rate in Japan. The relative stock inward-outward FDI figures also clearly indicate that Japan is an exception among major OECD countries, and this disequilibrium has grown in the 1980s and will continue to do so in the 1990s.

Technology flows as expressed in expenditures and payments for licenses, patents and royalties follow much the same regional distribution as FDI stocks because expenditures and payments mainly concern parent companies and subsidiaries (*see Table 4*). While Germany and Japan have a negative balance, the U.S. and the U.K. are the only two major OECD countries with a positive technology balance which, however, strongly reflects the long uninterrupted history of outward FDI flows from these countries.[9]

In the U.S., the U.K. and Germany about 3/4 of all technology payments accrue on a parent-affiliate basis, and services in industry that represent tacit know-how also are biased. With SDR 6.5 bill. and 0.2 bill. the USA and the United Kingdom each recorded a surplus in 1988, while Japan recorded the highest deficit in the technology balance of payments of OECD countries, namely SDR 2.5 bill. One may note, however, that the receipts from patents, inventions and copyrights increased much faster than the expenditures. This, of course, is related to the fast growth of Japanese FDI. Japan's stock of outward FDI in 1988 reached

$111 bill. while inward FDI stood at $ 10 bill. Less interesting than the balance is the low expenditure figure for U.S. technology imports which are - on a per capita basis - among the lowest in the OECD. In a world with a growing global division of know-how and "technology production" weak technological sourcing of the U.S. could explain a long term decline in the competitiveness of the U.S. economy and low U.S. productivity growth. In contrast to the U.S. major EC exporters such as Germany, Italy and France traditionally have relied upon the import of technologies and a partially world market-oriented diffusion of innovations.

Trade in goods or services is often parallel to direct investment flows, where restrictions to either can impede the prospects for the complementary flows.[10] The ratios of outward FDI to exports in the period 1970-79 for the U.S., the U.K., Japan, Germany and France was 13, 10, 3, 2.4 and 2.2 percent. The figures for the U.S. fell in 1980-87 to 8 %; in the other countries it rose to 14, 5.1, 2.7 and 3.9 percent, respectively (*Julius, 1990, p. 38*).

Table 4: Technology Balance of Payments for Selected Countries, 1985 and 1988
(Mill. of SDR)

		1985	1988
	Receipts	610	860
Germany	Expenditures	1200	2030
	Balance	-590	-1170
	Receipts	1063	1491
Italy	Expenditures	1742	2502
	Balance	- 679	-1011
	Receipts	508	850
France	Expenditures	967	1662
	Balance	-459	-812
	Receipts	298	532
Netherlands	Expenditures	721	925
	Balance	-423	-393
	Receipts	1144	1273
U.K.	Expenditures	793	1058
	Balance	351	215
	Receipts	5880	8000
U.S.	Expenditures	890	1530
	Balance	4990	6470
	Receipts	710	1210
Japan	Expenditures	2320	3740
	Balance	-1610	-2530

Source: IMF, 1989, Balance of Payments Statistics, Vol. 40, Yearbook, part 1, Washington.

Macroeconomic perspectives

Without implying any crude causality one may state that FDI-export ratios can reach magnitudes which are important for macroeconomic policies. Moreover, it would be useful to incorporate FDI in a modified IS-LM macro-model - with an investment function $I(r,r^*,q)$. As regards the balance of payments constraint, an interesting case is one when net exports X-qX* of goods and services go along with (net) real capital exports $J=J(T^*/T,..)$ such that the balance of payments constraint in a flexible exchange rate system is given by:

$$X(Y^*,q) - qX^*(Y,q) - J(T/T^*,..) + r^*K^{**} - F(i,i^*,f/e) = 0; \; \delta J/\delta T/T^* > 0$$

with q= terms of trade; X= exports; Y= real output; T= level of technology, * for foreign variables; K** stock of capital owned abroad; F=net purchase of foreign bonds/financial capital outflows; i(r)= nominal(real) interest rate; f,e =forward and spot exchange rates, respectively.

The equilibrium locus of the balance of payments curve will shift in r-Y space upwards if FDI outflows increase because of a rise in T/T*: for a given increase in Y which raises net imports of goods and services the rise in r, necessary to attract offsetting financial capital inflows, must be higher now than before.[11] If intra-company trade flows react differently to international relative price changes than unaffiliated trade, regional FDI patterns should affect the exchange rate and influence the J-curve effects.

If output abroad is determined by a Cobb-Douglas production function $Y^* = K^{*\alpha^*}L^{*(1-\alpha^*)}$ and profit maximization leads to $r^* = \alpha(Y^*/K^*)$ we obtain with Θ denoting the endogenous share of the capital stock owned abroad ($\Theta = K^{**}/K^*$; the share of foreign-owned assets in Table 3):

$$X(Y^*,q) - qX^*(Y,q) - J(T/T^*..) + \alpha^*Y^*/\Theta - F(..) = 0;$$

According to the preceeding analysis it is clear that (net) FDI outflows are determined not only by financing costs for investment and the terms of trade which determine profits in domestic consumption units but above all by the level of technology at home - say as expressed in patent applications - relative to that abroad.

3. European Impulses for Global Competition and International Trade

Eurogrowth

Supply-side economic policies in major Western European countries have contributed to overcoming Eurosclerosis and slow growth in the 1980s. Moreover, supranational EC policies that aim to create a single EC market and to limit protectionism are contributing to structural adjustment and growth as well as to changing international trade flows. EC-based firms as well as external firms - often motivated by the fear of Fortress Europe - adjust to the changes in the EC countries, where multinational companies directly shape the emerging new industrial landscape.

Being able to exploit static and dynamic economies of scale more easily in a unified and enlarged home market, the European industry might express a weaker demand for export promotion. However, as certain goods in high technology fields meet a critical minimum demand for exploiting learning curve effects only in a worldwide context and since global competition is expected to intensify, the demand for interventionist trade policies and subsidies is generally not reducing in Europe. The U.S. and Japan as well as other countries will react in the international subsidy race (*Welfens, 1990a; Ostry, 1990; van Tulder and Junne, 1988*).[12]

A new challenge is arising in Eastern Europe which offers new opportunities for private investment. The desire of most former CMEA countries to gain greater access to West European markets and even to join the EC confronts the Community with adjustment pressures which necessarily have major effects on the worldwide network of trade and production (Germany's unification already represents a specific enlargement of the EC).

In the new Europe the political East-West division no longer exists, but there is a deep economic divide along the German-Polish border. The economic division within Europe is accentuated by the growth effects of the creation of the single EC market and the dramatic systemic transformation in Eastern Europe. In the beginning of the opening up process Eastern Europe faces a depreciation of its industrial assets plus high transitory adjustment costs and hence a drop in real incomes. The long term growth potential of the East European economies and the USSR have, however, improved with the envisaged switch to market-based systems. Given the attractiveness of the EC market and of a future EC membership institutional reforms in Eastern Europe are likely to aim at EC compatibility.

3.1 Internationalization of Industry: A European Perspective

The globalization of competition is a rather new characteristic of the world economy. Certainly this simplifying view overlooks international technology gaps and the asymmetric structure of global trade with the 2/3 share of the OECD countries. Transatlantic trade is no longer dominating since Japan became a leading exporter in the 1980s. Having become a major trading power Japan entered the international competition stage with heavy foreign direct investment in the 1980s. Japanese activities included setting up transplants in the U.S., the NICs and Western Europe. Since network structures have become so important in industry, failure of local would-be suppliers to meet Japanese quality requirements has often resulted in an acceleration of Japanese FDI. Japanese suppliers of intermediate products followed the big companies abroad which facilitates meeting local content rules; an alternative strategy could be to acquire local suppliers. Japan's rapidly growing investment in U.S. industry - including the banking sector - has contributed to the internationalization of the U.S.[13] However, it also served to support increasing FDI in the U.K. and other EC countries where Japanese investments often attack the turf of U.S. subsidiaries whose parent companies failed to meet the Japanese challenge in North America.

While the perception of a Japanese challenge indirectly encouraged the economic integration process in Western Europe, the response from European industries was long a fragmented one. This fact was reflected in the failure to form "Euronationals". While pursuing outward foreign direct investment in North-America and the Third World, British, German, French and Dutch (as well as Swedish and Swiss) multinationals allocated minor funds in intra-EC investment projects; until the late 1980s, European M&As were mostly within the national framework. Moreover, state owned industries and banks in France, the U.K., Italy, Spain and Germany constituted a restricted European M&A menu. However, the supply-side revival of the 1980s in Europe and a wave of privatization schemes as well as the envisaged formation of a single EC market by 1992 changed this pattern.

The unifying EC markets called for larger firms. Since national M&A options were rapidly exhausted in view of more or less strict competition policies and because Euro-American M&As among leading companies were rarely feasible the formation of Euronationals became a much pursued option. Transatlantic industrial cooperation increasingly took the form of technology joint ventures and joint R&D projects between firms of complementary strength in core technologies (*Table 5*).

As regards the European reaction to EC 1992 firms emphasized both the need of greater cooperation in R&D and of greater use of the firm's resources; in addition to this the aim is to increase the size of production units and to tailor more specialized products which points to the need for product innovations as well as the desire to segregate markets in accordance with greater product varieties (*Welfens, 1990b*).

Table 5: Breakdown of Mergers/Takeovers/Acquisitions and New Joint Ventures of Majority Holdings in the EC
- figures in parantheses are in percent -

| | Mergers/Takeovers/Acquisitions by Type of Operation | | | |
	Domestic Operations	Community Operations	International Operations	Total
1983/84	101 (65.2)	29 (18.7)	25 (16.1)	155 (100)
1984/85	146 (70.2)	44 (21.2)	18 (8.7)	208 (100)
1985/86	145 (63.9)	52 (22.9)	30 (13.2)	227 (100)
1986/87	211 (69.6)	75 (24.8)	17 (5.6)	303 (100)
1987/88	214 (55.9)	112 (29.2)	57 (14.9)	383 (100)
	New Jointly-owned Subsidiaries by Type of Operation			
	Domestic Operations	Community Operations	International Operations	Total
1983/84	32	11	26	69
1984/85	40	15	27	82
1985/86	34	20	27	81
1986/87	29	16	45	90
1987/88	45	31	35	111

Source: EC Commission 1988, 1989. Reports on Competition Policy, Brussels .

There is the risk of a trade-off between free trade and free competition in the sense that the emergence of greater and more diversified "Euronationals" could reinforce the acceptance of free trade, while barriers to entry in Europe and elsewhere become more important.

In the EC the formation of Euronationals is to a large extent in response to the advance of Japanese multinationals - which rarely stand for international equity capital, but have a global market approach - and the increasing role of the NICs (*OECD, 1988*) in international markets. Another motivation to form Euronationals stems from the attempt to improve access to the huge national markets for government procurements and R&D subsidies in the EC. Finally, declining transportation and communication costs as well as improved robotics facilitate the spread of more complex multinational corporate structures that allowed the exploitation of scale economies of centralizing certain functions such as R&D and finance, while emphasizing at the same time decentralization, flexible specialization and intra-company competition in production and distribution.

In view of an ongoing EC integration process and the increasing role of multinationals worldwide, there are new opportunities for Europe's traditional leaders in international investment: the U.K., the Netherlands, Germany and France, where the first three are traditional advocates of free trade (along with Denmark); in the course of a restructuring of the

EC industrial landscape, the relative weight of protectionist and liberal forces might change in major European states. To the extent that trade and FDI go parallel, leading source countries of FDI can be expected to be promoters of both free trade in goods and in assets. Host countries play a role for the EC policy stance, too. Obviously, inward FDI which creates jobs and generates taxes is a factor influencing the acceptance of imported input factors: E.g. Japanese transplants in the EC serve not only the function of safeguarding against losing market shares in the context of potential import barriers; their presence can indeed create new two-way trade.

U.S.-based corporations are still the internationally most influential multinational companies because they not only organize a geographically diversified production but have doubled within three decades the relative financing of affiliates from non-parent sources and have thereby become more influential in international capital markets. U.S. companies' FDI represented in the late 1980s only 31 percent of the value of their affiliates' assets; at the same time - in contrast to Western Europe and Japan with 42.2. and 7.6 percent - the ratio of foreign sales to total sales had decreased to about a quarter in North-America in 1985 (*UNCTC, 1988, pp. 27, 36*). U.S. merchandise trade between U.S. parent companies and majority-owned foreign affiliates was particularly high for the Canadian case, and, to a certain extent in the European case. In contrast to low affiliated merchandise imports from the EC which had a percentage share (as a proportion of the respective U.S. trade) of 9.9 percent in 1985, the share of affiliated exports to Europe increased in the 1980s and reached a share of about 1/3 (*U.S. Department of Commerce, 1988, p. 32*). High affiliated exports to majority-owned affiliates in Europe imply a potentially high role for transfer pricing and some uncertainty with respect to exchange rate impacts on the volume of trade. In Germany, France and the U.K. export shares of foreign-owned manufacturing amounted to 24, 32 and 30 percent in the mid-1980s, whereas the figures for the U.S. and Japan were 23 and 2 percent, respectively; for the latter two import shares were much higher, namely 34 and 15 percent. [14]

Fear of Fortress Europe as well as anticipation of growing markets in Eastern Europe is accelerating U.S. and Japanese investment in the EC. The EC is not only the prime trading partner of the EFTA and the CMEA countries but also the greatest market for U.S. exports whose EC share is nearly 20 percent. With $ 620 bill. affiliates of U.S. multinationals in Europe recorded sales that were eight times the size of U.S. merchandise exports to this region, so that U.S. companies will benefit from rising incomes and growing intra-EC trade. Relatively high income and price elasticities for Europe (compared to Japan, but not in comparison with Canada) suggest that integration-induced increases of per capita incomes in the EC and declining dollar exchange rates will stimulate the American economy in particular (*Hufbauer, 1990; Cline, 1989*). However, a real depreciation of the dollar increases - in dollar terms - the profits from sales of European affiliates, and at the same time makes U.S. exports more profitable, so that the effect on the ratio of affiliated sales to U.S.-based exports is ambiguous unless higher output of subsidiaries goes along with increasing imports of capital goods and intermediate products from the parent company. Moreover, as pointed out by *Welfens (1990a)* and quantified by *Julius (1990)* ownership-based and resident-based trade flow analysis leads to different perceptions of the U.S. trade deficit in the 1980s. For the U.S. foreign sales (27 % of U.S. GNP in 1986) are almost six times as large as exports (5.3% of U.S. GNP in 1986), whereas foreign purchases are nearly three times as large as imports such that the American ownership-based trade balance was slightly positive as opposed to the U.S. trade balance deficit of $ 144 bill. in 1986; for Japan corresponding sales to export figures were 1.7 in 1986. Ownership-based figures indeed give a better measure of competitiveness of U.S., EC or Japanese companies as opposed to the competitiveness of firms operating in the U.S., the EC or Japan.[15]

The distinction between U.S.-based firms and U.S.-owned companies is indeed quite important if one is to assess the competitiveness of a country as compared to its firms. While the U.S. share of manufacturing exports fell considerably in past decades, the global share of U.S. multinational corporations was maintained since affiliates' gains compensated for parent companies' weakening positions (*Lipsey and Kravis, 1986*). Higher U.S. exports and sales could result from EC 1992, the creation of a European Economic Space (EC plus EFTA) and the opening up of Eastern Europe. A priori it is unclear whether U.S.-based firms or U.S. affiliates located in Europe would benefit more from this.

3.2 The Creation of the Single Market

The Community's 1992 program of EC-deepening - removing border controls, opening up public procurement and liberalizing services - will create a single giant market in Western Europe in which national and international companies compete in a more levelled EC playing field. However, the EC and the U.S. (or Japan) could generate a more distorted competition in third country markets, namely in the case that relatively increasing R&D subsidies in the EC and the new political leverage of the EC to obtain concessions abroad place EC firms in a better position than before. However, to the extent that R&D subsidies in combination with concentration effects lead to less static and dynamic efficiency in the EC the 1992 program might actually weaken the EC position. Finally, there is the issue of flexible exchange rates that raises problems of price rigidities in the sense that no full exchange rate pass-through in international trade can be expected. Indeed flexible rates can even generate conflicts over dumping when a firm that used to have a small profit margin abroad decides to respond to a currency depreciation in the export country with unchanged sales prices (in the foreign market) that could thereby fall under the price in the home market and the production costs incurred.

Technological progress that improves global communication and reduces transaction costs as well as national deregulation have increased exchange rate movements whose variance has become a distinct influence in international capital movements which are thus no longer mainly determined by different regional marginal products of real capital. Links between FDI and investment flows then imply a distortion of trade flows, too. With the rising share of services in national output of OECD countries and limited tradability of services, the role of FDI has increased in the service industry that is strongly influenced by government regulations or even shaped by public providers. Since modern service industries primarily provid services to the manufacturing sector distortions in the service industry indirectly affect trade in goods.

EC 1992 Principles

The EC 1992 principle of mutual recognition of technical standards and financial regulations brings a new element for international trade regimes. Particular problems in the field of the service industry and of FDI concern the application of the national treatment principle (treating foreign firms like domestic ones) which the EC has tried to link to the principle of reciprocity. In a transatlantic perspective the first principle in not very conflict-prone, except for the EC request to focus on procurement and investment policies of U.S. states in a similar way as the U.S. does with respect to national treatment in each EC country. Reciprocity is more conflict-prone since it raises the problem of different national regulations. Reciprocity could mean that e.g. all-finance banking common in Germany and other EC countries would be granted to EC banks in the U.S. because U.S. subsidiaries operating in the EC are not facing regulatory restraints that seperate commercial and investment banking in the U.S. Were EC banks' subsidiaries in the U.S. free to act without the restrictions faced by U.S. banks the American financial market would be characterized in effect by different regulations for foreign and domestic banks. Reciprocity considerations have indeed been used by EC banks and the EC to press for a deregulation of U.S. financial markets.

3.2.1 Dynamic Aspects of EC 1992

EC 1992 with the prospects of sharper competition in an enlarged "EC home market" offering considerable economies of scale means that all EC countries become potential locations for firms eager to serve the whole EC market and to generate or strengthen firm-specific advantages to be exploited by international direct investment in a global competition process. Moreover, the removal of capital controls and the envisaged hardening of the European

Monetary System will contribute not only to intensified competition in financial services but to intensified competition in the firms' financial sourcing and to increased pressure for adjusting corporate structures along new transnational lines. With higher European growth significant impulses for higher global trade could result as the traditionally strongly overproportional rise of world trade relative to world output suggests.

New transatlantic trade conflicts and conflicts between the G-7 countries could arise for various reasons. The EC and the U.S. trade deficits vis-à-vis Japan are of particular importance; the EC deficit might increase in the context of higher shipments from Japanese affiliates in the U.S. (e.g. Hondas from the U.S. that qualify as U.S. products). Major conflicts in U.S.-EC trade relations of the past decades concerned the sectors agriculture and fisheries and policy measures such as nontariff barriers and subsidies (*Hudec, 1988*). However, conflicts in high technology fields are likely to become more important in the future. The U.S. lead in high technology is no longer uncontested, where both EC countries and Japan have reduced the former technological gap. Japanese companies heavily rely on "technological sourcing" abroad - in particular in the EC and in the U.S.

With the rising role of EC R&D programs and the growing significance of innovation policy for international competitiveness in high technology, new conflicts in leading manufacturing industries are to be expected. Whenever national or supranational government provides public funding for creating firm specific advantages or supports those by discriminatory public procurement, not only future export opportunities but also prospects for foreign direct investment will be affected.

Recent developments in trade theory which emphasize the role of technology, scale economies and learning curve effects more than the traditional factor endowments - the strategic trade theory (*Brander and Spencer, 1983; Krugman, 1987; Baldwin, 1988*) - render the enlargement and unification of the European market in the context of the EC 1992 program particularly important. With major European firms acting in global markets, a single EC market is considered as a powerful home ground for exploiting economies of scale; and generous R&D expenditures allocated along with other subsidies by national and supranational governments offer new opportunities for EC competitors: namely, (i) to generate firm specific advantages, (ii) to shape comparative advantages, (iii) to lobby more effectively for interventionist export promotion vis-à-vis the U.S., Japan and Eastern Europe, (iv) to appropriate economic rents in the world market and (v) to adopt strategic pricing - in a first production stage below the going marginal costs - in foreign markets in which anticipated movements down the learning curve (as the accumulated output has increased) allow one to block market entry and raise long term market shares.[16]

EC 1992 and Imperfect Competition

With imperfect international competition standard models suggest that firms charge prices above marginal costs k', that is the relative price mark-up p-k'/p= 1/ß (ß is the elasticity of demand perceived by the individual firm). In a two-country model with firms n and n* in the domestic economy and a second country, market integration increases the individually perceived elasticities, even if the market elasticity E remains the same. With a higher number of competitors n + n* in the greater market firms' perceived ß increases and smaller mark-ups will result (*Smith and Venables, 1988*). Suppliers of intermediate goods that are induced to sell to EC producers at lower prices will contribute in some export fields to a better EC trade position, but exporting to foreign firms at lower prices will not necessarily generate higher export volumes.

The EC 1992 project suggests smaller mark-ups in the EC in the medium term, namely as long as induced cross-border M&A and national concentration tendencies do not dominate the competition increasing effects of the single market program. In the short and medium term a higher price responsiveness of market competition is to be expected in the EC which provides incentives for EC-based firms to cut costs and to increase intermediate input imports from countries with depreciating currencies. The dollar depreciation in the second half of the 1980s has already brought about significantly higher U.S. exports to Europe and slower growing EC exports to the U.S.

Exchange Rate Pass-Through

U.S. subsidiaries in the EC and their American parent companies - with considerable intra-firm trade and established information links - have developed some experience in effectively taking advantage of the dollar exchange rate flexibility which in fact is often determined by asset market/capital flows rather than by flows of goods and services. The proportionate change dp/p in reaction to a relative change of the nominal exchange rate e is unity only if the elasticity of foreign supply α^* (* for foreign variables) is infinity which can be seen from equation I (*Venables, 1990*):

(I) (dp/p)/de/e = $\alpha^* \sigma [\beta + \alpha^*(1-\sigma) + \alpha^*\sigma]$; σ= share of imports in the market

In a world of imperfect competition firms will charge different mark-ups in different countries; that is markets are segmented and exporters, aiming to maintain desired market shares s* abroad, are free to reduce the mark-up over marginal costs k' when the importing country's currency is devalued. With n domestic firms and n* foreign firms - all identical to each other, but different from the domestic firms - a simple Cournot oligopoly model results for the domestic firms in the profit-maximizing condition p = k'/(1-s/ß) and for the foreign firms in p(1-s*/ß) = ek'*.[17] For the case of constant k' the exchange rate pass-through is given by:

$$(I') \quad (dp/p)/de/e = \frac{1}{1 + n/n*}$$

This implies that markets with a dominant role of foreign supply (n* is high relative to n) will have an exchange rate pass-through close to unity. Most EC markets are characterized by a strong position of domestic producers.

The otherwise robust model above is doubtful if one introduces multinational subsidiaries producing both for the parent company and the host country market (here: domestic market). Profit transfers to the parent company fall in terms of the parent company currency when the currency of the host country depreciates. Transnationality affects international trade in the sense that foreign ownership or a mixed international ownership of industrial property rights changes the optimal regional structure of trade flows and, a fortiori, investment flows in the case of a growing world economy.

High sunk costs of FDI engagements - as opposed to recurrent fixed costs - make it rational for the firm not to reduce production and sales abroad (to raise prices in proportion with the devaluation rate) when exchange rates change in a way that profits are falling. This holds also if current price levels contain a bonus from acquired reputation abroad. Indeed, the increasing role of FDI worldwide - sometimes growing parallel to rising trade flows - affects the working of exchange rate regimes and trade regimes.

As regards innovativeness and dynamic efficiency in the EC an important question is to which extent there is a trade off between static and dynamic efficiency. If economies from mass production reduce the number of viable EC suppliers, tighter oligopolies in the EC could imply a loss of European innovativeness and impaired prospects for generating technology-based firm specific advantages. The view of some economists, such as *Porter (1989)* and, focussing on pharmaceuticals, *Thomas (1990)*, is that tough domestic environments are necessary to generate the pressure which makes diamonds. From this perspective any tendency of the EC Commission to adopt a French-style industrial policy, that is to promote EC champions as a strategy to maintain competitiveness for the global market, would be ill-suited.

3.2.2 Dumping Issues

The EC is - similar to the U.S. in some fields - an outspoken advocate of antidumping measures that are mostly directed against Japan and some NICs. The theoretical issue of dumping (*Ethier, 1982; Tarr, 1982; Takacs, 1982; Vermults, 1987; Gruenspecht, 1988*) has become a widely debated political issue in the 1980s. *Yamawaki (1989)* provides empirical evidence for the Japanese industry, which is quite successful in segregating markets, that demand fluctuations lead mainly to price responses in world markets; prices in home markets are kept stable as cyclical demand changes occur. There is little doubt that the associated cyclical dumping is relevant for U.S. and EC firms, too.

The role of antidumping actions in the EC has increased in the early 1980s, when the average ad valorem equivalent of the antidumping measures taken by the EC Commission against all countries is about 23 percent - high relative to the 7 percent EC post-Tokyo most-favored nation tariff in manufacturing or 4.2. percent in chemicals (*Messerlin, 1989*). The trade diversion effect of the antidumping approach becomes even more obvious when one takes into account that antidumping actions facilitate collusion and cartelization in the EC against which fines are miniscule. About one in four antidumping cases is coupled with anticompetition procedures under Article 85/86 of the Treaty of Rome. Dumping of EC-owned foreign firms is, however, hardly ever compensated by antidumping actions (usually on the ground that specialty products dumped do not inflict losses upon competitors in the EC) which clearly shows "ownership matters". A U.S.-based company owned by e.g. a German multinational therefore faces smaller export risks in Europe than an American firm. From a triangular capital-FDI-export (Japan-U.S.-EC) perspective, there is another aspect. From a strategic point of view one may assume that Japanese transplants in the U.S. whose products qualify as made in the U.S. enjoy a free rider position - that is, they benefit from U.S. free trade policy - namely in the sense that products exported from U.S. transplants to the EC are less likely to face antidumping measures than products made in Japan.

Distorting policy actions with considerable side effects upon trade and competition occur not only in labor-intensive fields (e.g. textiles) but in high-technology capital-intensive areas as well. As in the case of the U.S. antidumping strategy in the chip industry, international cartelization that reduces uncertainties about the distribution of market shares, profits and rents is often supported by voluntary export restraints that are not covered by the GATT framework but are employed as an effective substitute for antidumping measures. Governments in OECD countries are particularly eager to maintain strategic activities in their countries, namely R&D, financing and high-value added production lines.[18] Big countries with a relatively diversified economic structure can expect that trade effects during product cycles are neutral on average.

In 1990 GATT ruled against EC antidumping duties imposed on Japanese products assembled in the EC - in particular the EC could not impose duties if the products did not meet certain local content requirements. Consistency with GATT rules requires the EC to prove that EC producers have been harmed by dumping which is particularly difficult if import market shares fall, say because of an increasing market share of transplants. The transplants themselves could become a target of EC trade policy as they have already become in the case of switching from national quotas to EC-wide quotas in a post-1992 environment. Transplants might use intermediate products from Japanese firms in Asia (or in the future: in Eastern Europe) to which EC antidumping procedures could be applied.

In a world with many countries/production sites the question of policy consistency arises in the field of antidumping. Should there be a cross-dumping clause in the GATT framework (similar to cross-default clauses in international lending)? That is, if the EC rules that Japanese firms are dumping products from Japan on the EC markets, should the U.S. and other countries be automatically expected to open an antidumping case for the same Japanese products (or even automatically impose antidumping duties?).

In high technology fields highly spezialized products are typical, and these fields are hence not subject to effective antidumping controls. The relevance of international capital markets and foreign direct investment for trade flows has thus gained a new dimension. In a market as big as the EC the relevance of selective treatment of dumping is important because firms fully or partly owned by EC private or corporate citizens would enjoy indirect support against their competitors. Selective public procurement, antidumping measures as well as export promoting R&D subsidies are elements of the present EC policy whose trade-diverting impacts are likely to be tolerated by major partners as long as high income growth in Europe generates considerably higher import demand.

Imperfections of the markets for technological and organizational know-how are particularly conducive for FDI which is the basis for a full appropriation of economic rents from innovations. The globally increasing technology content of production is a structural element for the growth of FDI, while increasing markets by regional integration schemes could reduce FDI because firm-internal organization costs increase relative to the alternative to combine resources in the market process. One may expect a transitory period of higher intra-EC FDI which reflects the creation of a new European industrial landscape consistent with EC 1992 and the desire to segregate markets along income groups rather than across countries and currencies as done so far. In the long run greater FDI of EC-based companies in extra-EC countries can be expected, especially because EC firms that will increasingly consider the whole EC as a domestic market will tend to exploit accumulated firm specific advantages outside Europe. Relatively increasing market imperfections outside the EC imply relatively increasing FDI in the U.S., Japan, Eastern Europe and the Third World in the long term, if one follows the various internalization approaches of FDI (*Buckley and Casson, 1976; Dunning, 1979*).

3.2.3 EC Technology and Competition Policy

Increasing U.S. and Japanese investments in Western Europe could strengthen the desire of European-based firms to increase FDI within a counterattack mounted in oligopolistic global industries. The creation of the greatest regional market - with 345 mill. people - in the world brings new opportunities to set technological standards worldwide which is an important element of competition in global industries. It might also invite the pursuit of strategic trade policies based on increasingly exploited static and dynamic economies of scale that allow aggressive pricing in the stage of market entry abroad. The expectation of higher outward FDI as the result of a European counterattack - especially in a period of a dollar depreciation - would be consistent with the perception of investment rivalry in oligopolistic international markets (*Knickerbocker, 1973; Graham, 1978*). Opportunities for a counterattack may, however, be restricted for various reasons. Cultural traits, such as lifetime employment which makes hiring of qualified personell delicate in the case of greenfield investments, closed equity markets and relatively high capitalization ratios impair FDI in Japan (*Okimoto, 1987*). In Europe public ownership and government interference have long restricted inward FDI. While e.g. French multinationals - state-owned or private - have undertaken massive international investments in recent years, the French economy has been restricted for inward FDI; not least because the French government pursued an ambitious industrial policy that emphasized French competitiveness in high-technology.

Technology policies affect trade as well as asset prices in many ways. The EC's supranational programs have grown in volume, less so in the degree of success as problems in the EC computer and electronics industry have shown. Since the mid-1980s not only have EC R&D programs reinforced national R&D progams in Western Europe, but competition policy has been adjusted to facilitate joint R&D ventures of EC firms that face sharp U.S. and Japanese competition.

Block exemptions from the prohibition of collusion have become widespread in the 1980s in OECD countries. In the EC under Article 85 para. 3) group exemptions are granted which allow a group of firms not only to cooperate in R&D (in the pre-competitive stage), but also to jointly exploit the results of the R&D joint venture which may seem an acceptable pragmatic policy compromise among EC member states (*Jacquemin, 1988*). The current EC joint venture rule, adopted in 1985, gives a five year exemption; however, in the case of horizontal joint ventures - as opposed to conglomeral or vertical types - this exemption will only be given if the parties' combined market share does not exceed 20%. Similar to the case of the U.S. reform of 1985 the EC now allows cooperative R&D joint ventures, for which both the U.S. and the EC seem to be inspired by the Japanese example. However, while it is hardly debatable that in the pre-competitive R&D stage joint firm activities pose no serious problem for competition, the joint exploitation now possible under EC law represents a particular problem. It seems that important reasons for Japan's cooperative joint venture system are not well recognized in some Western political circles: namely, that the diffusion and inter-industry sharing of innovations would otherwise be extremely difficult in a system with seniority wages and life-time employment for many employees and hence a low inter-firm labor turnover rate in big industry. If the European labor market becomes more bureaucratized so that inter-firm knowledge exchange via a turn-over of skilled personell is difficult to achieve, only then does the enlarged EC block exemption seem to be appropriate.

The Japanese industry's strong position in the international diffusion of innovations could erode if U.S. firms' R&D projects become less oriented towards safe Pentagon subsidies but to the opportunities of earning uncertain economic rents in the world economy. Contradictions between the U.S. lead in high technology and the American trade performance have become obvious, where measures to increase the rate of diffusion offer prospects to better translate technological leadership into a strong international trading position (*Lawrence, 1990*). Moreover, in an integrated world economy the apparent hesitancy of the U.S. to import technologies points to pitfalls in the sourcing of foreign innovations. Efficient foreign sourcing can - as the Japanese example suggests - contribute to firm specific advantages and strengthen firms' competitive position in home, foreign and third-country markets. To adopt innovations abroad and to organize its diffusion within the whole network of a multinational firm is a major task which involves not only the use of advanced communication technologies but also the ability to adopt and appropriately modify "external" technologies to local organizational or cultural settings.

The EC's policy stance is most liberal and market-oriented in the field of the service industry. Removing intra-EC trade barriers and effectively eliminating impediments to factor mobility will strongly stimulate the competition in the service industry. However, when there is a close link with high-tech industries - as in the case of telecom and computers - then the EC's policy stance leads to distorted international competition because of high and increasing state R&D funding. R&D subsidies are granted both by regional and national governments as well as by the EC. The aim to restrict the benefits of tax-funded R&D subsidies to firms located within the Community implies that foreign (mostly U.S., Canadian and Japanese) firms of the respective industry have to resort to foreign FDI in Europe, if participation in e.g. advanced chip research programs is to be ensured (the U.S. Sematech program offers a similar problem).

The mix of national and supranational competition policy in the EC is a particular transition problem of institutional integration associated with market integration. Diverging national competition policy concepts have to be harmonized over time, and a consistent supranational merger policy will have to be developed. The egocentric view of national policy bodies and vested interests of bureaucracy render the internationalization of competition policy rather difficult. But nice compensation schemes for bureaucrats in excess supply might help to quickly cope with this problem.

A major danger for preserving strict competition and liberal trade rules stems from the fact that with the creation of a single EC market and - in some distant future - the introduction of au common currency, on the average more than half of each member country's external trade becomes intra-EC trade. This part of formerly GATT monitored trade will then be subject primarily to intra-EC competition laws, where at least some of the firms involved might speculate to benefit in recessions from increased EC state interference (e.g. regional policy schemes). Preserving allocation efficiency in the EC clearly requires that both internal and external transactions are subject to a consistent competition framework that allows new entrants, including those from the NICs or the CMEA, an unbiased competition process.

3.3 The Collapse of the East-West Antagonism in Europe

Japan's and some Asian NIC's rapid postwar economic development within the context of an export-oriented strategy finds its counter-model in the socialist CMEA countries with their gradual stagnation, autarkic trade orientation and absence of FDI.[19] Economic stagnation faced by the former CMEA countries for more than a decade can in principle be overcome by thorough internal changes - including institutional adjustments and innovations - and external reforms. The former CPEs are known for a low integration into the international division of labor, weak innovation and imitation dynamics as well as inefficient, albeit high, investments. Moreover, closed minds - rather than internationally-oriented business and policy strategies - were characteristic of the CMEA, where governments as well as private and corporate citizens therefore face tremendous adjustment problems. The system-specific weak innovativeness of socialist countries often entailed that firms from the technologically catching-up NICs crowded out suppliers from CMEA countries (*Poznanski, 1987; Welfens and Balcerowicz, 1988; Inotai 1988*).

Opening up Eastern Europe and achieving successful systemic transformation therefore requires a dramatic change of attitudes and policies towards foreign direct investment in the former CMEA countries which were characterized for many decades by currency inconvertibility, state-administered trade, capital controls and strong restrictions on private and especially foreign ownership.

While economic integration is being completed in Western Europe, institutional disintegration is observed in the CMEA country group in which Poland, Hungary and Czechoslovakia have embarked upon comprehensive market-oriented reform programs. Countries in Eastern Europe are now looking for closer ties with the EC. For U.S., Japanese and European firms operating in the EC this does not only imply new gains from increased West-East trade, but also the risk of getting more involved in the uncertainties of a complicated systemic transformation in Eastern Europe which has relied for decades on monopolistic economic structures coupled with insignificant international trade and the absence of multinational companies. In addition to this one may notice that the lack of outside FDI implies that (legal) international sourcing of technologies and the organization of production abroad have yet to be learned in Eastern Europe.

At the beginning of the 1990s the countries in Eastern Europe and the USSR are characterized by systemic market-oriented reforms and opening up strategies that are heavily oriented towards restoring historical economic ties in Europe. As a side effect of declining European ideological and military confrontation and because of the collapse of the socialist economic model in the CMEA countries, changes in the Third World are occuring. Developing economies whose systemic and policy orientation were - often motivated by anti-colonial sentiments vis-à-vis Western European countries - following socialist strategies are increasingly ready to embark upon market-oriented reforms and to reinforce economic ties with the Old World. Less dynamic LDCs are following an outward oriented liberalization strategy that was successfully adopted by the NICs. Successful strategies of Eastern Europe to cope with the problem of how to adjust the internal monopolistic structures of the economy in a stage of external liberalization will influence the internal adjustment process in LDCs for which the markets in the EC and its external trade policy are of prime importance.

Since per capita trade in the CMEA countries amounts to roughly 1/5 of OECD figures, the potential for greater trade is considerable in Europe. Trade creation will result from the demise of the East-West antagonism in Europe. This is true not only because Cocom rules have already been softened, but also because of a declining role of military expenditures and military R&D funds which traditionally are allocated within a national government-business relationship. Reducing ideological and military tensions can be expected in the developing countries, too, where former European colonies have turned towards marketization and liberalization, often inspired by the dynamic EC integration process.[20]

The countries of Eastern Europe and the Soviet Union which face self-imposed systemic transformation and reforms are to be integrated into the "world market economy". Entrepreneurial spirit, world market experience, modern technologies and management approaches as well as market consistent trade policies are at a premium in these countries. Investment and trade impulses from the OECD countries and from the NICs are needed for a rapid successful transformation.

Formerly command economy countries, not used to private property and internal competition, will face the challenge of not only accepting private property in industry but also foreign ownership of firms. Inward FDI of significant size requires in turn a free transfer of profits and currency convertibility so that the need to internationalize and modernize production generates its own reform impulses. With the shift from monopolistic economic structures to a market-oriented economy, growing intra-industry trade - so far an exception in the CMEA countries - will emerge and contribute to competition in a changing world economy. Economic structures in the OECD countries will also have to adjust to a new pattern if the external environment of Eastern Europe is not to impede the economic reform process in Eastern Europe and in the developing countries. Finally, all countries have to adjust to the evolving international division of technology. The technology factor in international production and hence the role of innovativeness and "Schumpeterian goods" is increasing, where policy shifts in the U.S. and Europe are most needed.

Major changes in Eastern Europe will be required if foreign technologies are to be used more efficiently. To accept inward FDI and to put less emphasis on joint ventures which typically represent both a low amount of paid-up capital and a lagged access to new technologies is necessary not only for raising incomes but for increasing international competitiveness as well. Western Europe is likely to support politically the stabilization and opening up process in Eastern Europe. From an economic perspective this makes sense because the EC has much to gain from prosperity and stability in Eastern Europe. Moreover, the EC 1992 program will increase intra-EC factor mobility and raise unit labor costs in the medium term and encourage FDI in labor intensive production in Eastern Europe.

The dramatic developments in the USSR which started under Gorbachev require radical politico-economic reforms as well as adjustments in the trade regime (*Wolf, 1988; Welfens, 1991c*). The smaller member countries of the disbanding CMEA have already envisaged or realized a strategy of systemic transformation which is based upon trade liberalization and price reforms, privatization of industry - including acceptance of inward FDI - and macroeconomic adjustments that aim at achieving currency convertibility and tariff reforms.[21]

4. Free Trade in a Unifying World?

With so many economies in Eastern Europe (and the Third World) opening up, the road to a unifying world market economy seems to be more accessible than ever. If the economic division of Europe could be overcome Eastern Europe's share in world trade which reduced in the period 1963-1986 by 1.3 percentage points to 10.8 % and reached only about 1/3 of the EC-10 share (*see Table 6*) could rise in the 1990s.

Table 6: Share in World Merchandise Exports, 1963-86 (figures are in percent)

	1963	1973	1981	1986
Developed countries	67.6	70.8	63.0	69.6
EFTA (1)	–	–	–	1.0
EC/EFTA(2)	–	–	–	7.7
EC***	33.7	36.7	30.9	34.5
Intra-EC (3)	15.2	19.8	15.8	19.7
Germany	10.3	12.5	9.4	12.2
Japan	3.5	6.4	7.8	9.9
U.S.	15.7	12.0	11.5	9.7
U.S./Canada** (4)	–	–	–	5.6
U.S./Mexico (5)	–	–	–	2.8
Other developed countries	14.6	15.8	12.8	15.6
Developing countries	20.3	19.2	27.6	19.5
Four ANICs	1.5	2.3	4.9	6.3
Other developing countries	18.8	16.4	23.4	13.3
Eastern trading area	12.1	10.0	9.4	10.8
Intra-area trade*(1+2+3+4+5)	–	–	–	40.1

Note: 4 ANICs = Asian newly industrializing countries: Hong Kong, Singapore, Taiwan and Republic of Korea. Eastern trading area percentage shares are probably overstated if world-market prices are applied which fell outside the CMEA area for many goods - except oil - traded among CMEA countries.
* includes Australia/New Zealand free trade in the context of the South Pacific Regional Trade and Economic Agreement (Sprectra) and defines the EC to be comprised of Spain and Portugal as well;
** The U.S. and Canada concluded a sectorial free trade agreement in 1965 which was generalized to a U.S.-Canadian free trade agreement in 1990;
*** not including Spain and Portugal.
Source: All data are from IMF (1988), Issues and Developments in International Trade Policy, Washington, Table A1 and Table A5.

There is the problem that rising East-West trade in Europe could reforce the tendency to create regional trading blocs that could impair global liberalization. Intra-EC, hypothetical Intra-NAFTA (US-Canada-Mexico) and EC/EFTA trade accounted for 20, 8 and 9 % of world exports, respectively. EC/EFTA free trade in industrial products was progressively established in the period 1972-84. As a transitory liberalization strategy intra-regional free trade could be conducive to global liberalization in the long term. The example of EC/EFTA free trade in industrial goods shows that a considerable trading volume can be kept free from protectionism in a pragmatic intra-European liberalization approach of different blocs.

The U.S. has been the leading advocate for free trade and free capital movements for many years; however, this position has eroded in the 1980s because of sustaining U.S. balance of payments problems that have led to a $ 1500 bill. U.S. foreign debt which therefore becomes more sensitive to foreign interest rate changes and because of reactions in the political arena that respond to new protectionist policies of other international actors.

4.1 GATT Negotiations

The question arises how to organize the free flow of goods, capital and technology in a world in which the stakes and roles in trade, investment and innovation are so asymmetric and in which the competition process is globalizing at the same time. For an efficient global allocation process it is indeed not appropriate to seek liberalization only for trade in goods and services. To date the GATT framework has provided a successful, albeit limited approach to establish and maintain an open multilateral trade network.

Interventionist policy orientations in Europe in combination with a more powerful and politically more influential EC industry constitute a new potential source for international trade conflicts - especially because U.S. dominance is no longer the accepted basis for the global trade regime. There is an increasing role of "club governance" as represented by G-7 meetings, OECD agreements, the GATT rounds and IMF activities. Finally, with the creation of the new European Bank for Reconstruction and Development there is a new supranational institution that aims to help overcome the economic divide of Europe.

A global free trade regime is utopian for the moment, but a reasonable guiding principle, despite the fact that existing distortions and external effects in many countries let free trade appear not to be an optimal solution at any point in time. With ongoing privatization in former CPEs and developing countries as well as in OECD countries the chances for more free trade have improved. In all major regions of the world the production of goods and services would predominantly be based on private enterprise, competition in interdependent markets and multilateral trade among economies which are open for multilateral trade in goods, investment and technologies. Free international exchange of goods, unrestricted investment flows and free trade in technologies might be envisaged as a feasible avenue for an increasingly prosperous world economy whose rules are mainly set by the GATT, the IMF and influential trading blocs.

From an optimistic point of view the international economic system seems to return to the liberal market system of the period after 1860 which witnessed a period of growing prosperity and increasing trade in the heyday of economic liberalism - as reflected in bilateral trade treaties, unilateral tariff reductions and, in some cases such as Switzerland and the Netherlands, the (transitory) abolishment of patent protection laws (*Dutton, 1984*). In the post-World War II period, leading innovators such as the U.S. and the EC seek a strengthening of intellectual property rights worldwide which is only reluctantly accepted by many developing countries. As became evident in the Uruguay GATT round concessions in the field of intellectual property rights and the removal of capital controls which so far restrict foreign competition in the service industry (and nontradable goods) can be expected from the South only if the North reduces agricultural protectionism and removes non-tariff barriers.

International trade liberalization is no longer based on bilateral trade agreements, but on multilateral regimes (GATT, WIPO) and regional trading blocks (EC, EFTA, CMEA, ASEAN, North American FTA); although the U.S. still has a decisive international impact that is comparable to the former British leadership, the world economy is shaped less by dominance than by "club governance" in a multipolar world (with Japan having a strong role), e.g. in the form of the G-7 meetings, the Group of Ten, the OECD or more informal groups such as the Cairns Group of major agricultural exporters formed in 1986. The present international economic system has been shaped by international organizations - institutionalized political clubs - which evolved after 1944. The existence of international organizations is in clear contrast to the institutional laissez faire approach of earlier economic liberalism.

Uruguay GATT round
There are four major ambitions of the Uruguay GATT round:
(i) to include trade in services in the GATT framework. Trade in services which so far accounts for only 20 percent of total global trade is low in view of the service industries' share of more than 50 percent in value-added in the OECD. This points to an insufficient international division of labor in the service industry, and the present attempts to include services in a GATT-type framework are therefore most important;

(ii) to improve the protection of trade-related intellectual property rights in a world economy in which technological know-how and innovations have become most important in the context of shortening product cycles and diversified preferences of consumers with their demand for product differentiation and innovations; high R&D costs can be recovered internationally only with low appropriation risks, that is with sufficient protection of intellectual property rights;

(iii) to reduce distorting trade-related investment measures, i.e. to promote the liberalization of international direct investment and hence to support the spread of multinational companies which account in the form of intra-company trade not only for about 30 percent of world trade but are also major sources and transmitters of technological progress. Although the mobility of service providers and users has risen because of technological progress and reduced transportation costs, the need to serve customers locally still implies that static and dynamic efficiency in the service industry can be obtained at an international level only if foreign direct investment in this industry is not restricted.

(iv) to limit the increased role of non-tariff barriers, such as technical standards, antidumping duties, local content rules, discriminatory rules of origin and voluntary export restraints (VERs) which have not been addressed within the GATT framework so far.

These topics constitute issues within a North-South context, but even more so create major conflicts among the leading industrial countries - U.S., Japan and the EC. The EC 1992 program is not only significant as an intra-EC trade liberalization attempt but is potentially associated with an increasing role of NTBs. Add to this aspect the fact that EC antidumping policies have resulted in so-called price undertakings in 3/4 of all 202 undertakings in the period 1980-88 (*Stegemann, 1990*): 60 antidumping cases ended with the imposition of countervailing duties on accused exporters, but in 202 cases exporters pledged to raise prices for sales to the EC in order to avoid material injury to EC producers of like goods. Besides fixing quantities in VERs and by quotas, the EC is heavily engaged in international "price management" that increases external producers' rents and bolsters their ability to divert part of their export potential to other regions. Trade diversion and trade creation effects caused by European developments will affect all regions of the world economy because the competition process is global.

Conflicting Positions of Major Countries

In the context of EC 1992 and the reforms in Eastern Europe Germany's geographical position at the dividing line between Western and Eastern Europe reinforces its role as a "silent and accepted trade giant". While recording a higher trade balance surplus relative to GNP than Japan, German trade never did become the subject of serious international disputes because the dominance of capital goods in German exports (50%) makes these goods valuable elements for reinforcing competitiveness in the importing countries. This holds even despite the fact that

West German trade surpluses reached with 4.5 percent of GNP nearly double the Japanese figure. In contrast to Japan with its highly visible exports of consumer goods, Germany's main export goods are rarely perceived by the public of importing countries, and they are often considered as vital inputs for maintaining jobs and incomes in the global competition process. Germany and Japan differ in their interest vis-à-vis the USSR and China. At the same time they share the risk that their traditional emphasis on and lead in civilian R&D will be matched by the U.S. in the 1990s provided that the East-West military confrontation is reduced permanently.

With the collapse of the East-West antagonism and the demise of socialism (except for China) the system design of developing countries is shifting towards economic and often political pluralism as well; the legacy of the international debt crisis of the early 1980s pressed - often in the context of IMF programs - many developing countries to promote exports, to liberalize imports in order to spur efficiency and growth, to privatize state-owned industries (often in connection with debt equity swaps) and to imitate outward-oriented development strategies of the NICs. Hence, the market economy model is spreading in two directions: to the South on the one hand, and, on the other hand, towards Eastern Europe. To support the reforms in the latter region the U.S., Japan and the EC countries (as well as other European countries) launched several aid programs and set up a new institution, the European Bank for Reconstruction and Development whose intellectual birthplace was the Paris G-7 1989 summit.

West European Aspects

Vis-à-vis Japan EC member countries adopted both VERs and - on the EC level - antidumping measures mainly directed against Japanese companies and firms from the Republic of Korea and Taiwan. The EC and Japan face common U.S. criticism in the case of agricultural trade which is not covered by the GATT and has witnessed a rise of protection rates of up to 40 percent while tariff rates for manufacturing goods came down to about 5 percent.

The service industry represents an area which is difficult to liberalize for various reasons. The principle of national treatment, namely that foreign companies should be treated equal to domestic companies, is guiding the U.S. approach, but reciprocity in some form is emphasized by EC countries which e.g. face the asymmetry of U.S. banks operating in all areas of financial business in Western Europe, while U.S. subsidiaries of EC banks have to narrow their fields of activities to the stipulations of the U.S. system with its division of commercial and investment banks. Adopting reciprocity obviously requires adjustments of the political system design, but to use this principle as an external leverage for political changes implies the risk of triggering both internal and external political conflicts. Generally, liberalizing services plays a decisive role because of the structural growth of this sector, the increasing tradability of the products offered and the importance of business-related services that are vital for manufacturing industry's competitiveness.

Transatlantic Conflicts

The Uruguay GATT round is focussing on agricultural trade, industrial property rights, the problem of temporary protection measures in the context of article XIX (VERs, OMAs etc.) and the insufficiency of the Code on Technical Barriers to Trade which is critical in view of its irrelevance for the private sectors' standard setting bodies in the OECD countries. In all problem areas the EC plays a core role, and its weight has increased because of anticipated closer links between the EC and Eastern Europe on the one hand, and, on the other hand, the envisaged European Economic Space to be formed with the EFTA countries. Due to the internationalization of industry and the bargaining trade-offs between North and South the European position is of particular significance. The agricultural exporters of the South and of Eastern Europe will accept liberalization of services and support tighter intellectual property rights demanded by the U.S. and the EC only if agricultural trade and trade in textiles - covered by the MFA - is liberalized; pending legislation proposals in the U.S. Congress which mean protectionism in favor of the domestic textile industry endanger the achievement of consensus in the Uruguay round. Moreover, for the first time Canadian-based industry would directly enjoy benefits of protectionist U.S. legislation, and this is all the more evident because before adopting the Free Trade Agreement Canadian import tariffs for shoes and textiles, respectively, amounted to 21.5 and 23.5 percent. Political action committees of Canadian subsidiaries in the U.S. might reinforce the protectionist lobby of U.S. firms producing textiles, clothes and shoes, and Canadian foreign direct investment in the U.S. could actually be influenced by the desire to buy into the political lobbying process of the U.S. A more protectionist policy stance of the U.S. would in turn encourage protectionist measures in Europe, where the main losers would be consumers in the North and producers in the South. This would not be the first case that the formation of a regional trading bloc is likely to have negative global repercussion effects. The Common Agricultural Policy (CAP) of the EC is another example. EC procurement rules, EC rules of origin (inducing U.S. firms' "forced investment" in EC chip production), and technical standardization create transatlantic conflicts. As regards services the U.S. and major EC countries have many common interests because the U.S., France, the U.K. and Germany are all leading traders of services, and their respective industrial competitiveness is relatively unaffected by a liberalization of services and their inclusion into a proposed GATT twin-organization General Agreement on Trade in Services (GATS); the conflict over trade in services is primarily a North-South problem on the one hand, and, on the other hand, it leads into the issue of the proper role of the state, namely to the extent that in many EC countries governments regulate the service industry and provide services that could be provided equally well or better by private industry. The US business community is concerned about state-owned or state subsidized EC service providers that could acquire U.S. firms which receive no government support. The EC's principle of liberalizing the service industry along the lines of "mutual recognition" and home country control in banking and insurance supports institutional competition in the EC and could help not only to create an efficient EC services industry but a more competitive EC manufacturing industry - relying on modern business services - too. The mechanism for the international diffusion of institutional frameworks that are conducive to static and dynamic efficiency in services could be the global competition faced by firms from manufacturing industry of all major economies.

Eastern Europe

The G-7 summit of Houston in 1990 did not bring coordinated action in favor of the reforms in the USSR and the smaller Eastern European countries, but de facto consensus that (unified) Germany could support the Soviet Union bilaterally and that Japan could resume credit financing for China. The pledge of the EC and major EC countries, respectively, to reduce agricultural subsidies were important as well, albeit not very credible. While support for the potential agricultural exporters USSR, Poland and Hungary was clearly not the intention of the U.S. emphasis on agricultural trade liberalization - domestic farm interests and the Western Hemisphere's export prospects were main motives - the really important effect of the U.S. initiative could lie exactly in the opening up of markets for Eastern Europe, where a modernization of agriculture (with 15-20 percent of the labor force employed in 1990) could lead to rapidly increasing exports.

The GATT round, facing a stalemate in late 1990, faces prospects for long-term success after the EC showed a greater willingness to reduce export subsidies for agricultural products and to cut production subsidies. The EC share of exports to the USSR and Eastern Europe, respectively, was around 1.5 percent which shows that the (former) CMEA countries play so far, given population figures and historical trade patterns, a disproportionally minor role as markets. A similar reasoning holds for the small EC imports from Eastern Europe and the USSR (*see Table 7*), let alone FDI-generated foreign sales which would require outward FDI of firms from the former CMEA countries. These countries face a difficult and time-consuming systemic transition towards market-based systems, where the difficulties encountered in the case of the former GDR - enjoying generous support from West Germany, but also facing the most rapid transition (*Welfens, 1991a*) - as well as in Poland and Hungary suggest that a longer time span and a broader liberalization concept might be required to overcome the intra-European economic divide. The problem is compounded by the sustaining unrest in the USSR whose instability and stagnation could impair prosperity and stability throughout Europe.

Table 7: Imports and Exports from the USSR and Central Europe in 1989 (bill. U.S. $)

	World	USSR	Bulgaria	Imports from CSSR	GDR	Hungary	Poland	Romania
Developed Countries	2219	25.2	0.8	4.1	2.9	4.5	6.0	3.7
W. Europe	1361	21.3	0.7	3.7	2.6	3.9	5.4	3.0
EC	1165	16.5	0.6	2.8	1.8	2.9	4.3	2.8
U.S.	493	0.8	.07	0.1	0.2	0.4	0.4	.09
Canada	114	0.1	.01	.06	.03	.04	.08	0.4
Japan	211	3.0	.05	0.1	0.1	0.1	0.1	0.2

	World	USSR	Bulgaria	Exports to CSSR	GDR	Hungary	Poland	Romania
Developed Countries	2108	27.8	2.4	3.6	3.1	4.6	6.1	1.2
W.Europe	1317	19.0	2.0	3.4	2.8	4.4	5.3	0.8
EC	1130	13.6	1.6	2.6	1.8	3.3	4.3	0.8
U.S.	364	4.3	0.2	.05	.09	0.1	0.4	0.2
Canada	116	0.2	.01	.01	.09	.01	.03	.04
Japan	275	3.1	0.2	.06	.02	0.1	0.2	.05

Note: Trade between the FRG and the GDR is not included.
Source: GATT (1990), International Trade 1989-90, Geneva, Appendix Tab. 1.

Germany plays a key role for the West-East liberalization of trade in goods, investment and technologies, and its historic trade orientation suggests at least to some extent that a liberalization for the whole of Europe would generate considerable West-East trade. Before World War I when all European economies were still market economies Germany's trade with Russia (then comprising Poland), Rumania, Austro-Hungary and Serbia was considerable, although not as important as trade with the U.S. and the U.K. (*see figures for 1913 in contrast to 1989 in Table 8*).

The CMEA countries must themselves realize the necessary internal changes that would allow the economies to successfully adopt an export-oriented growth strategy. For a transition period the question arises what the former CMEA countries could do as a group to improve resource allocation and the growth of trade. Free trade agreements for Central and Eastern Europe could play an important role in a transition period in which for internal politico-economic reasons neither the EC countries are eager to pursue EC-widening nor former CMEA countries willing to fully embrace the principles of EC 1992 as a prerequisite for EC membership. Moreover, a key EC 1992 principle, the free movement of persons, is difficult to accept for most EC countries as long as high West-East per capita income differences lead one to expect huge labor migration in a wider EC; at the same time the former CMEA countries find it difficult to accept foreign ownership and are often afraid that privatization, opening up of the economy and strong initial currency devaluations would amount to giving away domestic industrial assets at very low prices compared to long-term expected asset values.

Table 8: German Trade Orientations in 1913 and 1989*
(shares for merchandise trade with selected countries)

	Country Share in German Imports 1913	1989	Country Share in German Exports 1913	1989
USA	15.9	7.6	7.1	7.3
Great Britain	8.1	6.8	14.2	9.3
Russia**	13.2	1.7	8.7	1.8
(Poland)		0.7		0.7
Austria-		(A) 4.1		(A) 5.5
Hungary***	7.7	(H) 0.5	10.9	(H) 0.6
(CSFR)		0.5		0.4
Serbia****	0.1	1.3	0.5	1.1

* figures for 1989 are for West Germany; ** figures for 1989 refer to the Soviet Union.
*** figures for 1989 are comprised of the country shares of Austria, Hungary and the CSSR;
**** figures for 1989 are for Yugoslavia.
Sources: Statistisches Handbuch für das Deutsche Reich, Vol. II., Statistisches Bundesamt and Deutsche Bundesbank, own calculations.

Conflicts over strategies and how to achieve a broader trade liberalization are apparent in the issue of free trade. Multilateral solutions might often be more difficult to achieve in periods of internal adjustment pressures in many countries because politicians then face limited opportunities to support liberalization schemes with uncertain long-term pay-offs. Bilateralism can be an approach in its own right, but it can also serve as a model for later envisaged multilateral solutions. The U.S.-Canadian free trade agreement stands for such an approach.

North America

The U.S.-Canadian free trade agreement that entered into force in January 1989 is important not only qualitatively, namely because of the liberalization strategy of creating a regional trading bloc but because of the amount of trade involved, too. The inclusion of services and direct investment as well as new dispute settlement arrangements represent an institutional innovation. Representing new ideas and standing for a liberalization pact between partners of different economic size, the North American FTA could indeed work as an inspiring model for other countries or regions (*Schott and Smith, 1988; survey: Belous and Hartley, 1990*). If Mexico would be included in an extended NAFTA, this could be an encouraging model for Europe with its economic East-West divide.

Transpacific Conflicts

Of comparable size to the trade volume (exports plus imports) in North America is U.S-Japanese trade which, however, has yielded sustaining Japanese export surpluses of about $ 50 bill. p.a. and has created transpacific tensions rather than cooperation. The fact that the trade imbalance was relatively unsensitive to real exchange rate changes was a major reason for the U.S. administration to look for the removal of so-called structural trade impediments in Japan.

Flexible dollar exchange rates - not anticipated at the creation of GATT - translated in transatlantic trade into real exchange rate movements with considerable, albeit lagged adjustments in trade volumes. In the transpacific context flexible exchange rates seemed to work less satisfactorily. The U.S. pressured Japan for voluntary export restraints in the case of chips and automobiles. After Congress - based on the super 301 provision of the Omnibus Trade Act of 1988 - had named Japan together with Brazil and India in 1989 as unfair trading partners, bilateral trade negotiations between the U.S. and Japan (U.S. "Structural Impediments Initiative") followed, and they were successfully concluded.

If market access is improved firms from the EC countries will enjoy a free rider status in Japan. By further increasing their network of transplants in the U.S. and by raising the local contents appropriately Japanese companies could in turn enjoy a free rider status in transatlantic trade because EC countries will not dare to bloc Japanese products made in the U.S. Japanese-European conflicts have been limited so far, but Japan's first - successful - complaint in the GATT against EC local content rules and the spread of EC antidumping measures points to European trade conflicts.

4.2 Opening up East European CPEs

An important problem of liberalization concerns the phasing of various liberalization measures on the one hand, and on the other hand, the link between external opening up and internal adjustment - a problem that was much discussed for market economies and developing economies and emerges in modified form in Eastern Europe (*Corden, 1987; Choksi and Papgeorgiou, 1986; Edwards, 1989; Welfens, 1991b*). Many distortions encountered in East European CPEs are similar to those in certain developing countries that pursued inward-oriented (import-substituting) policies, relied on a large state-owned industrial sector and faced monetary instability, foreign debt problems and high budget deficits. However, many problems in opening up East European CPEs are distinct and require special treatment.

Of the many problems arising in the opening up of East European economies only three will be addressed here: (1) The problem of attracting FDI inflows is one element of improving the supply-side by modernizing the capital stock and imposing tighter competition on the one hand, and, on the other hand, by expanding output in so far neglected areas such as the service industry, especially banking, tourism and telecom. In Eastern Europe potential foreign investors face high risks with respect to the political stability of governments. Uncertainties could explain why even with sharp devaluations - reducing labor costs for foreign investors - undertaken to unify the official exchange rate and the black market rate CPEs do not attract significant FDI inflows in sectors with a high labor intensity of production. Given the enormous political problems in privatizing the monopolistic state industry FDI inflows are necessary to make the supply-side more flexible and more responsive to the price mechanism.

(2) There is the issue of the speed of opening up former CPEs to trade in goods and services. Suddenly opening the whole economy to import competition by way of trade liberalization reduces the monopoly problem in former CPEs drastically, but there is also a negative side-effect that is considerable and related to the fact that the CPEs's trade was highly specialized and primarily oriented to other CMEA countries. If former CMEA countries fully open up to Western imports better quality and richer product variety offered by OECD exporters is likely to inflict steep price discounts and rapid economic obsolescence of specific real and human capital in the former CPEs - a problem that could be reduced if a gradual but predetermined opening up strategy were adopted while replacing quotas with less distorting tariffs. Falling output and high unemployment could endanger the required monetary stabilization policies that are absolutely necessary to let the price system be a viable mechanism for efficient allocation. Moreover, only after inflation has been reduced to low sustainable levels can flexible exchange rates replace fixed exchange rates. The latter can serve in the immediate systemic transformation as a nominal anchor and generate pressure to avoid an inflationary policy that would erode the price-competitiveness of the economy. With rising FDI inflows and capital movements as well as with changing trade flows a flexible exchange rate is useful, especially since exchange rate expectations will influence capital flows which in turn offers government an incentive for policies that help to appreciate the currency and thereby reduce the excessive international wage differentials (e.g. in 1990 wage income was $ 180 in Poland).

(3) There is the problem of opening up in the presence of domestic monopolies which could pose a transitional problem for most former CPEs along the road to privatization. Assume that the transition to a market economy provides domestic firms with a monopolistic position in the home market whose new environment requires profit maximization. This leads us to the problem of price differentiation and the role of price elasticities (ß).

In general, firms which can separate markets regionally (say, on a country-by-country basis) will serve both markets at identical marginal costs; this is trivial in the case that goods sold are produced in only one country - this result is simply the implication of profit-maximizing firms which aim to minimize costs for a given share or amount of world demand. Marginal revenues will be equated across markets/countries in those industries where after-sale service, warranty conditions for durables or marketing investment allows the separation of markets. In a two-country world it holds - with * denoting foreign variables - that monopolistic price behavior leads to the equalization of marginal revenues at home, R', and abroad, R'* (k' = R' = R'*):

(1) k' = p - p/ß = p* - p*/ß* or, alternatively

(2) $k'(q+q^*) = p[1-1/\beta] = p^*[1-1/\beta^*]$; $\beta,\beta^* > 0$ (absolute value of the price elasticity), or

(2') $p/p^* = [1-1/\beta^*]/[1-1/\beta]$[22]

Fig. 1 highlights a special case ($\beta^* = $ infinity) where the firm considered acts as a monopolist in the home country and as a price taker in the world market so that p^* is exogenous.

Fig. 1: Political Economy of Trade Liberalization

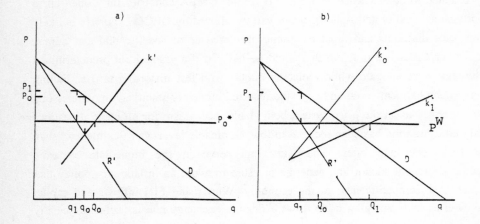

This diagram shows in panel a) what happens if an initially closed economy which is characterized by a monopolistic suppplier is affected by allowing trade. Initially, output q_0 is equal to domestic supply, where the price is p_0. Opening up markets for exports/trade leads, with a world market price p^*, to a reduction of output sold domestically - which makes liberalization in the presence of domestic monopolies difficult - and to an increase of total output. As the monopolistic firm realizes $p^* = R'$ the domestic supply is given by q_1 - sold at the increased price p_1 - while total output increases to Q_0, where Q_0-q_1 is exported. Those individuals who consume only goods supplied by monopolistic suppliers are worse off under export liberalization than before unless import competition shifts the cost curve downward sufficiently.[23] Until imports are totally liberalized and thus P^W becomes the offer price in the country under consideration, too, consumers can only benefit from trade if import competition leads to a higher induced rate of process innovations or brings price reductions for - now imported - intermediate goods. For a country with a monopolistic supplier the analysis suggests that opening up an economy could lead to price increases. This is a good example that free trade is not unambiguously beneficial to all countries and groups in the short term; moreover, it shows how essential it is for a policy strategy to reduce uncertainties about long term benefits of free trade. As panel b) shows, process innovations might be such that only foreign consumers and domestic/foreign capital owners benefit.

4.3 Prospects

New institutional approaches which take into account the links between trade in goods/services, the internationalization of industrial property rights and the significance of technology factors are appropriate if free trade in a broader sense is to be achieved. Agreement on a principle level seems to be feasible.[24] Emphasis should be given to transparency, most-favored nation treatment and a comprehensive dispute settlement mechanism. To merge the activities of the World Intellectual Property Organization with GATT/GATS could be one reasonable strategy; to gradually expand OECD membership and thereby broaden the basis of liberalization codes another. Main impulses for liberalization progress could come from Europe which faces adjustment needs both in Western Europe and in Eastern Europe. However, the EC could also become the source of new trade conflicts in which the internationally less influential players from Eastern Europe and the South are at a disadvantage while the U.S., Japan and the EC continue to develop mutually favorable solutions.

The GATT Uruguay round needs a successful completion. However, a new round is necessary in the near future since at the beginning of the Uruguay round nobody anticipated the systemic transition in Eastern Europe. Bargaining strategies of the major actors in the Uruguay round were developed without anticipation of the emergence of a new Europe. The old world needs time to sort out the problems that emerged in connection with the demise of the CPEs in Eastern Europe and the formation of the single EC market. Policy concepts for progressive and sustainable liberalization in the field of trade in goods, technology and assets are needed. The EC has become more influential in the design of the international trade regime and hence the attitude of the traditionally liberally oriented countries - (West)Germany, the U.K., the Netherlands and Denmark - is of particular importance. Germany plays a special role, not least because of the German unification process which not only implies enlarging the EC to include East Germany, but provides a welcome example for a fast systemic transformation. However, if transformation of East Germany would trigger recurrent conflicts, a more inward-oriented Germany could result in a weaker German commitment to free trade. With respect to the EC stance one may also note that British trade policy could become more protectionist if the economic recession in 1990 actually indicated renewed stagnation. The French trade policy is likely to be rather more protectionist in the future if as a result of German unification and fear of German industrial dominance French-Italian-Spanish M&As would strongly increase and thereby reinforce a parallel pressure in the business community to resort to old-fashioned protectionist attitudes in many EC countries. The intra-EC policy shifts could be decisive in a period in which aggressive bilateralism seems to be on the agenda in U.S.-Japanese trade relations which could erode global liberalization attempts. A renewal of the U.S.-Japanese chip treaty (expected in 1991) could be another sign that purely market-based allocation processes are not feasible in technology trade between major market economies. In a period in which East European countries are looking for orientation bilateral protectionism is not an adequate strategy.

Endnotes

1 More public funds - in Europe typically directed towards big business - would be necessary to maintain high innovativeness that otherwise could be expected from stricter competition policy and venture capital promotion.

2 On the international trading system see *Jackson 1989*.

3 The empirical evidence for links between exports, productivity and terms of trade is mixed: see *Marin, 1990*. For a survey on some empirical issues see *Richardson 1989*.

4 *Bhagwati (1987)* has argued that services have become more mobile on both the side of users and of providers.

5 Figures are taken from *GATT (1990)*.

6 In 1989 the USSR was No. 8, followed by the Netherlands, in the ranking of merchandise trade.

7 Figures are from *EC Commission (1990)*, Panorama of the EC Industry, Brussels, Table 3.

8 Spero dubbs the Japanese strategy to extract a foreign license in a core technology field "patent flooding"; according to his view Japan's big companies develop many patents in areas related to the core technology targeted and expect ιo get from the often smaller firms a highly valuable license for the core technology in exchange for licenses of minor technological advances for the Japanese market. See *Spero, D.M. (1990)*.

9 Expropriations of German and Japanese firms after World War II create a somewhat biased picture.

10 On the global service industry see *Nusbaumer, 1987 and Messerlin and Sauvant, 1990*.

11 In a long-term analysis FDI enters also on the supply-side and in the production function, respectively.

12 Subsidies for Airbus Industries met strong U.S. resistance in the 1980s.

13 On the internationalization of the U.S. see *Audretsch and Claudon, 1989*.

14 *EC Commission (1990)*, Table 1, based on figures from Julius and Thomsen.

15 Figures are from *Julius (1990)*, pp. 80-81.

16 The latter is a classical strategy of Japanese firms.

17 Firms choose sales in the domestic markets given the sales of other firms, and then price is determined from the demand curve. $ns+n^*s^* = 1$, and one can obtain the equilibrium price as $P = ß[nk' + n^*ek'^*]/[ß(n+n^*)-1]$; see *Venables 1990*.

18 In the context of international investment this leads to the problem of performance standards for FDI which pose interesting theoretical problems: see *Davidson et al. (1985)*.

19 The latter neglects so-called joint investment projects in the CMEA - mostly in the USSR - to which several member countries contributed - sometimes in exchange for cheap future imports from the new production facilities.

20 Developing countries are, however, facing considerable protectionism on the side of the EC, and the EC 1992 program has ambiguous effects upon these countries. See *Cable (1987) and UNCTC (1990)*.

21 Tariffs have been mostly moderate in the CMEA countries, but quotas were as distorting as different relative prices for tradables.

22 Assuming $ß^*$ and $ß$ to be rather large so that $1/ß$ and $1/ß^*$ is small, we can obtain a more convenient (approximative) expression by taking logarithms on both sides: $\ln p/p^* = (-1/ß^*) + (1/ß) = ß-ß^*/ßß^*$. The logarithms of $p/^*p$ is negative, i.e. $p/p^* < 1$, if $ß^* > ß$.

23 An additional problem enters if the economy is opened to capital inflows and foreign investors obtain along with part of the capital stock a share in monopolistic profits which - being higher than normal - imply a currency appreciation associated with the relatively higher price of assets to be acquired by foreigners, and this appreciation effect from capital inflows impairs export growth. If we assume that consumption, leisure and wealth are positive arguments in the individual utility function, there are ambiguous welfare effects of liberalizing trade in such a distorted environment - especially if privatization of state industry changes (perceived) private wealth which could raise or reduce the labor supply and will affect savings and output.

24 In Europe restrictions to foreign ownership were reduced in the late 1980s by both the reduction of capital controls and the EC's gradual restriction of multi-tier share structures (with unequal voting powers of various share types) that prevent hostile foreign take-overs. The EC rules in this area imply pressure on Sweden, Switzerland and other European non-EC countries to lift barriers for foreign ownership - otherwise these countries will not obtain full access (via free trade in goods and services) to the single EC market. With lower barriers to foreign ownership the respective country will face a currency appreciation, a switch to higher, i.e. normal stock price-earnings ratios, and an appreciation-induced slowdown of export growth. Economic growth need not be affected if with rising foreign ownership of industrial assets international technology transfers intensify; however, imports of goods and services are likely to rise with foreign ownership, in particular if foreign subsidiaries have a greater tendency to import capital goods (often from the same sources as the parent company) than domestic firms.

References

AUDRETSCH, D.B. and CLAUDON, M.P., eds. (1989) The Internationalization of U.S. Markets, New York: New York University Press.

AUDRETSCH, D.B.; SLEUWAEGEN, L. and YAMAWAKI, H., eds. (1989) The Convergence of International and Domestic Markets, Amsterdam: North-Holland.

BALDWIN, R. (1988) Evaluating Strategic Trade Policies, Aussenwirtschaft, Vol. 43, 207-230.

BELOUS, R.S. and HARTLEY, R.S., eds. (1990) The Growth of Regional Trading Blocs in the Global Economy, Washington: National Planning Association.

BERGSTEN, F. (1990) Rx for America: Export-Led Growth, International Economic Insights, Vol. 2, No. 1, 2-6.

BHAGWATI, J.N. (1987) Trade in Services and Multilateral Trade Negotiations, The World Bank Economy Review, Vol. 1, 549-569.

BHAGWATI, J.N. (1989) Is Free Trade Passé After All?, Weltwirtschaftliches Archiv, Vol. 125, 17-44.

BRANDER, B. and SPENCER, J.A. (1983) International R&D Rivalry and Industrial Strategy, Review of Economic Studies, Vol. 50, 707-722.

BUCKLEY, P.J. and CASSON, M. (1976) The Future of the Multinational Enterprise, London: Macmillan.

CABLE, V. (1987) The Impact of EEC Trade Policies on Developing Countries, in: GIERSCH, H., ed. (1987) 294-326.

CAVES, R.E. (1989) Exchange Rate Movements and Foreign Direct Investment in the United States, in: AUDRETSCH, D.B. and CLAUDON, M.P., eds., 199-228.

CHESNAIS, F., (1988) Multinational Enterprises and the International Diffusion of Technology, in: DOSI, G.; et al., eds., Technical Change and Economic Theory, London: Pinter, 496-527.

CHOSKI, A.M. and PAPAGEORIOU, D., eds. (1986) Economic Liberalization in Developing Countries, Oxford: Basil Blackwell/The World Bank.

CLINE, W.R. (1989) United States External Adjustment and the World Economy, Washington: Institute for International Economics.

CORDEN, M. (1987) Protection and Liberalization: A Review of Analytical Issues, IMF Occasional Paper No. 54, Washington, D.C.

DAVIDSON, C. et al. (1985) Analysis of Performance Standards for Direct Foreign Investments, Canadian Journal of Economics, Vol. 18, 876-890.

DUNNING, J.H. (1979) Explaining Changing Patterns of International Production: In Defence of an Eclectic Theory, Oxford Bulletin of Economics and Statistics, Vol. 41, 269-296.

DUTTON, H.I. (1984) The Patent System and Inventive Activity During the Industrial Revolution, 1750-1852, Manchester: Manchester University Press.

EDWARDS, S. (1989) On the Sequencing of Structural Reforms, NBER Working Paper No. 3138.

ETHIER, W.J. (1982) Dumping, Journal of Political Economy, Vol. 90, 487-506.

FAUST, K. (1990) Unternehmen als Patentanmelder in der Ifo-Patentstatistik, Ifo-Schnelldienst, Vol. 43, 15/1990.

GATT (1990) International Trade 1989-90, Geneva 1990.

GIERSCH, H., ed. (1987) Free Trade in the World Economy. Towards an Opening of Markets, Tübingen: Mohr.

GIERSCH, H., ed. (1988) Services in World Economic Growth, Tübingen: Mohr.

GRAHAM, E.M. (1978) Transatlantic Investment by Multinational Firms: A Rivalistic Phenomenon?, Journal of Post-Keynesian Economics, Vol. 1, 82-99.

GRILICHES, Z. (1990) Patent Statistics as Economic Indicators: A Survey, Journal of Economic Literature, 28, 1661-1707.

GRUENSPECHT, H.K. (1988) Dumping and Dynamic Competition, Journal of International Economics, Vol. 25, 225-248.

GRUNWALD, J. and FLAMM, K. (1985) The Global Factory, Washington: Brookings.

HILLMANN, A.L. and URSPRUNG, H.W. (1989) The Multinational Firm and International Trade Policy, discussion paper, University of Konstanz, mimeo.

HINDLEY, B. (1988) Integrated World Markets in Services: Problems and Prospects, in: GIERSCH, H., ed., Services in World Economic Growth, Tübingen: Mohr, 222-244.

HUDEC, R.E. (1988) Legal Issues in US-EC Trade Policy: GATT Litigation 1960-1985, in: BALDWIN, R.E.; HAMILTON, C.B.; SAPIR, A., eds., Issues in US-EC Trade Relations, Chicago: University of Chicago Press, 17-66.

HUFBAUER, G.C. (1990) ed., Europe 1992. An American Perspective, Washington: Brookings.

INOTAI, A. (1988) Competition Between European CMEA and Rapidly Industrializing Countries in the OECD Market for Manufactured Goods, Empirica, Vol. 15, 189-204.

JACKSON, J. (1989) The World Trading System, Cambridge: MIT Press.

JETRO (1990) Jetro White Paper on Foreign Direct Investment, Tokyo 1990.

JULIUS, D. (1990) Global Companies and Public Policy, London: Pinter.

KNICKERBOCKER, F.T. (1973) Oligopolistic Reaction and Multinational Enterprise, Boston: Harvard University Press.

KRUGMANN, P., ed. (1987) Strategic Trade Policy and the New International Economics, Cambridge, Mass.: MIT Press.

LAWRENCE, R.Z. (1990) Innovation and Trade: Meeting the Foreign Challenge, in: AARON, H.J., ed., Setting National Priorities, Washington: Brookings, 145-184.

LIPSEY, R.E. and KRAVIS, I.B. (1986) The Competitiveness and Comparative Advantage of U.S. Multinationals, 1957-1983, NBER Working paper No. 2051, Cambridge.

MESSERLIN, P.A. and K.P. SAUVANT, eds. (1990) The Uruguay Round. Services in the World Economy, Washington and New York: World Bank/UNCTC 1990.

MARIN, D. (1989) Trade and Scale Economies, in: AUDRETSCH, D.B.; L. SLEUWAEGEN, and H. YAMAWAKI, eds., The Convergence of International and Domestic Markets, Amsterdam: North-Holland, 29-56.

MESSERLIN, P.A. (1989) The EC Antidumping Regulations: A First Appraisal, Weltwirtschaftliches Archiv, Vol. 125, 563-587.

MURRELL, PETER (1990) The Nature of Socialist Economies, Princeton: Princeton University Press.

NUSBAUMER, J. (1987) Services in the Global Market, Boston: Kluwer.

OECD (1988) The Newly Industrializing Countries: Challenge and Opportunity for OECD Countries, Paris.

OECD (1989) Competition Policy and Intellectual Property Rights, Paris.

OKIMOTO, D.L. (1987) Outsider Trading: Coping with Japanese Industrial Organization, in: PYLE, K.B., ed., The Trade Crisis: How Will Japan Respond?, Seattle: Society for Japanese Studies, 85-116.

OSTRY, S. (1990) Governments and Corporations in a Shrinking World, New York: Council on Foreign Relations.

PORTER, M. (1990) The Competitive Advantage of Nations, New York: The Free Press.

POZNANSKI, K. (1987) Technology, Competition & the Soviet Bloc in the World Market, Berkeley: Institute for International Studies.

PRESIDENT'S COMMISSION ON INDUSTRIAL COMPETITIVENESS (1985) Global Competition. The New Reality, Washington D.C.

RICHARDSON, J.D. (1989) Empirical Research on Trade Liberalisation with Imperfect Competition: A Survey, OECD Economic Studies, No. 12, 7-50.

RIEDEL, J. (1990) The State of Debate on Trade and Industrialization in Developing Countries, in: RIEDEL, J. and PEARSON, C.S., eds., The Direction of Trade Policies, Cambridge, Mass.: Basil Blackwell, 130-150.

SCHOTT, J.J. and SMITH, M.G., eds. (1988) The Canada-United States Free Trade Agreement: The Global Impact, Washington, D.C.: Institute for International Economics.

SCHUHKNECHT, L. and URSPRUNG, H.W. (1989) Die Anti-Dumping Politik der EG und der USA: Ein Vergleich aus der Sicht der Neuen Politischen Ökonomie, paper presented at the symposium Neue Politische Oekonomie, Haus Rissen, October 11-13, Hamburg.

SIEBERT, H., ed. (1990) The Completion of the Internal Market, Tübingen (Mohr).

SMITH, A. and VENABLES, A. (1988) Completing the Internal Market in the European Community: Some Industry Simulations, European Economic Review, Vol. 32, 1501-1525.

SPERO, D.M. (1990) Patent Protection or Piracy - a CEO Views Japan, Harvard Business Review, Sept.-Oct. 1990, 58-69.

SPENCER, B.J. and BRANDER, J.A. (1983) International R&D Rivalry and Industrial Strategy, Review of Economic Studies, Vol. 50, 707-722.

STEGEMANN, K. (1990) EC Anti-Dumping Policy: Are Price Undertakings a Legal Substitute for Illegal Price Fixing?, Weltwirtschaftliches Archiv, Vol. 126, 268-298.

TAKACS, W.E. (1982) Cyclical Dumping of Steel Products: Comments, Journal of International Economics, Vol. 12, 381-383.

TARR, D.G. (1982) Cyclical Dumping of Steel Products: Another Look, Journal of International Economics, Vol. 12, 377-379.

THOMAS, L. G. (1990) Spare the Rod and Spoil the Industry: Vigorous Competition and Vigorous Regulation Promote Global Competitive Advantage, paper presented at the Meeting of the International J.A. Schumpeter Society "Entrepreneurship, Technological Innovation, and Economic Growth: International Perspectives", Airlie House, Va., June 3-5.

TRANSLINK (1990) European Deal Review, London and New York.

U.S. DEPARTMENT OF COMMERCE (1988) International Direct Investment. Washington.

UNCTC (1988) Transnational Corporations in World Development, New York.

UNCTC (1990) Regional Economic Integration and Transnational Corporations in the 1990s: Europe 1992, North American, and Developing Countries, Series A, No. 15, New York.

US DEPARTMENT OF COMMERCE (1986) International Direct Investment, 1988 Edition, Washington.

VAN TULDER, R. and G. JUNNE (1988) European Multinationals in Core Technologies, New York: Wiley/IRM.

VENABLES, A. (1990a) Macroeconomic Implications of Exchange Rate Variations, Oxford Review of Economic Policy, Vol. 6, No. 3, 18-27.

VENABLES, A. (1990b) The Economic Integration of Oligopolistic Markets, European Economic Review, Vol. 34, 753-773.

VERMULST, E.A. (1987) Antidumping Law and Practice in the United States and the European Communities: A Comparative Analysis, Amsterdam: North-Holland.

WELFENS, P.J.J. (1990a) Internationalisierung von Wirtschaft und Wirtschaftspolitik/Internationalization of the Economy and of Economic Policies, Heidelberg: Springer.

WELFENS, P.J.J. (1990b) Privatization, M&As and Inter-Firm Cooperation in the EC: Improved Prospects for Innovation?, paper presented at the Meeting of the International J.A. Schumpeter Society "Entrepreneurship, Technological Innovation, and Economic Growth: International Perspectives", Airlie House, Va., June 3-5.

WELFENS, P.J.J. (1990c) Economic Reforms in Eastern Europe: Problems, Options and Opportunities, prepared for Testimony before United States Senate, Small Business Committee, Washington D.C., March.

WELFENS, P.J.J., ed. (1991a) Economic Aspects of German Unification, Baltimore, forthcoming.

WELFENS, P.J.J. (1991b) Opening up East European Economies and the Sequencing Problem, AICGS/The Johns Hopkins University, mimeo.

WELFENS, P.J.J. and BALCEROWICZ, L., eds. (1988) Innovationsdynamik im Systemvergleich, Heidelberg: Physica.

WITZKE, H. von and HAUSNER, U., (1990) International Agricultural and Trade Policy Interdependency, in: SCHENK, H., ed., Jahrbuch für Neue Politische Oekonomie, Tübingen: Mohr, forthcoming.

WOLF, T.A. (1988) Foreign Trade in the Centrally Planned Economy, New York: Harwood.

WORLD BANK (1990) World Development Report 1990, New York.

YAMAWAKI, H. (1989) Export Price, Demand Disturbances, and Market Structure, Wissenschaftszentrum Berlin, discussion paper, Berlin.

Appendix

Table 9: Cross-Border Acquisitions in Europe

| | Acquisitions Made | | | | Acquisitions Recieved | | | | |
| | 1990 | | | 1989 | 1990 | | | 1989 | 1990 |
	Mill. ECU (1)	Number of Deals (2)	(3)	Mill. ECU (4)	Mill. ECU (1')	Number of Deals (2')	(3')	Mill. ECU (4)	Deal Value Ratio (1)/(1')
France	10,599	263	166	9,625	6,536	211	192	5,534	1.9
Sweden	9,395	173	119	1,382	2,991	66	34	762	3.1
U.S.	9,223	177	182	13,803					
U.K.	7,380	245	281	5,512	15,723	277	238	20,833	0.5
Japan	2,460	54	55	1,482					
Germany	1,967*	111	128	6,647	4,812	206	215	5,534	0.4
Netherl.	1,787	93	47	619	2,465	96	99	1,883	0.7
Belgium	1,199	31	27	1,016	1,678	70	62	1,236	0.7
Italy	963	60	51	1,505	2,669	132	103	4,122	0.4
Norway	729	21	13	660	527	41	31	210	1.4
Denmark	566	18	13	393	653	37	33	544	0.9
Switzerl.	559	113	83	926	3,343	52	43	91	0.2
Austria	460	21	14	18	85	26	24	376	5.4
Finland	435	36	35	714	37	18	12	314	11.8
Spain	371	19	18	295	3,576	142	127	2,689	0.1
Ireland	217	24	22	305	331	20	12	174	0.7
Portugal	1	1	0	0	426	31	19	346	-
Luxembourg	0	2	10	12	0	4	3	1	-
Liechtenst.	0	2	2	144	-	-	-	-	-
Greece	-	-	-	-	17	7	7	263	-
Iceland	-	-	-	-	1	1	0	0	-
EUROPE++	125	4	0	0	EU+2207	24	10	315	-
Total					48,438	1467	1266	45,059	

+ incl. targets with business locations spread among several European nations where national allocations could not be estimated.
++ incl. acquisitions made in European nations by US and Japanese companies as well as acquisitions between European nations.

Note: The industrial breakdown was as follows (bill. ECU in 1990): Automotive 6.2; Paper: 5.8; Food: 5.4; Electronics: 4.7, Insurance: 3.7, Banking: 3.3; Drinks: 3.1; Construction: 1.9; Airlines: 1.6; Engineering: 1.6, Pharmaceuticals: 1.4, Oil & Gas: 1.2, other were below 1 bill. ECU.

* reduction mainly due to German unification (deal value ratio in 1988: 1.2)
Source: The European Deal Review

Table 10: Anti-Dumping Investigations in the EC, 1984-1988

a) Anti-Dumping Actions of the EC, 1980-1988

	Investigations opened	Definitive duties	Price un- dertakings	Total	No measu- res appl.
1980	25	7	46	53	12
1981	47	10	6	16	14
1982	55	7	35	42	9
1983	36	19	27	46	10
1984	48	4	27	31	10
1985	36	8	4	12	19
1986	24	4	25	29	18
1987	39	9	8	17	4
1988	39	18	0	18	8

Cumulative figures 1980-89: complaints: 449, initiations: 378, measures taken 279 (of which definitive duties: 96; price undertakings: 183; findings of no dumping (no injury): 34 (63), measures in force in 1989: 120 (1985: 166)

b) Anti-Dumping Investigations by Type of Country, 1980-88

	Number of investigations	percent	% change in value of imports 1980-88
Industriali- zed countries			
EFTA	15	4.3	+87
Portugal	2	0.6	n.a.
Spain	18	5.2	n.a.
Other W.Eur.	34	9.7	+197
North America			
USA	25	7.2	+42
Canada	6	1.7	+31
Japan	27	7.7	+193
Other	5	1.4	+79
	---	----	---
	132	37.8	+82
Dev. countries			
4 Asian NICs	30	8.6	+145
South Am. NIEs*	24	6.9	+39
OPEC	5	1.4	-59
Other	17	4.9	+34
	---	----	---
	76	21.8	-11
State trading area			
Eastern Europe	119	34.1	+19
China	21	6.0	+252
Other	1	0.3	-7
	---	----	---
TOTAL	349	100.0	+36

* Argentina, Brazil, Mexico, Venezuela (not incl. in OPEC)

Source: EC Commission, 7th Annual Report of the Commission on the Community's Anti-Dumping and Anti-Subsidy Activities (COM (90)229), Brussel 1990; EC Commission.

COMMENTS ON: INTERNATIONALIZATION OF PRODUCTION, INVESTMENT AND EUROPEAN INTEGRATION

Claude Barfield

Paul Welfens' paper successfully tackles a number of the most important questions relating to the internationalization of production and investment, coincidental with the integration of the European economy. It is solidly rooted in the most important historical and recent economic literature and thus provides an up-to-date source for understanding mainstream economic consensus in these areas.

For this reviewer, the strongest sections of the paper include the explanations of the links between trade, multinational firms and innovation; the analysis of the phenomena behind the creation of a European single market; the description of transatlantic conflicts; and the analyses -- occurring throughout the paper -- of the problems and challenges facing East European economies. There is also a very clear discussion of the anti-dumping issue from a European perspective.

Conversely, for this reviewer, the paper would have been considerably strengthened by additional analysis in three areas: the place and role of Japan in any equations relation to the internationalization of production and investment; a more detailed discussion of strategic trade theory as it relates to European technology and trade strategies; and a more systematic analysis of the issues presented by the economic structural differences - highlighted first in the U.S.-Japan Structural Impediments Initiative -- for the international trading system and the EC in particular.

No discussion of the U.S.-EC trade and investment relations can be complete without inclusion of Japan. Japan's industrial strategy is being copied by both EC and U.S. companies, and often U.S. and EC policies aimed at defending home markets against allegedly unfair Japanese competition end up having a greater impact on EC or U.S. companies than they have on Japanese competitors (i.e., EC anti-dumping and rules or origin actions).

Europe is now at a crucial point in deciding how - or whether -- to attempt to salvage some of its high-tech sectors, particularly in the field of electronics. A closer look at the specific lessons - and cautions -- gleaned from strategic trade theory would have rendered the paper more timely and relevant.

Finally, the next round of multilateral trade negotiations is likely to address a series of structural issues that previously have not been considered trade-related -- such as impact of financial market organization, trust and tax policies and technology policy. Though the paper contains a useful section on competition policy, it does not deal with the issue as a part of a new continuum of previously domestic policies that will increasingly become part of the policy agenda for the international trading system.

MULTINATIONALS AND PRICING TO MARKET BEHAVIOR

Michael M. Knetter

1. Introduction

The amplitude and frequency of fluctuations in currency values since the early 1970s have complicated the pricing decisions of firms exporting to foreign markets. The recent behavior of the dollar vis-à-vis the Deutschemark illustrates the point quite dramatically. In early 1985 the dollar traded at roughly 3.4 DM. By 1987 it had fallen to about 1.7 DM. If German firms exporting to the U.S. market had held DM prices of their goods constant over this period, the dollar price paid by U.S. importers would have doubled in a span of two years. Nearly all of this change would represent relative price change, since the inflation rate in the U.S. was under 5% per year at the time.

Obviously, prices of German-produced goods selling in the U.S. did not change by nearly 100%. There are a number of possible explanations for why price adjustment was less than proportionate to changes in the exchange rate. Among them are the following: (1) German costs of production changed in a manner that offset the impact of the dollar depreciation, (2) the dollar depreciation weakened demand for German goods such that German profit margins and export prices were reduced to all buyers, and (3) German firms reduced export prices to U.S. buyers to cushion the impact of the dollar depreciation, while leaving prices unchanged to other markets.

Recent research has attempted to determine the relative contribution of these three factors in explaining incomplete pass-through of exchange rate changes to goods prices. *Knetter (1989), Marston (1989)*, and *Gagnon and Knetter (1990)* present evidence that price discrimination exists either across export destinations or between export and domestic markets. *Paul Krugman (1987)* refers to such price discrimination, triggered by exchange rate movements, as "pricing to market". *Knetter (1990)* also finds industry-level evidence to support the idea that either costs or world demand conditions were sufficiently related to movements in the dollar that German auto export prices to all destinations were affected by the dollar swing of the 1980s.

While the causes of incomplete pass-through are of interest themselves, so are the rather disparate findings of these papers for the pattern of export price adjustment across industries, source countries, and destinations. Industrial organization theory provides a number of reasons for industry level differences. Industry differences in the shape of demand schedules, returns to scale in production, durability of the product, conduct among firms, and other aspects of market structure could easily account for observed differences across industries. It is less obvious why pricing to market patterns might differ across source countries or destinations. *Gagnon and Knetter (1990)* find that in the automobile industry, the export pricing behavior of German, Japanese and U.S. exporters is quite different, even to common destination markets. Japanese export prices are adjusted to almost fully offset changes in the value of the yen, thereby maintaining stable prices in the importers' currency. This pattern of adjustment is less pronounced for German export prices and non-existent for U.S. exports. Explaining these differences in source country behavior in the automobile industry is the focus of this paper.

Section 2 of the paper presents a simple static model of export pricing behavior. Section 3 covers the specification and estimation of a fixed effects model of export pricing. The model is estimated on 7-digit export unit values for the U.S., Japan, and Germany. Both of these sections draw heavily from *Gagnon and Knetter (1990)*. Section 4 interprets the results of estimation with reference to the locational pattern of production by auto makers in the three countries. Section 5 offers some concluding remarks.

2. Theory

The empirical methods used in this research are most easily motivated by a model of a monopolist selling in a number of foreign markets which may be segmented by national boundaries. The monopoly assumption is not essential to the analysis, but makes the exposition simpler. What is essential is that the firm or industry under consideration sell to multiple foreign markets and that the marginal cost of output sold to each destination market moves in proportion to the marginal cost of output to other destinations, apart from a random error term.

Consider a monopolist producing a good for sale in n separate destination markets. The domestic currency profits, π, of the firm are given by:

(1) $\pi(p_1, p_2, \ldots, p_n) = \Sigma p_i^* q_i(e_i^* p_i) - C(Q, w)$

where p denotes price in the exporter's currency, q is quantity demanded which is a function of the import price (written as the product of the export price and the exchange rate, e (units of the destination market currency per unit of the exporter's)), C is the cost function which depends on total quantity produced, Q, and the domestic factor price, w. Q will be a function of the export prices and exchange rates as well. The subscript i indexes destinations.

Profit maximization for the monopolist implies that marginal revenue in each foreign market is equal to the common marginal cost. This condition can be written in elasticity form, which expresses the price charged to each destination market as a markup over the common marginal cost:

(2) $p_i = c*(\epsilon_i/(\epsilon_i - 1))$

where c is the common marginal cost and ϵ denotes the elasticity of demand.

This form of the first order condition clearly reveals the channels by which an exchange rate movement can influence export price: by affecting marginal cost of production or by influencing the elasticity of demand and thus the markup over marginal cost. The former effect can occur through several distinct channels. An exchange rate change could in principle affect marginal cost by altering the quantity produced (provided marginal cost is not independent of output) or by affecting input prices (as in the case of an imported input). Changes in the markup over cost will occur if the elasticity of demand is not constant along the import demand schedule. The constant elasticity demand function has the special property that markups are invariant to changes in cost. Demand schedules with less convexity than a constant elasticity demand schedule (such as linear demand), imply that markups will fall with increases in cost. Under certain conditions, namely very convex demand, it is possible that markups actually increase as costs rise. (For details on the effect of functional form on export price adjustment, see *Knetter (1990)*.)

Equation (2) suggests a very simple fixed effects model for analyzing the export price adjustment process. A natural approach to analyzing the data is to control for the common factor using time dummy variables and control for time invariant destination-specific factors (e.g., trade policies, industry structure, etc.) using dummy variables for each destination. Consider the following model:

(3) $\ln p_{it} = \Theta_t + \tau_i - \beta_i \ln e_{it} + u_{it}$

Destination-specific export prices depend on a common factor, Θ_t, and an idiosyncratic factor, τ_i. Exchange rates are introduced as a covariate in the model to capture destination-specific effects they have on export prices via import demand. The impact exchange rates have on marginal cost (if any) should already be accounted for by the common factor in the regression. Errors in the equation, u_{it}, arise because of factors not accounted for by the model.

In an integrated world market, price changes over time should be entirely accounted for by the common factor. No destination-specific price differences should exist, thus the destination-specific intercept and the coefficient on the exchange rate should be zero. If the world market is not integrated and price discrimination is possible, then the destination specific coefficients may be non-zero. The destination intercepts reflect the average markup over marginal cost (at least relative to a base country). The ß coefficients reveal destination-specific changes in the markup that are related to exchange rate movements. In the monopoly case, these coefficients depend on the convexity of market demand schedules.

A few caveats are in order before proceeding with the empirical implementation of this model. The monopoly model is an oversimplification. The demand elasticities in equation (2) should not be thought of as market demand elasticities, but rather as elasticities of residual demand schedules faced by exporters. Thus, they include the typical reaction of other firms to price changes. A second shortcoming of the model is that it is static. Demand side dynamics may further cloud the interpretation of the elasticities in equation (2) in the empirical implementation. Consequently, the empirical method will be unable to distinguish between several factors that affect the pattern of price adjustment: the shape of market demand schedules, the mode of conduct between firms, and demand dynamics. Nonetheless, it is possible to measure the response patterns of firms to exchange rate changes and make comparisons across industries, source countries, and destination markets.

3. Specification, Data, Estimation, and Results

3.1. Specification

This section of the paper will present the main empirical facts on export pricing adjustment in the automobile industry by U.S., German, and Japanese exporters. The results parallel those presented in *Gagnon and Knetter (1990)*. The equation we estimate is similar to equation (3) above, but includes an additional restriction. This restriction is motivated in detail in *Knetter (1990)*. The intuition for it is quite simple. Other things equal, a 10% increase in marginal cost should leave the exporter in the same position as a 10% exchange rate appreciation with respect to any particular market. Consequently, the effect of cost and exchange rate changes on export price adjustment should be symmetric. The symmetry result holds independently of the shape of the demand schedule. The specification that incorporates this restriction is given by:

(4) $\ln p_{it} = (1-\beta_i) \, \Theta_t + \tau_i - \beta_i \ln e_{it} + u_{it}$

If demand is less convex than a constant elasticity demand schedule, then ß is greater than zero (i.e., markups of price over cost fall with an increase in cost), while if demand is more convex than constant elasticity, ß is less than zero. It is natural to think that demand curves with less convexity than constant elasticity are more plausible than demand curves with greater convexity. Furthermore, the phenomenon of PTM, as described by Krugman, implicitly assumes that demand curves are less convex than constant elasticity. In the empirical results of this paper, estimates of ß near 1 suggest exporters adjust prices in units of their own currency to preserve a stable price in the buyers currency as a result of exchange rate movements. This is considered "complete pricing to market". Estimates of ß near 0 indicate an absence of pricing to market, although they may not preclude price discrimination across destinations. Theory does not rule out cases in which ß is less than 0.

It is important to remember that measures of PTM are not strictly related to measures of the "pass-through" of exchange rates to import prices. Pass-through typically refers to the overall effect of an exchange rate change on a country's import prices. The pass-through of an exchange rate change might be incomplete either because of pricing to market (henceforth, PTM) by foreign producers or because the foreign producers' marginal costs were affected by the exchange rate. This paper focuses on only the former effect.

3.2 Data

Equation (4) is estimated using annual export unit values for selected 7-digit categories within the automobile industry. There are three source countries for auto exports: the United States, Japan, and Germany. For each source country, there are f.o.b. values and quantities of exports to several major destinations. The data are taken from government publications of the respective source countries and are typically collected by customs agents in those countries. The exchange rates are annual average spot exchange rates divided by the wholesale price index in each destination market. The rationale for dividing by foreign price levels is that the foreign demand curve, q(ep), is presumably a function of a real price rather than a nominal price. The estimation period is 1973-87 for Japanese and U.S. exports, and 1975-87 for German exports. During this period there was tremendous variation in exchange rates, which ought to enable identification of the extent of PTM very precisely.

3.3 Estimation

Estimation proceeds by pooling the data on export prices to a cross-section of destination markets for a single source country and product category. The model is estimated using non-linear least squares. The non-linearity arises because of the interaction of estimated coefficients ß and Θ in equation (4). The model is estimated in logs of the variables and first-differences of the logs. The standard errors of coefficient estimates are reported only for the regressions using first-differenced data. This is because the data in logs are non-stationary, which implies non-standard distributions for the coefficient estimates. The main results of the paper, however, are not at all sensitive to the choice of specification. Both the linear model in equation (3) and the non-linear model in equation (4) give similar results for the regressions in levels and first differences. This is verified in *Gagnon and Knetter (1990)* and *Knetter (1990)*.

The fact that unit values, as opposed to actual prices, are used in estimation introduces an additional source of measurement error into the equations. The destination-specific intercepts will capture differences in the average quality of goods, in addition to differences in markups. The time-specific intercepts common to all destinations will capture quality change that is common to all destinations. The problems normally associated with the use of unit values are mitigated considerably in cross-section, time series analysis. As long as destination-specific quality changes are not systematically related to exchange rate changes, the estimates of pricing to market will be unaffected by the use of unit values. It should be added that destination-specific price indices do not exist, so that unit values are the only data suited to this study.

3.4 Pricing to Market in the Automobile Industry

The results for automobile exports are in Tables 1-6 and Figures 1-8. For each of the three source countries - Germany, Japan, and the United States - two equations are estimated for each product category, one in log levels and one in log first differences. The levels results are in Tables 1-3 and the first difference results are in Tables 4-6.

Table 1: German Exports of Automobiles Estimates of ß in Equation (4)

(4) $\ln p_{it} = (1-\beta_i)\,\Theta_t + \tau_i - \beta_i \ln e_{it} + u_{it}$

Destination	1500-1999 cc	2000-2999 cc	3000 cc and over
Canada	0.24	-0.08	-0.20
United States	0.59	0.12	-0.15
Japan	-0.64	0.90	0.09
United Kingdom	0.05	0.37	0.00
France	0.52	0.45	-0.79
Sweden	0.31	0.44	-0.68

Table 2: Japanese Exports of Automobiles Estimates of ß in Equation (4)

(4) $\ln p_{it} = (1-\beta_i)\,\Theta_t + \tau_i - \beta_i \ln e_{it} + u_{it}$

Destination	0-1000 cc	1001-2000 cc	2001 cc and over
Canada	0.79	0.80	
United States	-1.66	0.79	0.81
United Kingdom	0.95	0.82	0.91
Germany	1.03	0.83	0.91
Norway		0.86	
Sweden		0.82	
Switzerland	0.98		
Australia	0.35		

**Table 2A: Japanese Exports of Automobiles Split
Sample Estimates of ß in Equation (4)**

(4) $\ln p_{it} = (1-\beta_i) \Theta_t + \tau_i - \beta_i \ln e_{it} + u_{it}$

Destination	1001–2000 cc		2001 cc and over	
	1973–80	1981–87	1973–80	1981–87
Canada	0.58	0.86	0.66	0.69
United States	0.53	0.85	0.48	0.67
United Kingdom	0.19	0.86	-0.28	0.76
Germany	0.02	0.89	0.18	0.75
Norway		0.67	0.60	
Sweden	0.44	0.85		

**Table 3: U.S. Exports of Automobiles Estimates of ß
in Equation (4)**

(4) $\ln p_{it} = (1-\beta_i) \Theta_t + \tau_i - \beta_i \ln e_{it} + u_{it}$

Destination	6 cylinders or less	over 6 cylinders
Canada	-0.04	0.11
Japan	0.05	-0.02
Germany	-0.0ɔ	0.00
United Kingdom	0.16	-0.21
Sweden	0.10	0.00
Italy		0.02
Australia		0.24

Table 4: West German Exports of Automobiles Estimates of ß from First Difference (d) Version of Equation (4)

(4b) d $\ln p_{it} = (1-\beta_i)\,\Theta_t - \beta_i\,d\,\ln e_{it} + u_{it}$

Destination	1500-1999 cc	2000-2999 cc	3000 cc and over
Canada	0.13 (.33)	-0.26 (.54)	-0.09 (.07)
Japan	-0.31 (.29)	0.17 (.32)	0.20 (.20)
United Kingdom	0.54 (.33)	0.60 (.17)	-0.45 (.22)
United States	0.72 (.11)	0.24 (.19)	-0.13 (.11)
France	0.14 (.29)	0.75 (.13)	-1.93 (1.00)
Sweden	0.21 (.14)	0.06 (.34)	-0.86 (.65)

Note: Standard errors are in parentheses.

Table 5: Japanese Exports of Automobiles Estimates of ß from First Difference Version of Equation (4)

(4b) $d \ln p_{it} = (1-\beta_i) \Theta_t - \beta_i \, d \ln e_{it} + u_{it}$

Destination	0-1000 cc	1001-2000 cc	2001 cc and over
Canada		0.63 (.08)	0.73 (.16)
United Kingdom	0.75 (.27)	0.42 (.14)	0.47 (.36)
United States	-1.64 (1.87)	0.66 (.08)	0.71 (.18)
West Germany	0.90 (.17)	0.48 (.15)	0.79 (.19)
Australia	-0.58 (.87)		
Switzerland	0.88 (.16)		
Sweden	0.49 (.12)		
Norway			0.58 (.31)

Note: Standard errors in parentheses.

Table 6: U.S. Exports of Automobiles Estimates of ß from First Difference Version of Equation (4)

(4b) d $\ln p_{it} = (1-\beta_i)\,\Theta_t - \beta_i\, d\, \ln e_{it} + u_{it}$

Destination	6 cylinders or less	over 6 cylinders	over 6 cylinders*
Canada	0.64 (.16)	0.94 (.11)	0.40 (.15)
Japan	0.34 (.26)	0.59 (.32)	-0.29 (.45)
United Kingdom	0.37 (.25)	0.77 (.31)	-1.15 (.67)
West Germany	0.23 (.29)	1.15 (.30)	-0.43 (.31)
Sweden	0.04 (.46)	0.76 (.31)	0.23 (.35)
Italy		-1.40 (1.90)	
Australia		2.06 (.80)	

Note: Standard errors in parentheses.

* The third column presents results for exports of large cars when Italy and Australia were excluded from the sample. The reason for excluding these countries is that there were several "outlier" observations for each of them that caused the time dummies to be estimated imprecisely.

Table 1 shows the estimates of ß for equation 4 for German exports of autos in three engine sizes - 1500-1999 cubic centimeters, 2000-2999 cc, and 3000 cc and over - to six destination markets - Canada, Japan, the United Kingdom, the United States, France, and Sweden. Somewhat surprisingly, the estimated PTM is most pervasive in the two smaller engine size categories. For exports of small cars to the United States and France, the estimated coefficients are .59 and .52, respectively. The implication is that a 20% depreciation of the dollar, all else constant, would elicit a 12% reduction in the DM price charged to U.S. buyers. The dollar price would rise by only 8%. The DM price faced by other buyers would remain unchanged provided their exchange rates had not changed. The extent of pricing to market is less pronounced for other destinations.

In the second category, the estimated magnitude of pricing to market is about 40% for France, Sweden, and the United Kingdom. It is 90% for Japan, and close to zero for the United States and Canada. For the largest auto category, the point estimates of the PTM coefficient have the negative sign. For the United States, for example, the estimate of b implies that all else equal, a 20% depreciation of the dollar leads to a 3% increase in the DM price charged to U.S. buyers. Thus, the dollar price rises by 23% - even more than the depreciation itself. For France and Sweden, the effect is even more extreme.

The pattern of export pricing for Japanese auto exports is much clearer (*see Table 2*). All but one coefficient estimate implies that price adjustment will have a stabilizing effect on the price in the buyer's currency in the face of an exchange rate shock. The only exception is small car exports to the United States. The overwhelming majority of the point estimates suggest that 80% to 90% of the impact of exchange rate changes are offset by adjustment of the yen export price for all destinations. In the absence of any change in marginal cost, a 20% appreciation of the yen against the dollar would increase dollar prices by only 4% for autos over one liter in engine size.

For U.S. auto exports, the price adjustment pattern is equally clear - although much different in character (*see Table 3*). The correlation between destination-specific price movements and exchange rates is virtually zero for all destination markets. Export price adjustment appears as likely to increase the variability of price in the buyer's currency as to reduce it. Over half of the estimates lie between -.05 and .05. This stands in stark contrast to the German and Japanese auto exporters' behavior.

We were concerned about the possibility of structural change in these relationships, particularly due to the imposition of voluntary export restraints (VERs) on Japanese auto exports to Canada and the United States in 1981. Due to nonstationarity of the data, we could not run a standard Chow test. However, we did estimate equation 4 for Japanese auto exports over two subsamples, 1973-80 and 1981-87. The results are presented in Table 2A. One would expect that binding quantitative restrictions would be associated with a stable price in the destination market, and hence, a high degree of observed PTM. Indeed, the measure of PTM in Table 2A does tend to rise after 1980. For the United States and Canada, which imposed VERs on Japanese autos, the estimated increase in PTM is modest. For Germany and the United Kingdom, the apparent increase in PTM is striking. We are puzzled by this result. There was no substantial evidence of structural change by U.S. and German exporters over this sample.

Figures 1-8 provide convincing evidence of the differences in PTM for Japanese exports of autos and U.S. exports of autos. The evidence also shows that the measured export unit values behave quite sensibly given the inflation and exchange rate movements of this period. Figure 1 plots the log of the unit values of Japanese exports of autos between 1000 and 2000 cc to the United States and Germany as well as the estimated time effect (THETA) from the regression of equation (4). The time effects behave very much as expected, with their change over time closely approximated by an average of the price changes. The evidence of PTM is quite clear during the 1980s in this figure. The unit value of shipments to the United States rises much more rapidly than the German counterpart during dollar appreciation. Then when the Deutschemark strengthens against the dollar from 1985 onward, German unit values rise abruptly and U.S. unit values fall.

Further evidence can be seen in Figures 2 and 3, which plot the unit values to each destination (after subtracting their means) against the price-level-adjusted exchange rate (also net of their means). A fall in the exchange rate series of 0.1 means that with no change in the yen export price, the dollar price would fall by 10%. It is quite clear in Figure 2 that the unit value to the United States is negatively correlated with this exchange rate series. The unit value rises rapidly during periods of dollar appreciation and actually falls during the dollar depreciation of 1986-87. Figure 3 also shows how unit values to Germany rise most when the DM is appreciating and vice-versa. Figure 4 plots the adjusted exchange rate series for several destination markets. The main message of the figure is that the ability of the data to identify PTM is greatest in the 1980s, when there are divergent movements in several of the series.

Figure 1. Export prices of Japanese autos (1-2L.) to the U.S. and Germany.

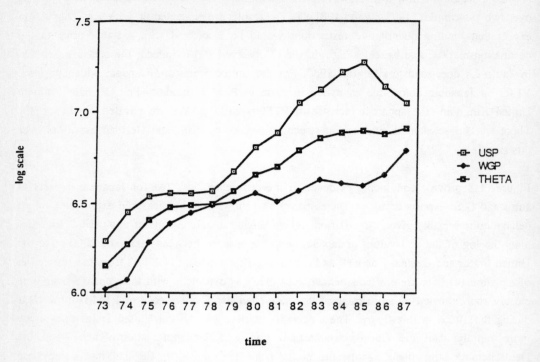

Figure 2. Export price to U.S. in relation to the price-level adjusted exchange rate.

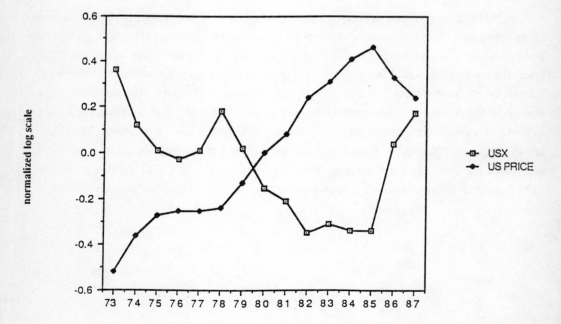

Figure 3. Export price from Japan to Germany in relation to the price-level adjusted exchange rate.

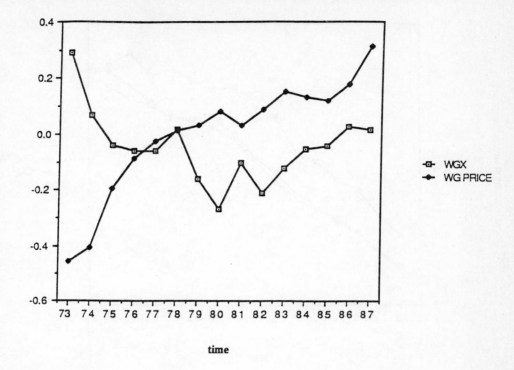

Figure 4. Price-level adjusted exchange ates against the yen for four countries.

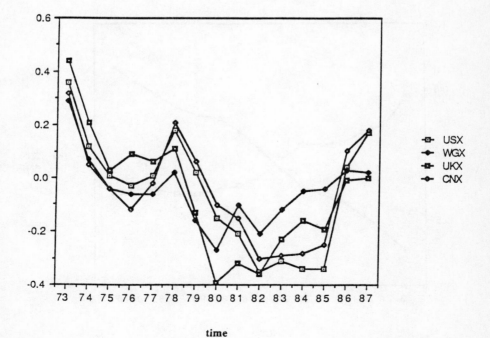

Figure 5. U.S. export price to Canada and the U.K. for autos under 6 cylinders.

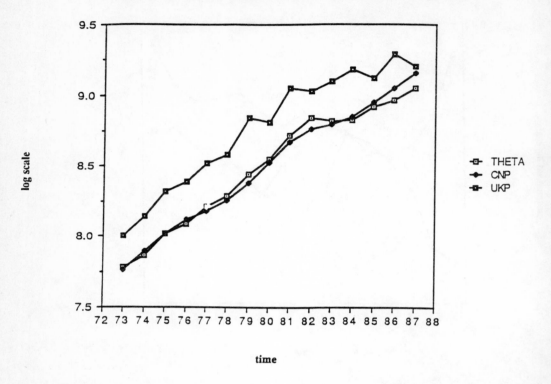

time

Figure 6. Price of exports to Canada in relation to the price-level adjusted exchange rate.

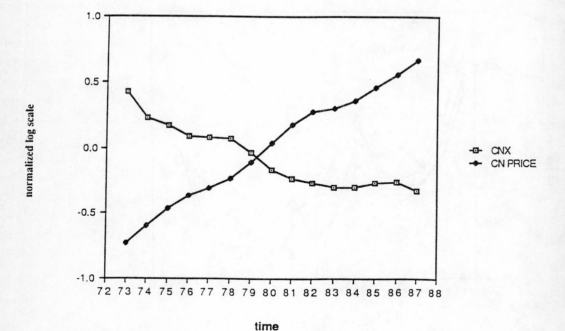

time

Figure 7. Price of exports to the U.K. in relation to the exchange rate.

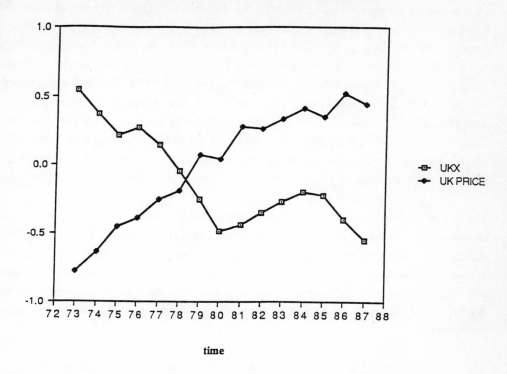

time

Figure 8. Price-level adjusted exchange rates against the dollar for four countries.

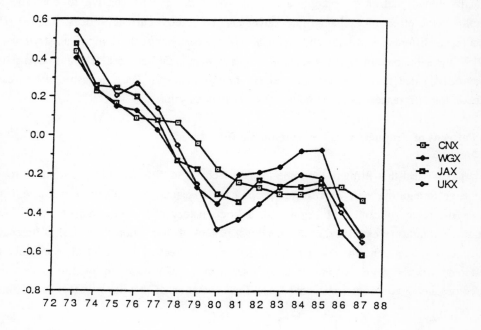

time

Figures 5-8 are the corresponding evidence for unit values of U.S. shipments of autos under 6 cylinders to Canada and the United Kingdom. The unit value series grow together quite closely, which leaves little scope for PTM. The time effects are centered around the Canadian unit values since Canada is the country without a fixed effect in the regression. Figure 8, which plots the price-level-adjusted exchange rate for several U.S. destination markets shows that the best chance of identifying PTM is during the two swings in the dollar/pound rate in the 1980s. Figure 7 shows there to be very little effect on the upward trend of unit values of shipments to the United Kingdom during either the fall of the pound between 1980 and 1985, or its subsequent rise. Figure 6 plots the rise of unit values to Canada, which proceeds quite steadily, with little apparent relationship to the exchange rate, especially in the 1980s.

The results of the first difference regressions are very similar. In general, the coefficient estimates tend to be slightly smaller in magnitude. This probably reflects the fact that adjustment to exchange rate changes takes more than a single period. Part of the adjustment to a change in the environment occurs in the next period, so the correlations are weakened slightly. Nonetheless, the same basic findings persist. The standard errors, which are reliable due to the stationarity of the differenced data, indicate that many of the coefficients are indeed significant.

The finding that the U.S. exhibits a markedly different pattern of price adjustment relative to other trading countries conforms to other evidence from different data samples. *Mann (1986)* actually found that profit margin adjustment on U.S. exports relative to domestic sales amplified the effect of exchange rate movements on foreign currency prices. *Knetter (1989)* documents differences in U.S. and German exporter behavior at the 7-digit industry level that follow the same pattern as the automobile industry data presented here. The auto data is more convincing since the product categories are nearly identical. Thus, industry effects cannot explain the differences, as might be the case in previous studies.

4. Patterns of Production in the Automobile Industry

It is paradoxical that firms in the same industry behave so differently in exporting to roughly the same foreign markets. This section proposes an explanation for the observed asymmetries in export price adjustment. I begin with a brief history of the development of the world automobile industry emphasizing the locational pattern of production. The stark differences in pricing to market behavior documented in the previous section are matched by equally stark differences in the degree of international diversification of production by auto makers in the three producing countries considered here. The contention of this paper is that diversification in the location of production by U.S. producers accomplishes the equivalent of pricing to market that we observe for Japanese producers.

Multinationalization of production facilities has a long history in the automobile industry. In 1902 the German firm Daimler acquired an Austrian subsidiary. Ford Motor Company of Canada was formed in 1903. Ford established facilities in the U.K. and France shortly thereafter. General Motors began its drive into foreign production in the 1920s. The rationale for foreign production facilities at this point in time was threefold: (1) to reduce shipping costs, (2) to avoid tariff barriers, and (3) to reduce wage costs in some cases. European firms did not develop multinational production apart from small projects in other European countries. In general, the American firms had tremendous cost advantages during this period due in part to the large domestic market which enabled more rapid development of production technology. This probably deterred the Europeans from entering the market on a large scale.

The post-World War 2 period saw expansion of European production facilities owned by U.S. firms. New factors were providing the incentives for foreign direct investment, including the strong dollar in the immediate post-war period, tighter import restrictions of the economically troubled region, and the preference for smaller, more fuel efficient vehicles due to higher real oil prices in Europe. Local content laws in many foreign countries required production to go well beyond merely assembly plants. European expansion was confined primarily to neighboring countries, apart from a few plants being set up in developing countries. No European plants were built in the U.S. due to the strong dollar, high wages and the relatively low tariff barriers in the U.S. The U.S. market was served by European exports, with the first substantial shipments hitting the market in the mid 1950s. The early entrants were smaller vehicles that had little competition from the big U.S. domestic producers. In fact, the initial response of the U.S. industry to the new European challenge was to introduce captive imports (sales of cars produced by U.S. firms abroad) to the domestic market. These captive imports have remained a non-trivial share of U.S. imports. Captive imports represented 5% of U.S. firms' sales in the domestic market and were nearly equal in magnitude to exports by German firms to the U.S.

Japan's auto industry emerged in shambles from the war. After the war, severe restrictions were placed on both imports and foreign investment in order to protect the domestic industry from outside competition. After a period of slow growth in the industry, assembly plants were allowed in the early 1950s and were gradually subjected to local content laws. Furthermore, licensing agreements with foreign firms required Japanese ownership. In conjunction with a protected domestic market, these policies spurred rapid growth in the Japanese auto industry.

By the mid 1960s the Europeans and the Japanese made inroads into the U.S. market. The share of imports exceeded 10% by 1968 and would never fall to single digits again.

The pattern of development in the automobile industry thus led to dramatic differences in the location of production facilities for the major producers of the U.S., Japan, and Germany. U.S. firms tended to produce autos in the markets in which they were sold, relying very little on exports from domestic production. This resulted from the early development of the U.S. auto industry (transportation costs were still relatively high when U.S. multinationals were born) and the relatively high wages in the U.S. Japanese firms relied exclusively on domestic production until only very recently. This is because the modern Japanese industry did not develop until the late 1950s. By then, transportation costs were low enough to make exports feasible on a large scale. Furthermore, domestic labor was cheap and foreign markets - at least the U.S. - did not have stringent restrictions against imports. Likewise, the German production facilities were based primarily at home. There were modest investments in neighboring European countries and South America. In 1978 Volkswagen built the only German-owned plant in the U.S, but U.S. production accounted for only one third of U.S. sales by VW in 1987.

In 1987, GM and Ford combined produced nearly 1.5 million vehicles in Germany. Over half of the total, about 900,000 vehicles, were exported to other markets and 600,000 were sold in Germany. Total exports from the U.S. to Germany were miniscule by comparison. They exceeded 20,000 in 1979 (when the dollar was relatively weak), fell to just over 2,000 in 1985 (when the dollar was strong) and have grown only slightly since then.

Over most of the sample period considered in this paper, all sales by Japanese firms in the U.S. market were imports from Japan. In the 1980s, led by Honda, the Japanese began producing in the U.S. The incentives for producing in the U.S. came in part from the Voluntary Export Restraint agreement and the implicit threat of further trade restrictions. The volatility of exchange rates since 1973 may have also played a role in stimulating foreign direct investment. Nonetheless, production in the U.S. by Japanese firms was still small by comparison with total sales in that market. In 1987, total sales by Japanese firms in the U.S. were 2.2 million vehicles. Less than 500,000 of these vehicles were produced in the U.S., with the remainder still exported from Japan.

While Volkswagen was the first foreign firm to begin producing in the U.S., no other German firm has followed. As of 1987, German firms sold 430,000 vehicles in the U.S. Just over 60,000 of these were VWs produced in the Pennsylvania plant. The remaining 370,000 were exported to the U.S. from West Germany.

Clearly, the U.S. industry is unique in terms of its extensive international production facilities. Models that are expected to gain significant shares in foreign markets tend to be produced in those markets - not exported from the U.S. Exports of U.S. made autos to foreign markets consist of specialty items, unlikely to become big sellers abroad. The exports of Germany and Japan, however, represent mainstream models that are intended to capture significant market shares in the foreign market. As a result, fluctuations in currency values require adjustment of the price (in units of the exporter's currency) in order for German and Japanese firms to remain competitive in foreign markets.

The vigorous pricing to market pursued by Japanese and, to a lesser extent, German exporters in the U.S. and elsewhere accomplishes what multinational production does for U.S. firms. It provides the product at a stable price in the local currency, which in turn establishes a growing clientele provided the product is successful. Why is market share so important in automobiles? In which other markets might pricing to market be observed as a substitute for multinationalization? In automobiles, the dealership and service network is essential to sales. Dealerships and service centers need continual commitment by the exporter in order to remain viable. Pricing to market establishes that commitment in much the same way as foreign direct investment does. By maintaining steady sales through pricing to market, exporters guarantee steady business at service centers and dealerships.

Is the U.S. at a relative advantage for dealing with exchange rate volatility? Perhaps so in autos, due to the international diversification of production. This diversification makes possible the shifting of production to lower cost countries as exchange rates fluctuate. Of course, production shifting may not be possible without a fair amount of standardization of the product. One would expect production shifting to occur across plants that typically produce for export. This might include Germany, Spain, and Brazil. Whether such production shifting has in fact occurred will be considered in future research.

5. Conclusions

Several conclusions can be drawn from this paper. The world market in autos is characterized by global production, although the consumer markets appear to be segmented by national boundaries. Common currency price differentials of apparently similar products are greatly affected by exchange rate fluctuations. Japanese export prices are particularly sensitive to the buyers exchange rate, evidenced by the pattern of price discrimination across the U.S. and German markets during the dollar swings of the 1980s. This reinforces the finding by *Marston*

(1990) that domestic prices in different industries are more closely related than foreign prices in the same industry. In other words, goods markets may not be very well integrated.

Secondly, the pattern of pricing to market in automobiles differs dramatically across source countries, but seems easily explained by the degree of diversification in location of production facilities. The international automobile market is segmented by national boundaries. Consequently, common currency prices differ across markets. Firms that serve their markets by exporting must price discriminate across markets, and the common currency price differentials will vary with movements in exchange rates between the destination markets. Firms that produce in the markets of final sale and do very little exporting, such as the U.S. firms, are unlikely to exhibit a similar pattern. However, both pricing to market and foreign production should not be viewed as anti-competitive practices. Together they suggest the industry is dynamically competitive within an environment that contains barriers to arbitrage including transportation costs, tariffs, product safety regulations and buyer preferences.

The automobile industry will not necessarily be typical of other manufactured goods industries. There is evidence of different patterns of pricing to market across source countries in other industries. It is not clear that such differences will be as easily explained as they are in automobiles.

References

GAGNON, J. and KNETTER, M. (1990) Pricing to Market in International Trade: Evidence from Panel Data on Automobiles and Total Manufacturing, Dartmouth College Working Paper, August, 1990.

KNETTER, M. (1989) Price Discrimination by U.S. and German Exporters, American Economic Review, March 1989, 198-210.

_____(1990) Exchange Rate Pass-Through: An Industrial Organization Approach, Dartmouth College Working Paper, 1990.

KRUGMAN, P.(1987) Pricing to Market When the Exchange Rate Changes, in S.W. ARNDT and J.D. RICHARDSON, eds., Real-Financial Linkages Among Open Economies, Cambridge: MIT Press.

MANN, C. (1986) Prices, Profit Margins and Exchange Rates, Federal Reserve Bulletin, June 1986, 366-79.

MARSTON, R. (1989) Pricing to Market in Japanese Manufacturing, National Bureau of Economic Research Working Paper No. 2905, March 1989.

MARSTON, R. (1990) Systematic Movements in Real Exchange Rates in the G-5: Evidence on the Integration of Internal and External Markets, National Bureau of Economic Research Working Paper No. 3332, April 1990.

COMMENTS ON: MULTINATIONALS AND PRICING TO MARKET BEHAVIOR

Robert Lawrence

Knetter uses an ingenious strategy of having period dummies which capture common effects and country dummies which capture institutional effects so that what remains is a coefficient which captures the country specific exchange rate effects of pricing to market. The idea is that the effects of exchange rates on marginal costs have already been controlled through the common factor in the regression so that what remains are the effects of exchange rates that operate via import demand.

The results of the paper are that automakers differ dramatically. The Japanese price to market most strongly; the Americans do not while the Germans fall somewhere in between - in small cars there is pricing to market in the US and France; in larger cars much less PTM in the USA and Canada. In the final part of the paper, Knetter offers an explanation for these differences: they can be explained by patterns of production. The United States doesn't export much. It services local markets with local production and therefore can keep prices stable through this means; the Japanese do not, however, and therefore have to price to market.

The paper is clear, carefully written and qualified and provides microfoundations for the modelling. I found the empirical analysis convincing. I am much less convinced by the explanation for the differences and certainly the degree of rigor in laying out the hypothesis and testing the production explanation differences from that of the pricing behavior itself.

First on the testing of price behavior. While the test is admirable, I must confess dome doubt that the complex strategic pricing behavior in an oligopoly can be adequately captured by a single coefficient when one might expect different responses over time and markets and would expect such behavior to be dependent on the strategic responses of other participants. It would also be useful to have the production explanation formally tested and then related back to the original elasticity coefficient in a rigorous fashion. It seems to me that Germany presents a problem for the explanation. Germany does not produce large cars in the US, yet it does not price to market. In addition, the more recent changes in Japanese production location in the form of so-called transplant operations in more recent years is not taken into account. This should be exploited, as should information on Japanese production in other parts of the world - i.e. those destinations which have large local content requirements.

It is interesting, for the Japanese, that the period of VRAs makes very little difference. I must say here that it is very important to distinguish who got the rents from the VRAs - dealers versus manufactures. Because Bhagwati argued that the VRAs were a major reason for the failure of the US trade balance to adjust. But the evidence actually suggests that the US dealers actually picked up the rents from the VRAs initially and only later, when the yen appreciated did the Japanese automakers seek to restore their profit margins by pricing these rents away from the dealers.

I would also like to suggest perhaps more could be done to exploit the unit value data on the issue of luxury versus other types of cars. I am less happy by the simple splitting of the sample into engine size. BMWs are not Toyotas. Finally, it may be interesting to lower the price of the car but will raise it when they have no choice.

FOREIGN DIRECT INVESTMENT OUTFLOW FROM THE UNITED STATES: AN EMPIRICAL ASSESSMENT

Michael W. Klein and Eric Rosengren

1. Introduction

The correlation between real exchange rates and foreign direct investment (FDI) has encouraged researchers to examine possible macroeconomic motivations for FDI. Previous research has provided empirical support for the exchange rate influencing FDI through its effect on relative wages (*Cushman, 1985, 1987; Culem, 1988*) and through its effect on relative wealth (*Froot and Stein, 1989; Klein and Rosengren 1990*). *Klein and Rosengren (1990)* find evidence that relative wealth rather than relative ages seems to best explain FDI into the United States. If relative wealth is an important determinant of FDI we should find evidence in both inward and outward FDI. This paper tests the relative wage and the relative wealth hypothesis on outward FDI data and concludes that as with inward FDI, there is greater support for the relative wealth hypothesis.

Studies which have examined macroeconomic motivations for FDI find that exchange rates can have significant effects, primarily through its impact on relative labor costs (*Cushman, 1985, 1987; Culem, 1988*). The theory underlying this relationship is that currency depreciation makes labor relatively cheap causing an inflow of capital. As long as changes in exchange rates are an important source of movements in relative labor costs between developed countries, depreciation of a country's currency should be associated with greater foreign investment.

Whether the relationship between exchange rate movements and foreign direct investment can be attributed to relative labor costs is not firmly established. The relative labor cost differences between developed countries is small compared to the wage gap between developed and less developed countries. Thus, capital for products where labor costs are important should flow to less developed countries rather than to countries which have recently experienced currency depreciation. Furthermore, given the volatility of exchange rates, investors would have no guarantee that current labor cost advantages would not be offset by future exchange rate movements. Even if a country experienced what was perceived as a permanent exchange rate depreciation that reduced relative labor costs, this would be an incentive for increased investment but not necessarily increased foreign investment. Given the impediments for foreign investors one might expect that domestic investors would have an advantage in exploiting lower labor costs created by currency depreciation.

An alternative explanation for the relationship between exchange rate movements and foreign direct investment is provided by *Froot and Stein (1989)*. They present a model where information asymmetries prevent acquisitions from being entirely financed by external debt. If external debt is costly, financing an acquisition from the wealth of the acquirer can reduce the cost of an acquisition. Consider two firms with equal wealth, one domestic the other foreign, which are bidding for a third firm. Any change in the exchange rate will provide the firm with appreciated currency an advantage in the auction since the value of their equity will increase, increasing the potential price they can offer at the auction. Thus, unlike the relative wage hypothesis, the wealth hypothesis can explain why foreign investors would have an advantage over domestic investors when their currency appreciates.

Klein and Rosengren (1990) test whether the exchange rate affects FDI through a wealth effect in a study of foreign direct investment into the United States. They find that wealth is a significant determinant of inward FDI and that relative wages are not a significant determinant after controlling for wealth. However, they did not explore whether wealth could also explain foreign direct investment out of the United States.

This paper analyzes whether the determinants of FDI from the United States is similar to the determinants of FDI into the United States. The first section provides an overview of the data. The data for outward FDI is not as comprehensive as inward FDI data. Inward and outward FDI are compared and the data problems are discussed. The second section examines the macroeconomic determinants of outward FDI. While the results are not as strong as those found by *Klein and Rosengren (1990)* for inward FDI, they do provide further support of the importance of wealth as a determinant of FDI. The final section concludes that relative wealth rather than relative wages appears to be the major mechanism for exchange rates to affect FDI.

2. Overview of the Data

The auction model implies that investors with increased wealth are more likely to win an auction for existing firms. To test this theory we would ideally want data that separates plant expansions and reinvested earning from acquisitions of existing assets. This data is available for inward FDI from the Acquisition and Establishment Survey (AES) conducted by the Bureau of Economic Analysis and from a survey of public sources conducted by the International Trade Administration. Unfortunately, comparable data is not available for outward FDI. The only available data source for foreign direct investment out of the United States is the increase in equity capital from the Balance of Payments Accounts (BPA) calculated by the Bureau of Economic Analysis. Our tests analyze the BPA data for outward FDI from the United States to Canada, Germany, France, Japan, the Netherlands, Switzerland

and the United Kingdom. These 7 countries were used in Klein and Rosengren's study of inward FDI and account for 36% of outward foreign direct investment to all countries and 69% of outward foreign direct investment to developed countries from 1979 to 1988. These same countries accounted for 73% of all foreign direct investment into the United States over the same sample period. The difference is accounted for by less developed countries who are the recipients of FDI from the United States but compose relatively little of the FDI into the United States.

The BPA has two major problems that are not encountered when using the AES data. The AES data covers acquisition of new and existing plant and equipment and therefore excludes reinvested earnings and plant expansions. The BPA measure of foreign direct investment excludes reinvested earnings, but includes plant expansions. The second problem is the treatment of acquisition financing. With the AES data the total outlay to acquire a firm is included regardless of how the investment is financed. In contrast, the BPA data only includes outlays by the foreign parent group. For example a Canadian company's purchase of an American company with its own cash would be included as inward FDI by both the BEA and the BPA. However, if the Canadian company purchased the American company with funds borrowed from an American bank, it would be included as FDI in the AES but not in the BPA.

Because of the potential problems with the BPA data it is important to contrast this measure of FDI with alternatives that are closer to the definition that we would ideally like to use. Table 1 provides the correlation of inward FDI from the AES and ITA data sources used in the Klein and Rosengren study (1990) with inward BPA data. If the inward BPA is not correlated with the AES measure of FDI, we would be concerned with using outward BPA data for measuring potential wealth effects in this study.

Table 1 shows that the BPA measure of FDI is highly correlated with the AES and International Trade Commission measures of FDI despite the significant differences in definitions. The correlation between AES and BPA is 0.62, while large, is still smaller than the correlation between the AES and ITA data.

Table 1: Correlations of Alternative FDI Measures

	AES	Total	M&A	BPA
AES	1			
Total	0.82	1		
M&A	0.87	0.91	1	
BPA	0.62	0.60	0.67	1

AES: BEA measure of foreign direct investment from
        acquisition and establishment survey
Total: ITA measure of foreign direct investment
M&A.   ITA measure of mergers and acquisitions
BPA: BEA measure of equity capital from the balance
        of payments accounts

These correlations are weighted averages of each countries correlation of FDI measures, where the weights are the average level of FDI from the U.S.

While the alternative measures of inward FDI are highly correlated with the BPA measure, it is possible that the measurement problems for outward FDI using the balance of payments definition would be more acute. Inward FDI grew significantly in the 1980s and the BPA measure is likely to be dominated by acquisitions of establishments rather than expansion of existing companies. The opposite is true for outward foreign direct investment which is likely to be dominated by plant expansions rather than new acquisitions since American firms established significant foreign operations well before the 1980s. Therefore, the BPA outflow data may principally reflect plant expansions rather than new acquisitions. Despite its success in describing FDI inflow, we might expect the wealth variable to perform less successfully in describing FDI outflows because of the lack of new acquisitions.

Table 2 provides summary statistics on capital outflows for the 7 countries in our study. The table provides the maximum, minimum and average outward FDI over the ten year period for which outward FDI is available (1979-1988). By far the largest two destinations for American capital are the United Kingdom and Canada. While the same is true for capital inflow data there are two important differences. First, the magnitude of the outflows is much smaller than the inflows. For example, over this 10 year period capital inflows averaged $8 billion from the United Kingdom to the United States while capital outflows to the United Kingdom from the United States over the same period averaged only 1.7 billion. In recent years the disparity between capital inflows and capital outflows is most apparent with Japan. While capital inflows from Japan have increased significantly in recent years, capital outflows to Japan remain relatively modest. The average, maximum and minimum capital outflows to Japan are all below that of the other six countries, despite the Japanese economy being much larger than the other countries in our sample. Second, while inflows from most countries increased significantly at the end of the sample, outflows do not show a positive trend for most countries.

Table 2: Capital Outflow by Country (Millions)*

	Minimum	Maximum	Average
Canada	614.9	2605.2	1165.8
France	130.4	641.8	297.4
Germany	150.8	772.1	350.7
United Kingdom	288.0	3180.0	1675.8
Switzerland	35.3	816.0	226.7
Japan	34.8	498.9	218.1
Netherlands	66.0	748.1	264.7

* Constant 1988 dollars, deflated by implicit price deflator.

Table 3 provides the cross-country correlations of outward FDI. No clear pattern emerges except for outflows to Japan which are negatively correlated with outflows to every other country in our sample except Switzerland and Canada.

Table 3: Cross-Country Correlations of FDI (Outflows)

	Can	France	Germany	Japan	Neth	Switz	UK
Canada	1						
France	0.64	1					
Germany	0.01	0.07	1				
Japan	0.03	-0.27	-0.10	1			
Neth	-0.03	0.26	0.79	-0.41	1		
Switz	-0.35	0.13	-0.15	0.48	-0.15	1	
UK	0.48	0.56	0.10	-0.56	0.61	-0.48	1

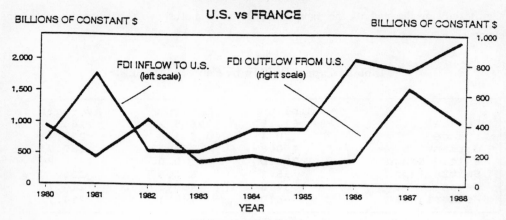

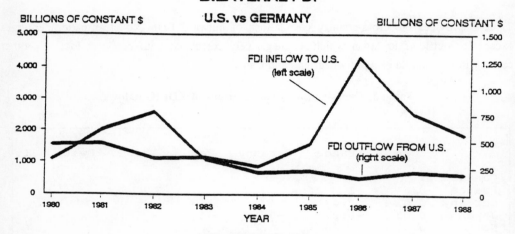

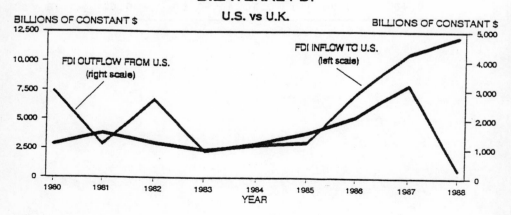

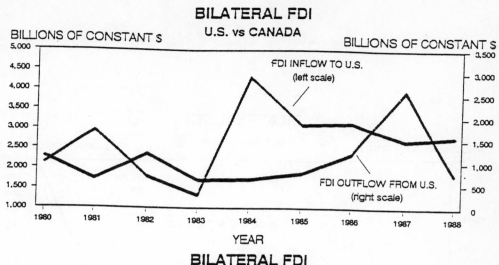

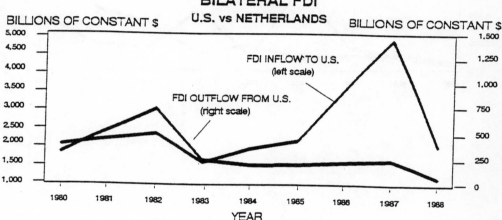

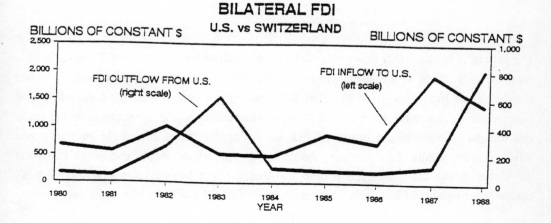

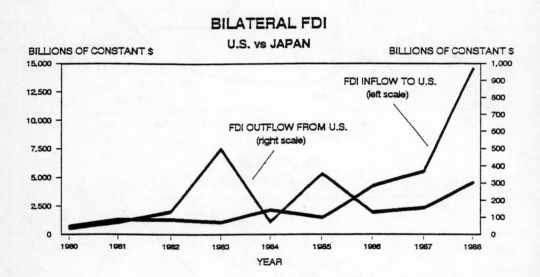

The pattern of bilateral FDI flows with each of the countries are shown in the 7 charts. In each chart the FDI inflow to the United States and the FDI outflow to the United States is shown for the period from 1980 to 1988. The BPA measure of FDI is used for both inflow and outflow data. The charts have several common characteristics. For most countries the peaks and troughs of outflow and inflow of FDI do not appear coincident. If the exchange rate affects relative wealth, periods where the dollar has appreciated should encourage FDI from the United States but discourage FDI to the United States from foreign investors. For all countries the volume of FDI inflow was much larger than FDI outflow during the 1980s.

3. Determinants of FDI from the United States

Klein and Rosengren (1990) using FDI inflows found the correlation between exchange rates and FDI is best explained with wealth rather than relative labor costs. We want to examine whether this relationship also occurs in the FDI outflow data. Following the convention in the empirical literature we scale foreign direct investment by the GNP of the host country. Normalizing outward FDI by some measure of net worth of foreign companies would be an alternative specification. Unfortunately, such information to our knowledge is not available.

The two most important variables are our measures of wealth and relative labor costs. Our measure of relative wealth, $Stock_{it}$, is the dollar value of the United States stock market divided by the dollar value of the stock market in country i at time t. The stock market data is from the Morgan Stanley Capital International Perspective which is a weighted index of stocks representing approximately 60% of each country's market capitalization. The expected sign of the wealth variable is positive, as American investors are wealthier; either because of dollar appreciation or a relative increase in the value of American stocks, they should be less wealth constrained when bidding for foreign companies.

The measure of relative labor cost, $wage_{it}$, is the index of United States manufacturing wages divided by the dollar valued index of manufacturing in country i at time t. The source of the wage indices is the International Monetary Fund's International Financial Statistics. The expected sign of the relative wage variable is positive. As United States wages become relatively more expensive with dollar appreciation, investors prefer to invest abroad to reduce their labor costs.

In addition we include several variables to control for factors not captured by a relative wealth or relative labor cost hypothesis. A trend variable is included to control for secular changes in FDI outflow. While a clear upward trend for inward FDI is apparent from the charts, no clear pattern appears for outward FDI so the sign is indeterminate. DIFGDP is the annual growth rate of GDP in the foreign country minus the annual growth rate of GDP in the United States. If foreign countries are growing much faster than the United States, investment prospects should increase FDI outflow so the expected sign is positive. Country specific intercept dummies are included to allow for different intercepts across countries. Equation 1 is estimated on annual data from 1979 to 1988 for outflows to Canada, France, Germany, Netherlands, Switzerland, Japan and the United Kingdom.

1) $FDI_i = B_0 + B_1 \ln(Stock_{it}) + B_2 \ln(Wage_{it}) + B_3 Trend_i + B_4 DifGDP_{it} + \sum_{j=1}^{6} a_j$ [

The subscript i refers to countries and the subscript t refers to time. The dependent variable is a 1x68 stacked vector of 7 countries' FDI, each with 10 annual observations except Netherlands which has only 8 observations because of two years of suppressed data to maintain confidentiality. The regressions are estimated by OLS. Two tests for the presence of autocorrelated error terms were conducted. The first ran individual country regressions without the country specific dummy variables and the Durbin Watson was checked. The second regressed the error on the lagged error term after dropping the first observation of each of the seven countries. Both tests failed to reject the hypothesis of no serial correlation.

The results of estimating equation 1 are reported in Table 4. The first column is equation 1 with the relative wage variable omitted. The second column is equation 1 with the relative stock variable omitted. The third column is equation 1. When the relative wage variable is omitted, relative stock has the expected sign and is significant at the 95% level of confidence. The difference in GDP and the trend are not significantly different from 0. When relative stock is omitted, relative wage has the correct sign and is significant at the 90 percent level of confidence. When both relative stock and relative wage are included, both have the correct sign but neither is significantly different from 0. The coefficient on relative wage in the full equation is much lower while the coefficients on relative stock and the other independent variables is unchanged.

As was noted earlier, capital outflows to Japan have been quite small relative to the size of their economy. In addition, Japan experienced an unprecedented increase in their stock market in the 1980s. Such an increase in their stock market relative to the United States should increase Japanese inflows into the United States and discourage United States outflows to Japan. As shown in the chart presented earlier, Japanese inflows have risen sharply while outflows to Japan have not changed noticeably. If cultural, economic, and governmental barriers have already made capital entry into Japan quite difficult, capital outflows to Japan may be unresponsive to changes in relative wealth.

Table 5 presents two modifications to equation 1. The first includes an interactive dummy variable for Japanese stock. The dummy variable is equal to the relative stock price of Japan for the Japanese observations and 0 otherwise. The second modification excludes Japan entirely. Both modifications result in an increased coefficient on relative stock and an increase in the t-statistic of the coefficient. When equation 1 is run with an interactive dummy for Japan, relative stock is significant at the 90% level of confidence while the relative wage variable remains insignificantly different from 0. When Japan is excluded altogether relative stock is significant at the 95% level of confidence while relative wage is insignificantly different from 0.

Table 4: United States Outward FDI

	equation 1	equation 2	equation 3
Relative Stock	0.85 (0.38)**		0.73 (0.52)
Relative Wage		0.88* (0.52)	0.23 (0.69)
Trend	0.00 (0.03)	0.01 (0.0;)	0.00 (0.03)
Differences in GDP	0.02 (0.04)	0.02 (0.04)	0.02 (0.04)

Regressors not reported here are the constant and six country-specific dummy variables. Numbers in parentheses are standard errors. The dependent variable is outward FDI scaled by GDP of the target country.

*significant at 10%; **significant at 5%*

Table 5: United States Outward FDI

	Interactive Japan Dummy	Excluding Japan
Relative Stock	1.08 (0.59)*	1.13 (0.56)**
Relative Wage	0.28 (0.69)	0.25 (0.66)
Trend	-0.01 (0.03)	-0.01 (0.03)
Differences in GDP	0.03 (0.04)	0.04 (0.04)
Interactive Japan Dummy	-0.99 (0.79)	
R^2	0.74	0.65

Regressors not reported here are the constant and six country-specific dummy variables. Numbers in parentheses are standard errors. The dependent variable is outward FDI scaled by GDP of the target country.

*significant at 10%; **significant at 5%*

Tests were conducted to see if the coefficient on relative wages was sensitive to the choice of countries. Exclusion of countries did not affect the finding of relative wages having no significant effect on capital outflows after controlling for wealth.

4. Conclusion

Previous research has found that relative wealth is an important determinant of FDI into the United States. This paper finds that relative wealth is also an important determinant of FDI out of the United States. While studies of this link are hampered by the lack of data related directly to acquisition and establishments that are available for inward FDI, a significant link appears when Japan is excluded from the sample. The wealth effect may be of little relevance to outward FDI to Japan because of the significant barriers to entry into the Japanese capital market.

The link between FDI and relative labor costs appears more tenuous. After controlling for wealth, relative labor costs are not a significant determinant of outward FDI in any of our regressions. It is possible that relative labor costs would be an important determinant of FDI in a broader sample of countries that included less developed countries. However these labor cost differentials are likely to be more affected by relative stages of development rather than exchange rate fluctuations whose effect on long-term labor costs are uncertain.

This article ignores the many industrial organization arguments for foreign direct investment. This omission is not because industrial organization motivations for FDI are irrelevant, but rather, because these effects are difficult to test using aggregated data.

The macroeconomic motivations for FDI examined in this paper are often omitted in studies examining industrial organizational motivations for FDI. Our findings show that relative wealth may be an important determinant of FDI. Future studies should consider whether the wealth effect that appears in macroeconomic data continues to be important in studies using disaggregated data that can better control for industrial organization motivations for FDI.

References

CULEM, C.G. (1988) The Locational Determinants of Direct Investments Among Industrialized Countries, European Economic Review, 32, 885-904.

CUSHMAN, D.O. (1985) Real Exchange Rate Risk, Expectations, and the Level of Direct Investment, Review of Economics and Statistics, 297-308.

CUSHMAN, D.O. (1987) The Effect of Real Wages and Labor Productivity on Foreign Direct Investment, Southern Economic Journal, 174-185.

FROOT, K.A. and STEIN, J.C. (1989) Exchange Rates and Foreign Direct Investment, An Imperfect Capital Markets Approach: N.B.E.R. Working Paper, 2914.

KLEIN, M.W. and ROSENGREN, E. (1990) Determinants of Foreign Direct Investment in the United States, Clark University Working Paper 90-3.

COMMENTS ON: FOREIGN DIRECT INVESTMENT OUTFLOW FROM THE UNITED STATES: AN EMPIRICAL ASSESSMENT

Edward M. Graham

Drs. Klein and Rosengren's paper is an extension of work that they did to test the hypothesis of Froot and Stein that correlations between exchange rate changes and foreign direct investment flows into the United States can be accounted for by wealth effects induced by exchange rate changes. They found that such wealth effects are significant in explaining these inflows.

In the present paper, Klein and Rosengren look at wealth effects as a determinant of US outward direct investment. They do find significant effects when Japan is excluded from the list of host nations, but insignificant effects when Japan is included. They conclude that Japan has significant barriers to direct investment inflows (and to foreign acquisition of domestic firms in particular, we might note), and hence that the wealth effect hypothesis can be accepted.

Their results, however, are never as robust as were the earlier ones for inward direct investment. There are substantial reasons, in fact, to question the hypothesis as regards US direct outward investment to Europe. Perhaps the most substantial of these is that US multinational firms have long established presences in Europe, and indeed hold significant portions of their assets in Europe. Thus, any wealth effect deriving from exchange rate changes would be at most a net effect; if, for example, the dollar depreciated relative to European currencies, the effect would be that any US-based multinational firm's European assets would rise in value relative to its US ones. In net, the total resulting increase in the dollar value of this firm's assets (as a percentage of the initial dollar value of these assets) would be less than the increase (again, in dollar value) of a purely European rival. How great would be the relative increase in the wealth of the European rival would, of course, depend upon the proportion of the total assets of the US-based firm held in Europe.

The point here is that relative wealth changes induced by exchange rate movements is attenuated by the diversified nature of the assets held by multinational firms. Combined with possible capital market "hysteresis" in the face of exchange rate volatility, one can begin to question whether the Froot and Stein hypothesis would be valid for established multinationals.

So why then are Klein and Rosengren able to report significant relationships between measures of US outward investment to Europe and exchange rate movements not attributable to relative labor costs? One possibility is that, the preceding remarks notwithstanding, wealth effects are significant. But another is that the correlations are spurious.

One factor weighing in favor of the latter is that because Klein and Rosengren used balance of payments data for FDI, they might not have used data that adequately capture wealth effects. This data includes equity increases used to finance plant expansion, which presumably is not responsive to wealth effects, or at least not to the same extent as acquisitions. Klein and Rosengren acknowledge this possibility.

An "out-of-sample" reason to question their results stems from the fact that US-based firms in Europe have been on something of an acquisitions binge in 1989 and 1990, as part of an overall expansion and rationalization of their capacity in response to Europe's prospects for growth in the wake of the 1992 program and other initiatives to make Europe a more integrated market. The period 1989-1990 is not covered in Klein and Rosengren's data, and it is not clear whether inclusion of this period would alter their results. I suspect it would. The nation in which the largest number of acquisitions have been recorded is the United Kingdom. But this binge has occurred during a period when on trend the dollar has been falling against European currencies in general and especially against the pound sterling. This, on the face of it, is contrary to the Froot/Stein hypothesis.

The best test of the Froot/Stein hypothesis for US investment in Europe would be to determine whether currency-induced wealth effects could explain merger and acquisition activity by US nationals in Europe, and data on this activity are now becoming available (e.g., from *Translink's 1992 M&A Monthly*). Alas, however, the data are available for recent years only, and the series may be too short to enable robust statistical testing. The bottom line thus may be simply that the Froot/Stein hypothesis, as regarding US direct investment in Europe, can be better addressed several years from now than at the present time.

TECHNOLOGY-BASED TRADE AND MULTINATIONALS' INVESTMENT IN EUROPE: STRUCTURAL CHANGE AND COMPETITION IN SCHUMPETERIAN GOODS

Henning Klodt

1. Introduction

The patterns of international trade between developed and less developed countries are rapidly changing. Especially in high-tech industries, industrial countries are facing intensified competition from abroad, in particular from newly industrializing countries of South-East Asia. The production and export of modern consumer electronics, data processing equipment and sophisticated textiles are no longer an exclusive domain of rich and research-intensive countries (*Figure 1*).

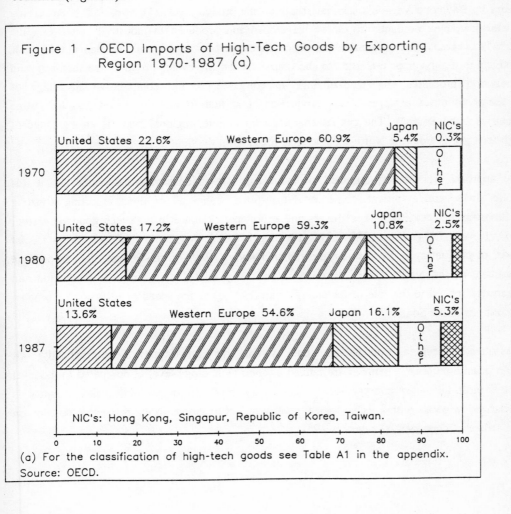

Figure 1 - OECD Imports of High-Tech Goods by Exporting Region 1970-1987 (a)

NIC's: Hong Kong, Singapur, Republic of Korea, Taiwan.

(a) For the classification of high-tech goods see Table A1 in the appendix.
Source: OECD.

These developments are challenging the conventional wisdom of textbooks on international trade and the product cycle. In the following text, it is argued that the shifts in the composition of inter-industry trade are mainly reflecting shifts in the international transfer of technology. For a formal analysis of these shifts a simple Ricardian model with one production factor, two countries and three types of goods is developed. The model explicitly takes into account sectoral differences in the transaction costs of technology transfer (Section 2). Subsequently, it is examined whether the predictions of the model are in accordance with the structure of international trade (Section 3). A summary is provided in Section 4.

2. Determinants of Comparative Advantage in High-Tech Industries
2.1 Product Cycle Models

The development and diffusion of product innovations was integrated into international trade theory by Raymond Vernon's seminal article on the product cycle (*Vernon, 1966*). According to his view, new products are chiefly developed and produced in industrial countries ("the North") because R&D capacities are concentrated in this region and the demand for new products is highly income-elastic. In the course of the life-cycle, products are maturing and production processes are standardizing. In consequence, the comparative advantage of industrial countries disappears and production is shifted to less developed and low wage countries ("the South"). The central characteristic of inter-regional trade is an exchange of high-tech goods from the North for low-tech goods from the South.

This approach immediately attracted the interest of international trade theorists;[1] and it was applied in several empirical studies on North-South trade, all of them reporting a strong relationship between R&D expenditures and export performance in high-tech goods (*Keesing, 1967; Hirsch, 1974; Horn, 1976*). Nevertheless, it took more than a decade before a formal model of product cycle trade was presented (*Krugman, 1979*). In this model, the comparative advantage of the North in new products is positively related to the rate of innovation and negatively related to the rate of technology transfer, i.e. to the speed of diffusion of product innovations to the South.

Subsequently, Krugman extended the model by replacing the two types of countries and goods by an infinite number. Countries are ranked by their technology level as compared to the level of the most advanced country - the "technology gap". In this version, each country is specialized in goods with a technological quality that corresponds to the respective position on the "ladder of countries" (*Krugman, 1985*).

The concept of the product cycle was further developed by Gene Grossman and Elhanan Helpman. In the Krugman models, the rate of innovation in the North and the speed of technology transfer from North to South are exogenous. Grossman and Helpman, by contrast, argue that both innovation and imitation are costly and that entrepreneurial decisions on these activities depend on expected discounted values of future profits arising from the introduction of new goods in the North and from transferring technical knowledge to the South (*Grossman and Helpman, 1989a, 1989b, 1989c, 1990*). They still adhere to the assumption that product innovations can only occur in the North, but the whole product cycle is now endogenously determined.

As a common feature of all product cycle models, there is a monotonic hierarchy of countries and products with respect to their technology intensity. In consequence, the predictions on international specialization are very similar to the original Vernon version: If innovation exclusively takes place in the North, the South will never be able to gain a comparative advantage in high-tech products. In other words, these models are unable to explain the success-stories of the Asian NIC's, which are mainly based upon exports of specific high-tech products.

2.2 Mobile and Immobile Schumpeter Industries

Understanding the ongoing shifts in high-tech trade presumably requires a closer look at the specific properties of the international transfer of technology in research-intensive industries (hereafter: Schumpeter industries). Due to imperfections in the market for technical knowledge, most of this transfer takes place within multinational firms. By and large, research and development activities are concentrated in industrial countries, but the resulting know-how is often transferred as a head-quarter service to foreign affiliates in low-wage countries. The increasing importance of such transactions may reduce the explanatory power of traditional product cycle models (*Vernon, 1979*).[2]

The crucial factor for the profitability of multinational activities in Schumpeter industries are the transaction costs that are associated with the geographical separation of R&D and production. If these transaction costs exceed the wage differential between the South and the North, a shift of production to the South will not pay. In traditional product cycle models, it is implicitly assumed that the transaction costs of technology transfer in Schumpeter industries are prohibitively high, i.e. the establishment of production sites for high-tech goods in the South is not feasible at all.[3] In reality, however, it can be expected that there are substantial differences across Schumpeter industries:

- In some industries, like non-electrical machinery or the aerospace industry, R&D is an integral part of the whole production process. Here, successful development of new products depends on intense personal contacts between scientists, engineers and production workers and often it is even impossible to distinguish between research and production departments. Separating R&D from production would involve a loss of synergy effects or economies of scope that would probably more than outweigh the labor cost advantage of producing abroad. Since it is very unlikely that such industries will shift their production of high-tech goods to less developed countries, they may be labelled as "immobile Schumpeter industries".

- In other industries, like pharmaceuticals or biotechnology, the links between research and production are much weaker, but production itself requires the availability of a well-trained labor force. Since high-skilled workers are in general not available in low-wage countries, the comparative advantage of industrial countries in these industries is not endangered. They can also be included, therefore, in the category of immobile Schumpeter industries.

- The production of computers and other microelectronic appliances may serve as a third example. In this industry, the development of new products is in general concentrated in specific research departments with their own scientific and technical research staff. Formal and informal links to production departments are of minor importance. Hence, a geographical separation of R&D and production is technically feasible. Since the qualification requirements in production are rather low, it is often profitable to carry out R&D in an industrial headquarter country and to shift production of new goods from the beginning to foreign affiliates in low-wage regions. Such industries may be called "mobile Schumpeter industries".

The dynamics of comparative advantage in Schumpeter industries presumably result from technical progress in information and communication technologies. In the past two decades, new developments in microelectronics facilitated communication across long distances by providing a variety of new techniques and by substantially reducing the costs of transmitting information. Monitoring and supervising the production of foreign affiliates is less expensive, therefore, than in previous periods. This increased potential for an internationalization of production can be best exploited by mobile Schumpeter industries. It can be expected, therefore, that competition from low wage regions in high-tech products concentrates on this field.

The next section presents a formal model that is intended to catch the main features of shifting comparative advantages in different Schumpeter industries.

2.3 A Modified Product Cycle Model

In Ricardian models of international trade, the comparative advantage of countries are determined not by different relative factor endowments but by different technology levels. These differences can most easily be handled in a one-factor model, since in this case technology differences reduce to differences in productivity[4]. In order to take account of the considerations on sectoral differences in technology transfer, three types of industries are distinguished: industries with standardized technology (s), immobile Schumpeter industries (i) and mobile Schumpeter industries (m).

It is assumed that the "best-practice" technology for each sector is improving with a constant rate p over time t. The development of the "best-practice" technology can be expressed as the development of the sector-specific input coefficient (a^*)[5]:

$$(1) \quad a_z^* = e^{-p_z t} ; \quad z = s, i, m$$

The sector-specific rate of technical progress p_z can be interpreted as a measure of the technology intensity of sector z.

Different technology levels of countries show up in different technology gaps to the "best-practice" technology. This gap can be modelled by the time-lag (l) between innovation in the most advanced country and imitation in the country under consideration. The input coefficient of country j in sector z is given by

$$(2) \quad a_z^j = e^{-p_z(t-l_z^j)}$$

The productivity advantage of country j vis-a-vis country k in industry z depends on the ratio of input coefficients:

$$(3) \quad a_z^k / a_z^j = e^{-p_z(t-l_z^k)} / e^{-p_z(t-l_z^j)}$$

$$= e^{p_z(1_z^k - 1_z^j)} \quad ; \quad 1_z^k > 1_z^j$$

In a logarithmic form, (3) reads as follows:

$$\ln a_z^k - \ln a_z^j = p_z(1_z^k - 1_z^j)$$

Since this expression is always positive (i.e. productivity in country j is higher than in country k), country j faces an absolute advantage over country k in all industries. This advantage increases with the technology level p_z and the difference in imitation lags.

An explicit formulation of comparative advantages would require an inclusion of the demand side into the model. If there are no impediments to trade, however, then a country will face a comparative advantage in industries with an above-average absolute advantage or a below-average absolute disadvantage. The average itself is the production-weighted absolute advantage or disadvantage of all industries of that country against foreign countries.

In this general form of the model, various constellations of comparative advantages and disadvantages can occur, depending on sector-specific technology intensities and imitation lags. In order to derive unequivocal conclusions, some further restrictions must be introduced. In the following, it is assumed that the technology intensities of both types of Schumpeter industries are identical:

$$(4) \quad p_h = p_i = p_m$$

Furthermore, the imitation lags within countries are assumed to be the same for standardized industries and immobile Schumpeter industries:

$$(5) \quad 1_s^j = 1_i^j = 1^j$$

The imitation lag in mobile Schumpeter industries is given as a fraction r of l:

$$(6) \quad 1_m^j = rl^j \quad ; \quad 0 \le r \le 1$$

Equation (6) implies that imitation in mobile Schumpeter industries is always easier than in other industries but that advanced countries are in a better position for imitation than less advanced countries.

For the three types of industries, the absolute advantages are now determined as follows:

$$(7) \quad \ln a_s^k - \ln a_s^j = p_s (1^k - 1^j)$$

$$(8) \quad \ln a_i^k - \ln a_i^j = p_h (1^k - 1^j)$$

$$(9) \quad \ln a_m^k - \ln a_m^j = p_h r (1^k - 1^j)$$

From $p_s < p_h$ it follows that developed countries (j) have a comparative advantage vis-a-vis less developed countries (k) in immobile Schumpeter industries. If $r = 1$, the advantages of developed countries in mobile and immobile Schumpeter industries are identical. With declining r, the comparative advantage of industrial countries in mobile Schumpeter industries deteriorates and eventually turns into a comparative disadvantage, that may be even more distinct than in standardized industries.

In this model, p, l, and r are exogenously determined. It can be argued, however, that p and l depend on the R&D activities in advanced and less advanced countries respectively and that r is mainly influenced by the development of information and communication technologies. The catch-up of some less developed countries in Schumpeter industries can be ascribed, therefore, to a narrowing of the technology gap (to a shortening of the imitation lag l) or to an increased potential for an internationalization of production in mobile Schumpeter industries (a decline in r).

In conventional product cycle models, it is impossible for developing countries to specialize in high-tech goods. In the version presented in this section, by contrast, such shifts of specialization are very likely when the costs of transmitting information across long distances are substantially decreasing. In the remainder, it is examined whether the patterns of inter-industry trade are in accordance with the predictions of the model.

3. Changing Patterns of Inter-Industry Trade

Statistics on international trade are in general organized by product groups, not by industry. For an empirical investigation, the three types of industry under consideration must be identified by their corresponding headings of the Standard International Trade Classification (SITC). The products of Schumpeter industries can be distinguished from the products of standardized industries by a variety of different lists that are mainly based upon the so-called Kelly's list of the *OECD (1969)*, which was repeatedly refined and revised[6].

Discerning the subcategories of mobile and immobile Schumpeter industries requires additional information on the links and economies of scope between R&D and production. That kind of information can be derived from engineering estimates or from the extent of multinational activities in different industries. Within Schumpeter industries, it can be expected that the internationalization of production will be a predominant strategy in mobile Schumpeter industries. Hence, statistical information on the relative importance of multinational enterprises can serve as a guideline for separating mobile from immobile Schumpeter industries *(Klodt, 1987)*.

Based on a list of products of different types of industries *(Table 4* in the appendix) the export and import values of industrial countries were calculated from OECD trade statistics. The comparative advantages of countries were evaluated by the concept of revealed comparative advantage (RCA), i.e. by comparing the export/import ratio of specific industries to the export/import ratio of the whole country:

$$RCA_z = \ln (x_z/m_z : \Sigma\, x_z/\Sigma\, m_z) \cdot 100$$

x_z and m_z denote the exports and imports of industry z. Positive RCA values indicate a comparative advantage, negative values a disadvantage. In a world of free trade, this concept is equivalent to the concept of comparative advantage in the above described product cycle models. The results for seven major industrial countries (Table 1) disclose a comparative disadvantage of most of them in standardized industries (except Italy). In immobile Schumpeter industries, by contrast, the RCA-values for most of these countries have been and still are positive. And they are in general substantially higher than the RCA-values in mobile Schumpeter industries. Presumably, these differences can be attributed to the comparably low impediments to international technology transfer in mobile Schumpeter industries.

**Table 1: Revealed Comparative Advantage of Seven OECD Countries
1970-1987**

	1970	1980	1987
United States			
Standardized industries	-64.9	-54.0	-67.9
Mobile Schumpeter industries	53.4	33.0	35.8
Immobile Schumpeter industries	37.2	27.8	20.6
Japan			
Standardized industries	19.6	-35.4	-82.5
Mobile Schumpeter industries	-17.8	-2.6	28.3
Immobile Schumpeter industries	-25.1	54.8	68.1
West Germany			
Standardized industries	-45.3	-41.0	-36.3
Mobile Schumpeter industries	5.0	- 2.4	-15.4
Immobile Schumpeter industries	65.1	56.3	50.3
France			
Standardized industries	- 3.8	-11.8	-11.9
Mobile Schumpeter industries	-15.2	-13.1	- 1.3
Immobile Schumpeter industries	14.7	25.5	15.6
United Kingdom			
Standardized industries	-29.9	-22.1	-10.2
Mobile Schumpeter industries	-20.7	6.4	0.0
Immobile Schumpeter industries	67.2	25.7	13.1
Italy			
Standardized industries	3.5	25.2	33.5
Mobile Schumpeter industries	-24.0	-52.5	-60.2
Immobile Schumpeter industries	10.0	- 5.4	- 5.6
Sweden			
Standardized industries	- .9	- 3.3	0.6
Mobile Schumpeter industries	-22.5	-30.7	-34.5
Immobile Schumpeter industries	15.8	21.9	18.4

Source: OECD; own calculations

The major beneficiaries of an intensified international transfer of technology are those countries that are wide open to foreign direct investment. Since the technology of mobile Schumpeter industries is largely conveyed by the establishment of foreign affiliates of multinational enterprises, liberal capital markets are a prerequisite for attracting mobile technical knowledge. In this respect, the NIC's of South-East Asia probably provided the most favorable conditions for shifting the production of high-tech goods to low wage regions.

In the course of the past two decades the Asian NIC's turned into serious competitors of industrial countries. They are no longer restricted to the export of standardized labor intensive goods. In immobile Schumpeter industries, their importance is still rather low, but they increasingly take advantage of the new opportunities for internationalizing production in mobile Schumpeter industries (Table 2).

It can be expected that the NIC's of the first generation will continue to specialize in mobile Schumpeter industries and that the Asian NIC's of the second generation (like Malaysia, the Philippines or Thailand) will soon follow this path. The decisive step in this direction seems to be an opening of domestic capital markets for foreign investors, since the inflow of technology is closely related to the inflow of fixed capital.

In the future some CMEA-countries will probably join the Asian NIC's. Especially Poland, Hungary and the CSFR are opening their capital markets and are increasingly attractive for foreign direct investment. Up to the late eighties, however, this potential was not exploited. Despite rapidly changing world market conditions the export structure of CMEA-countries was rather stable - clearly indicating sluggish central planning (Table 3).

With respect to factor endowment, the CMEA-countries are in a position quite similar to the Asian NIC's: an abundant supply of labor, a well-developed educational system, and a comparably low level of their own R&D activities. In South-East Asia, the import of modern technology was mainly achieved by attracting technology intensive multinational enterprises. In past years, the CMEA-countries have not been able to adopt a similar strategy since their currencies were non-convertible, capital markets were almost non-existent, and external trade was a state monopoly[7].

In years to come, it can be expected that Poland, Czechoslovakia, and Hungary will no longer specialize in resource and labor intensive industries and will be able to gain significant market

Table 2: Structure of South-East Asian Exports to the OECD
1970-1987

Country	Export shares (percent)		
	1970	1980	1987
Hong Kong			
Standardized industries	87.8	82.6	75.3
Mobile Schumpeter industries	11.7	15.3	21.8
Immobile Schumpeter industries	.5	2.1	2.9
Singapore			
Standardized industries	50.4	31.9	19.6
Mobile Schumpeter industries	47.9	57.3	69.8
Immobile Schumpeter industries	1.7	10.8	10.6
Republic of Korea			
Standardized industries	91.7	79.4	62.6
Mobile Schumpeter industries	7.8	18.5	27.1
Immobile Schumpeter industries	.5	2.1	10.3
Taiwan			
Standardized industries	74.7	71.2	62.6
Mobile Schumpeter industries	23.8	23.2	28.9
Immobile Schumpeter industries	1.5	5.6	8.8

Source: OECD; own calculations

Table 3: Structure of CMEA Exports to the OECD 1970-1987

Country	Export shares (percent)		
	1970	1980	1987
Czechoslovakia			
Standardized industries	62.4	63.3	64.4
Mobile Schumpeter industries	10.0	14.1	15.3
Immobile Schumpeter industries	27.6	22.6	20.3
Hungary			
Standardized industries	71.7	62.3	62.4
Mobile Schumpeter industries	16.7	21.6	21.5
Immobile Schumpeter industries	11.6	16.1	16.1
Poland			
Standardized industries	73.1	66.1	67.5
Mobile Schumpeter industries	13.8	10.6	15.4
Immobile Schumpeter industries	13.1	23.3	17.1
Soviet Union			
Standardized industries	78.3	53.3	57.6
Mobile Schumpeter industries	8.9	27.9	23.2
Immobile Schumpeter industries	12.8	18.8	19.2

Source: OECD; own calculations

shares in mobile Schumpeter industries. Within this category, they will not necessarily specialize in the same niches as the Asian NIC's, i.e. in products related to microelectronics. Perhaps, their traditional industry structure will be more favorable to technological cooperation with the West in sophisticated chemicals or other mobile Schumpeter industries.

Whatever the case may be, Western industrial countries should be ready to face an intensified competition in this segment of the high-tech market. They will be forced to strengthen their position in immobile Schumpeter industries and to shift at least part of their production factors from manufacturing to sophisticated services.

4. Summary

The previous analysis suggests that structural change in international trade of high-tech goods is increasingly influenced by international technology transfer. The catch-up of less developed countries is not evenly distributed over industries. Instead, new patterns of specialization are emerging.

The new patterns cannot be depicted in conventional models of the product cycle. Innovations are no longer trickling down the ladder of countries, but less developed countries are often in a position to produce high-tech goods from the first date of innovation onwards. The new opportunities for and internationalization of high-tech production mainly arise from the development of modern information and communication technologies that facilitate the transmission of information across long distances. Especially in those industries where a geographical separation of R&D and production is feasible without a loss of efficiency (mobile Schumpeter industries), the increased potential for international technology transfer has reduced the comparative advantage of industrial countries. The central determinants of shifting comparative advantages are analyzed in a modified product cycle model, which explicitly takes account of sectoral differences in the transaction costs of international technology transfer.

By and large, structural change of world trade in the past two decades is in accordance with the predictions of the model. The position of Western industrial countries in high-tech goods is no longer unaffected by the competition from low-wage regions. Especially the NIC's from South-East Asia have gained substantial market shares in mobile Schumpeter industries. Up to the present, the CMEA-countries have not been able to participate in the international diffusion of mobile technical knowledge. It can be expected, however, that the opening of capital markets will improve their competitiveness in producing technology intensive products.

According to the predictions of trade theory and to empirical experience of the past, such a stimulation of the international division of labor will be beneficial to all participants.

Endnotes

1 See, e.g., the contributions to *Vernon (1970)*.
2 See also *Giddy (1978); Vernon (1982); Helpman (1984)*.
3 For an attempt to include multinational activities in product cycle models see *Grossman/Helpman (1989a)*.
4 It should be noted that the product cycle models of Krugman, Helpman, and Grossman are also one-factor models.
5 The input coefficient is the inverse of the factor productivity, which is - in a one-factor model - equivalent to the level of technology.
6 For a survey of such lists see *Donges (1985)*. The main criterion for separating high-tech from low-tech goods is the research intensity of the corresponding industries.
7 See *Kostrzewa (1988)*.

References

DONGES, J.B. (1985), Trotz des Exportbooms besteht Anpassungs- und Investitionsbedarf bei den deutschen Unternehmen. Kiel Discussion Papers, 108, April.

GIDDY, I.H. (1978), The Demise of the Product Cycle Model in International Business Theory. The Columbia Journal of World Business, Vol. 13, 90-97.

GROSSMAN, G.M. and E. HELPMAN (1989a), Product Development and International Trade. Journal of Political Economy, Vol. 97, 1261-1283.

-------, ------- (1989b), Endogenous Product Cycles. The David Horowitz Institute for the Research of Developing Countries, Working Paper 2/89, Tel Aviv, March.

-------, ------- (1989c), Quality Ladders and Product Cycles. NBER Working Paper No. 3201, Cambridge, December.

-------, ------- (1990), Trade, Innovation, and Growth. American Economic Review, Papers and Proceedings, Vol. 80, 86-91.

HELPMAN, E. (1984), A Simple Theory of International Trade with Multinational Corporations. Journal of Political Economy, Vol. 92, 451-471.

HIRSCH, S. (1974), Hypotheses Regarding Trade Between Developing and Industrial Countries. in: Herbert GIERSCH, ed., The International Division of Labor, Problems and Perspectives, Tübingen: Mohr, 65-82.

HORN, E.-J. (1976), Technologische Neuerungen und internationale Arbeitsteilung. Kieler Studien, 139, Tübingen: Mohr.

KEESING, D. B. (1967), The Impact of Research and Development on United States Trade, Journal of Political Economy, Vol. 75, 38-48.

KLODT, H. (1987), Wettlauf um die Zukunft: Technologiepolitik im internationalen Vergleich. Kieler Studien, 206, Tübingen: Mohr.

KOSTRZEWA, W. (1988), Verpaßt Osteuropa den Anschluß auf den Weltmärkten? Kiel Discussion Papers, 144, September.

KRUGMAN, P. (1985), A "Technology Gap" Model of International Trade, in: Karl JUNGENFELT, Douglas HAGUE (eds.), Structural Adjustment in Developed Open Economies. Basingstoke, London.

--------------- (1979), A Model of Innovation, Technology Transfer, and the World Distribution of Income. Journal of Political Economy, Vol. 87, 253-266.

OECD (1969), Gaps in Technology. Final Report. Paris.

VERNON, R. (1966), International Investment and International Trade in the Product Cycle. Quarterly Journal of Economics, Vol. 80, 190-207.

------------ (1979), The Product Cycle Hypothesis in a New International Environment. Oxford Bulletin of Economics and Statistics, Vol. 41, 255-267.

------------ (1970), (ed.), The Technology Factor in International Trade. NBER Conference Series 22, New York.

------------ (1981), Technology's Effects on International Trade: A Look Ahead, in: Herbert GIERSCH (ed.), Emerging Technologies: Consequences for Economic Growth, Structural Change, and Employment, Symposium 1981, Tübingen 1982, 145-166.

Table 4: Product Categories in the Standard International Trade Classification (SITC)

SITC rev.2	SITC rev. 1	Division headings (abridged)
		Standardized industries
53	53	Dyeing, tanning and coloring materials
55	55	Essential oil and perfume materials
56	56	Fertilizers, manufactured
57	57	Explosive and pyrotechnic products
61	61	Leather, leather manufactures
62	62	Rubber manufactures
63	63	Cork and wood manufactures
64	64	Paper, paperboard
65	65	Textile yarn, fabrics, rel. products
66	66	Non-metallic mineral manufactures
67	67	Iron and steel
68	68	Non-ferrous metals
69	69	Manufactures of metals, n.e.s.
793	735	Ships, boats
81	81	Sanitary, heating and lighting fixtures
82	82	Furniture and parts
83	83	Travel goods, handbags
84	84	Apparel and clothing accessories
85	85	Footwear
88	861.1,861.2 861.4,861.5 861.6,862 863,864	Photographic apparatus, optical goods, watches and clocks
89	89	Miscellaneous manufactured articles, n.e.s.
		Mobile Schumpeter industries
51,52	51	Organic and inorganic chemicals
58	58	Artificial resins and plastics
59	59	Chemical material and products,n.e.s.
75	714	Office machines, computers
76,77	72	Telecommunication equipment, consumer electronics, electrical machinery
		Immobile Schumpeter industries
54	54	Medicinal and pharmaceutical products
71-74	71(excl.714)	Non-electrical machinery
78	732,733	Road vehicles
791	731	Railway vehicles
792	734	Aircraft and parts
87	861.3,861.7 861.8,861.9	Professional, scientific and controlling instruments
5-8	5-8(excl.52)	Manufactured goods

COMMENTS ON: TECHNOLOGY-BASED TRADE AND MULTINATIONALS' INVESTMENT IN EUROPE: STRUCTURAL CHANGE AND COMPETITION IN SCHUMPETERIAN GOODS

Claudio R. Frischtak

1. This paper addresses an important issue, namely, the rise of newly industrializing countries' share in world exports of relatively sophisticated (non-standardized) goods, and the inability of traditional models of innovation and trade in accounting for this phenomena. In particular, the composition of these countries' exports seems to contradict Vernon's well-known and seminal product cycle story and the conclusions of a rigid technological and trade pecking order derived from both Vernon's concept and the more formal models which it inspired.

2. The paper, however, fails to articulate a convincing alternative due to a few key shortcomings. First, its basic proposition, namely that developing countries that have been "wide open to foreign investment" are "often in a position to produce high-tech goods from the first date of innovation onwards" does not appear to be factually correct. In very few instances one can point out examples of multinational enterprises "globally scanning the horizon" (incidentally, a major departure from the product-cycle notion by Vernon himself that the author failed to acknowledge) to allocate production resources on an immediate post R&D basis (IBM might possibly be an exception that might fit the story the author has in mind.) Much more often, the need to continuously improve still unproven designs and production methods and not global cost minimization considerations drive these firms' decisions at the post-R&D stage, and conspire to delay an eventual locational separation of R&D and production.

3. Moreover, when such separation takes place, it is at a point when innovative products are becoming mass-produced, low value-added and thinly-profitable commodities, competing in buyer's markets. Whether these products are then "high-tech" (an expression the author never defines well) or not, is of secondary importance. A 20 megabyte hard-disk or a dot matrix printer, a standard modem or a 386-based PC, are increasingly standardized commodities, and in this sense no different (from an economic standpoint) than a ton of flat steel or polyethylene. In fact, the author's notion of "high-tech" is no different than Vernon's, except that whereas Vernon in his 1966 article might be thinking of toys, textiles and basic intermediates, in the present article the author is focusing on chemicals, plastics, consumer electronics, telecommunications equipment, electric machinery and related products ("mobile schumpeter industries").

4. The more interesting question is what is driving newly industrializing countries (NICs) increasingly into certain niche markets of specialty products of higher value added and greater R&D content. The answer is clearly their quest to sustain their competitive position in industry, qua industry, over time. These efforts, undertaken with particular intensity in East Asia, are being spearheaded often by domestic producers in cooperation with Governments (as in S. Korea and Taiwan). Multinational enterprises are also being prodded to move up the "value-added chain" (as in the case of Singapore). However, by and large, direct foreign investment has played a secondary role in this upgrading movement. Even within the author's definition of high-tech goods, the role of direct foreign investment in South East Asian NICs' export capabilities has been uneven, being the least important in South Korea and quite critical in Singapore and Hong Kong (with Taiwan in between). In any case, there is no evidence to support the statement that for these countries, most technology transfer has taken place within multinational firms (as the author seems to suggest).

5. The conceptual and factual weaknesses of the author's basic proposition are neither overcome by the model that purports to capture the newness of NICs' high-tech exports nor by the evidence presented by the paper. The model itself is at best illustrative of the possibilities of a shifting composition of NICs' exports towards "mobile Schumpeter goods" under certain circumstances. But no testable proposition can be derived from it. It is a set of definitional relationships under exogenously determined constraints. No economic behavior is driving it, and no predictions can be ascribed to it.

6. The evidence itself the paper presents is unconvincing. Its categorization of industries into standardized, mobile Schumpeter and immobile Schumpeter appears highly arbitrary, and not very useful at that level of aggregation. Among immobile Schumpeter industries, for example, one could argue that most categories that make it up are in fact mobile and some highly so (such as non-electric machinery and pharmaceutical products). More generally, most industries seem to be comprised of mobile and immobile segments and products; similarly, most products that appear quite "immobile" (for example aircraft) are increasingly composed of quite "mobile" parts.

7. The weakness of the categorization is paired with contradictory evidence presented on the evolution of different industries over time. Among seven major OECD countries, for example, results are moderately consistent only with respect to the "revealed comparative disadvantage" (RCA) of these countries with respect to "standardized" industries (although even in this case, only Japan and France appear to fit the idea that such disadvantage is growing over time). On the other hand, shifts in RCA in mobile and immobile Schumpeter industries do not present any intelligible pattern. Some countries lose in both (U.S., W. Germany, Italy), one gains in

both (Japan), whereas others even gain in mobile and lose in immobile Schumpeter industries (such as U.K.). Thus no conclusion can be derived from OECD country evidence.

8. The same can be said with respect to the structure of South East Asian NICs' exports (it is unclear, incidentally, why the author failed to use the same measure of comparative advantage, namely RCAs, for these countries). All that can be said is that the share of "standardized" industries exports is falling, and that of Schumpeter industries is growing. Clearly, the share of "mobile Schumpeter industries" is quite significant by 1987. But this only shows that goods from the electronics and chemical complexes play a significant role in their exports; the nature of those goods (if mere commodities or not) and their economic significance remains unclear.

9. In sum, we still miss a conceptual frame and supporting evidence explaining the relative success of some industrializing countries in moving beyond the product cycle rigid hierarchy of nations. All we can suggest at this point is that the answer has less to do with direct foreign investment in production and export of "high-tech" commodities, and more with growing domestic efforts in the acquisition and effective deployment of technological and marketing capabilities undertaken by national firms, and supported by an effective institutional infrastructure.

II. MULTINATIONALS IN ACTION

FOREIGN DIRECT INVESTMENTS IN REFORMING CMEA COUNTRIES: FACTS, LESSONS AND PERSPECTIVES

Andras Inotai

1. Introduction

In recent years, foreign direct investment (FDI) has become the basic avenue of globalization of the international economy. Between 1983 and 1988 FDI worldwide rose by more than 20 percent annually, four times faster than world trade that had been considered for a long time as the basic engine of growth. After two decades of sometimes emotionally loaded discussions and controversial host country policies towards FDI, its contribution to growth, employment, structural change, technological modernization, exports and general economic performance has been widely acknowledged. The overwhelmingly positive attitude of a number of national economies vis-a-vis FDI is a convincing proof of the fundamental changes taking place in the assessment of this vital factor of production. At the same time, the response by FDI to various legal, institutional, economic and political conditions established by potential capital-importing countries is a reliable mirror of how the present and prospective performance of different countries is viewed on the international scale.

Also Central (Czechoslovakia, Hungary, Poland) and Eastern European (Bulgaria and Romania) countries and the Soviet Union have increasingly recognized the economic reasons for attracting FDI. After the first and generally weak steps of a few countries in the seventies, all of them have elaborated the legal framework that has been updated several times until very recently. Beyond the importance of the ideological and political changes, opening up to FDI helped or started to reverse a basic and paradoxical economic process of four decades. Eastern European economies that after 1948 shifted into the position of net direct capital exporters, returned or are returning to their centuries long economic development pattern, characterized by substantial net direct capital imports.

2. Main Development Trends
2.1 Basic Figures

The number of joint ventures registered in the European CMEA countries and Yugoslavia soared to 3345 by the end of 1989, a dramatic increase compared to less than 200 ventures at the beginning of 1988 (without Yugoslavia). A recent unpublished OECD study indicates that by mid-1990 their total number increased to more than 5400 with nearly US $5 billion invested (*The Financial Times, June 26, 1990*). The Economic Commission for Europe reports US $6.5 billion by the end of September 1990, from which US $3.14 billion was in the Soviet Union and US $1.2 billion in Yugoslavia (*Scott, 1990*). While there is a wide gap between registered and functioning joint ventures in the Soviet Union where only about 10 percent of the ventures in manufacturing are operational, substantial development took place in some smaller Central European countries. According to national data, there are about 2000 ventures in Hungary with foreign capital exceeding US $1 billion. In Poland, 1145 joint ventures were granted licenses for business activity. The registered foreign assets amounted to US $187 million until March 1990 (*Foreign Trade Research Institute, 1990*). As a result of rapid economic unification with the Federal Republic of Germany, the German Democratic Republic also reported 600 ventures in the first half of 1990 (of which West German firms had a 96 percent share). Slower progress was made in Czechoslovakia (about 120 ventures with some US $30 million in foreign capital) and practically no new activity was reported from Bulgaria (about 35 firms) and Romania (5 firms) (*Table 1*). Due to data availability and the "critical mass of experience" accumulated, the present paper concentrates on cooperation with FDI in Hungary and Poland.

2.2 Expectations and Realities

Despite impressive growth of joint venture activities in some countries, FDI still exerts a very modest impact on the macroeconomic performance of host countries. Detailed calculations are only available from Poland where firms with foreign capital had a share of 1.9 percent in total output, 1.6 percent in employment and 3.7 percent in hard currency exports (*Nawrocki, 1989; Foreign Trade Research Institute, 1990*).

For most of the period, registered capital per venture remained rather low and much behind expectations. Small- and medium-sized companies prevailed as partners, and internationally operating large firms, even if they revealed some interest in investing, mostly established "experimental" units. Although there was an impressive increase of capital inflow to Hungary due to a few large investments in the last year, average registered foreign capital per firm is still about US $500,000, and excluding large investments, even much smaller. The average figure for Poland is US $163,000, and for Czechoslovakia about US $250,000 (before the "small privitazition" that substantially reduced this average).

Poland reported only 5 companies with a registered capital of more than US $5 million, being the Kvaerner Gdynia Shipyard (US $17.5 million with Norwegian capital) and Interdell (US $10 million, with Sweden) the most important ones. In comparison, from among the 11 joint ventures with the highest registered capital in Hungary between 1974 and 1988 (more than US $10 million each) seven were established in the last year of the period. *(Inotai, 1989)*. In 1989 and early 1990, accompanied by hundreds of very small ventures (below Ft 5 million or US $80,000) that made use of the favorably changing legal and financial rules, some really relevant and internationally reported transactions also occurred. Tungsram was sold to General Electric for US $150 million; Ford, General Motors, Suzuki and Daewoo announced investments between US $80 and 200 million each. These deals are expected to create the necessary demonstration effect to increasingly attract transnational companies to Hungary.

Not only foreign companies, but also Hungarian and Polish firms interested in joint ventures overwhelmingly belonged to the group of small-sized state-owned enterprises and cooperatives. Signs of a changing pattern emerged, however, in 1989. On the one hand, the number of privately owned joint companies skyrocketed. On the other hand, large enterprises, previously not very much interested in cooperating with foreign capital, suddenly realized that their future cannot be guaranteed by generous state subsidies or by the Soviet market with its low-quality standards and aggravating liquidity problems. Using their newly created larger maneuvering room and seeking adequate response to the new challenges, first of all to those originating from the collapse of the CMEA and the abolition of domestic subsidies, they increasingly turned to the possibility of establishing mixed companies or selling parts of the enterprise to foreign buyers.

FDI started everywhere in the service sector. Low capital requirement and low risk, accompanied by unsatisfied or growing internal demand for the products of this relatively underdeveloped sector motivated investment decisions. While between 1974 and 1981 the share of service sector made up 71 percent and between 1982 and 1984 still made up 50 percent of the joint ventures established in Hungary, between 1985 and 1988 almost three quarters of the newly established mixed companies belonged to the manufacturing industry. New regulations supporting small-scale activities in 1989 generated a boom in some service sectors (retail and foreign trade). Similarly, industrial activities also kept their momentum. As of November 1989, there were 346 joint ventures in manufacturing compared with 566 units in services (38 and 62 percent), with the registered capital more evenly distributed between the two main areas (51 and 49 percent).

Also, most of the so-called Polonia ventures (firms established by people of Polish origin) are involved in services and retail trade. However, recently the involvement of foreign capital in manufacturing activities, concentrated in food processing, wood processing and manufacturing of building materials has been strengthened. Slightly more than 50 percent of the ventures are working in industrial activities although their sectoral (and sub-sectoral) orientation still considerably differs from the sectoral priorities formulated by the Polish Government in order to restructure the economy with the help of FDI (*Misala, 1990*).

Further complaints were expressed both in Poland and Hungary concerning the negligible or far less than expected impact of FDI on the inflow of modern technology, increasing efficiency, higher level of employment and exports to convertible currency area. Nevertheless, the contribution of FDI both to hard currency exports and to hard currency import substitution, as expressed in their total output value, is higher than the national industrial average of both countries.

In sum, differences between ambitious expectations of planners and economic policy makers in the CMEA countries and reluctant, slow and "experimental" behavior of foreign capital have been a major issue since FDI was allowed to flow to the region. Emerging new trends after 1988, particularly in Hungary, can only partly be attributed to fundamental changes in the political and partly economic conditions in this region. A critical mass of experiences, as a result of a longer learning process, as well as appropriate changes in the treatment of foreign capital and clear economic policy orientation are the necessary prerequisites of bridging the gap between expectations and realities.

3. Major Changes in the Environment of Foreign Direct Investment

Central and Eastern European experiences, very much in harmony with those made by other capital-importing economies, highlight three critical areas of improving the conditions for attracting FDI.

3.1 The Legal and Institutional Framework

The legal and institutional framework - although major changes were made in almost all countries of the region during the last years - keeps on showing clear differences. (For a comparison of some basic features see *Table 2*.) The tax system, the repatriation of profits, the approval procedures and the network of international legal guarantees are still widely diverging from country to country. Here only some crucial areas will be identified that for a long time had not been recognized or were barred by ideological considerations.

The possibility of establishing majority- or wholly-owned foreign companies, prohibited or permitted in exceptional cases in the seventies and most of the eighties, became legalized in the last years. Hungary and Poland played the leading role, but, as a result of recent changes in the national legislation, Czechoslovakia, Bulgaria and Romania also allowed full foreign ownership. The laws of the Soviet Union that did not explicitly permit full foreign ownership, although they nowhere prohibited it, where "streamlined by the end of October 1990. Only the former GDR insisted on foreign minority rules until the last minute of its existence.

By the end of 1988, 61 percent of the mixed companies in Hungary had national majority, in 19 percent equity capital was evenly shared (50:50), and 21 percent revealed foreign majority. Considering only new establishments in 1988, foreign majority-owned ventures amounted to 28 percent and 50:50 ventures to another 23 percent, with 49 percent being Hungarian majority-owned companies. Preliminary data on recent developments clearly show a rapidly increasing share of majority- or wholly-owned foreign firms in the total number, and even more, in the total assets of newly established joint ventures. Also in Poland, where ideological and psychological barriers substantially limited FDI activities in the early eighties (only FDI by ex-Poles had been made possible and only for a ten year contractual period), dramatic reorientation took place in the late eighties. As a result, and also due to the substantial devaluation of Zloty assets against foreign contributions, in more than 700 companies out of the total of 1145 firms with foreign capital (63.6 percent), the foreign partner's share exceeded 50 percent (and in 243 firms the share was between 91 and 100 percent) by March 1990 (*Foreign Trade Research Institute, 1990*).

The impressive general liberalization of the legal treatment of FDI should not, however, conceal that a number of sectoral prohibitions still remained effective. Activities of foreign capital in banking and financial services are barred or seriously restricted (with the exception of Hungary). In most countries, land cannot be sold; uncertainty about property ownership prevails; and the employment of foreign manpower in the management of the company is restricted. Probably more for ideological and political than for economic reasons, there are also limitations in involving foreign capital into the privatization process where working councils seem to be strong factors in the decision-making process. In Poland, for example, foreigners are allowed to acquire only 10 percent of the shares in a Polish enterprise after which they need specific approval.

The internationally predominant trend is that about 85 to 90 percent of all FDI is in existing firms and only 10 to 15 percent flows into new ventures; therefore, the buying out of existing companies has to be permitted by appropriate laws. Hungary presented the first - and in practice rather controversial - transformation and privatization legislation, followed by Poland. Czechoslovakia started this process in April 1990 and most recently the Soviet Government has also enacted legislation allowing the establishment of joint-stock companies and the sale of stocks and bonds to Soviet and foreign investors. In the territory of the former German

Democratic Republic, the adoption of the laws and regulations governing the West German market economy does not require the elaboration of specific rules, although the transformation of the large state-owned companies is likely to pose a number of legal and economic difficulties.

Profit remittances in convertible currency are absolutely free from Hungary, even if part of the profit has been generated in inconvertible currencies, as a result of sales in the domestic or in the CMEA market. In the Soviet Union, remittances in convertible currency have to be earned by the joint company in hard currency. In Poland and most recently in Romania, profits earned in convertible currency can be transferred freely, and a modest share of profits made in domestic and intra-CMEA business (15 percent in Poland and 8 percent in Romania) can also be exchanged for convertible currency by the entitled national banks. However, taxes on profit transfer apply. Czechoslovakia, which tends to manage this problem in the framework of creating the internal convertibility of the national currency by 1991, still obliges the foreign company to sell a part of its foreign currency proceeds (according to a separate law, about 30 percent) to the State.

An extensive net of bi- and multilateral agreements on the protection of foreign property and on the avoidance of double taxation exists in Hungary and Poland. Czechoslovakia is preparing the appropriate legislation. However, the acceptance of OECD recommendations on dealing with foreign direct investments, adhesion to international agencies settling investment disputes and participation in MIGA are important steps still to be done for most countries. At present, Hungary and Poland are members of MIGA, while Czechoslovakia's membership is expected to be ratified in a short time. Also the main capital exporting countries can contribute to the higher level of investment security by guaranteeing national investors against political risks and by increasing the confidence would-be host countries badly need. OPIC guaranteed the General Electric's deal in Hungary. The British Export Credit Guarantee Department has extended its activities to the Central European reforming countries and insured British investments of about US $20 million, mostly in Poland.

3.2 The Economic Environment of Foreign Direct Investment

While most CMEA countries still are working on improving the legal and institutional factors of importing direct capital and some of them firmly believe that, by simply changing the legal conditions, major positive shifts can be achieved in the orientation of FDI, in reforming Central European countries it has become a commonplace that - beyond political stability and long-term expectations - the decisive element of attracting foreign direct capital consists in the generally favorable economic environment. Evidently, improved legal treatment can exert a positive impact on foreign capital, but only after the favorable economic environment has been created. Even the most generous legal treatment is unable to compensate for uncertainties, low performance or un(der)developed factor markets in the capital-importing country. On the contrary, such a policy tends to aggravate structural rigidities, creates new monopoly rights to be enjoyed by foreign companies and increases the social and political tensions between foreign capital and actors of the national economy. In other words, it may become counterproductive both in political and economic terms.

Policymakers should be very much aware of the fact that it is not the role of FDI to put in order, reform or restructure the host economy. Of course, FDI does play an important role in attaining the main economic objectives of a country if the country's economic policy appropriately influences the foreign capital by creating the necessary preconditions. According to international experience, FDI is usually interested in exploiting the profit-making possibilities offered by the host economy. Therefore, it can both support the government's main economic reforms and deepen structural and financial imbalances, depending on the economic policy pursued in the host country.

Although foreign direct capital has some specific features, it is just one of the various production factors. Its effectiveness largely depends on the "absorption capacity" of a national economy, and not on the special treatment granted. If an economy makes use of its different production factors (capital, labor, skill, raw materials, etc.) on a rather low level of efficiency, foreign capital - as an additional production factor - will also tend to be used inefficiently.

Transparent economic policies are required in order to enhance the effectiveness of FDI. In Central and Eastern European countries it includes at least three basic requirements:

(a) The opening up of the economy by eliminating export and import licenses, by demonopolizing foreign trade and by rapidly liberalizing the flow of internationally traded goods and services. Foreign trade monopolies have largely been eliminated in Poland, Hungary and most recently also in Czechoslovakia. The liberalization of 40 percent of Hungarian imports in convertible currency in 1989 and that of another 30 percent in 1990 is one of the many factors explaining the rapidly increasing number of joint ventures in the last years. Import and export requirements imposed on joint ventures (domestic content rules and minimum export shares in total production) are generally counterproductive.

(b) As long as convertibility of the national currency cannot be created, big differences between the official and the unofficial exchange rates are to be avoided in order to attract foreign capital. More importantly, unrestricted profit transfer can introduce virtual convertibility for companies operating in the Central and Eastern European economies.

(c) In the longer term, the utilization of potential beneficial impacts of FDI depends on the effectiveness of an economic policy creating the forward- and backward-linkages in the national economy. Here, conditions for strengthening the local entrepreneurial capacities, education and training, infrastructural developments, the establishment of an efficient financial system (stock exchange, commercial banks) and changing mentality can be considered as crucial factors.

3.3 Size of the Potential Market

While the above mentioned three main components of improving the attractiveness of the economic environment largely fall into the scope of the host country's activity, a fourth element, namely the size of the potential market, is mostly beyond its competence. International direct capital flows are predominantly influenced by two basic considerations: the comparative advantage of various factors of production and the size of the market. All Central and Eastern European countries, with the notable exception of the Soviet Union, have a limited and in the last years stagnating domestic market. Due to economies of scale considerations and the reorientation of economic strategy (opening, export-orientation), market access becomes a crucial element in general, and in attracting FDI, in particular. In the past, the small CMEA countries were unable to play any meaningful role as potential locations for subsidiaries of international companies producing on the world market. The potentially almost infinite Soviet (CMEA) market remained inaccessible due to the inconvertibility of the transferable rouble.

Simultaneously, a number of trade barriers (from quantitative restrictions to relatively high tariffs) stood in the way of export expansion to the OECD countries. As a result of recent, mostly politically inspired developments and of consistent efforts of economic diplomacy of the Central European countries, the terms of access to various developed markets have been improved. The granting of GSP (general system of preferences) by the United States, Japan or Austria to Hungary and also by the European Communities to Hungary and Poland, as well as the elimination of several QRs, the substantial increase of export quotas, including sensitive sectors as textiles or steel in Hungary's and Poland's exports to the EC (and from January 1991 also to Bulgaria, Czechoslovakia and Romania), are expected to increase both direct exports and the interest of FDI in starting new ventures at least in some countries of this region.

There is no doubt that the latest larger investments by foreign companies in the Hungarian industry and strong interest in further deals are motivated by changing trade conditions, too. Better market access to the EC of Hungarian-made products very likely was a key factor in investment decisions by Suzuki and Ford in favor of Hungary. The EC's strict rules of origin can only be avoided if at least 5O percent of the corresponding product (e.g. Suzuki cars) will be made in Hungary. Any strengthening of this rule by Brussels may have serious repercussions on the investment location and business strategy of foreign (multinational) firms.

4. Some Critical Areas and Attitudes

Experience with FDI, particularly in the last two years, and new challenges both from domestic developments (economic and political reforms) and from the international community, put on the agenda a number of issues that will substantially influence the general environment of FDI in the region.

4.1 Treatment of Foreign Versus Domestic Investments

Several instruments, such as preferential taxes and tax holidays, exemption from wage limitations, terms of credit availability, etc., as specified in the Hungarian and Polish laws on FDI, have the clear intention of providing special advantages to foreign capital. In contrast, Czechoslovakia stresses that foreign and domestic companies should be treated equally. Also Romania, in its new joint venture legislation, returns to this principle, after several years of clearly discriminating against FDI. The two apparently very different approaches are rooted in the substantial time lag and institutional development in the individual countries. Hungary and Poland, with quite essential experiences in how to attract FDI and how to assess its behavior and short-term reactions, after a decade of very modest results considerably widened the privileges to be granted to FDI. Czechoslovakia and Romania still do not have sufficient experience and may consider equal treatment from the beginning as a promising measure. It cannot be ruled out that the presently diverging positions will move from the two extremes towards less dissimilar approaches. As a first sign of it, both Hungary and Poland indicated that at least some of the unilateral advantages are likely to be reshaped in the next period in order to provide better investment opportunities also for domestic entrepreneurs. Two fundamental concepts dominate the discussion. One major view sustains that temporary special treatment of foreign direct capital is necessary in a relatively underdeveloped, capital-poor economy. Basic handicaps originating from this underdevelopment and additional handicaps attributed to past but in the major capital exporting countries still not forgotten political and ideological patterns (communism, expropriation, state ownership, command economy, etc.) should be counterbalanced by more generous and internationally competitive regulation.

According to the other opinion, sound economic policy and not tax policy considerations should be the decisive factor of attracting FDI. Generous tax policy granted exclusively to foreign capital or to national capital linked to foreign capital in joint ventures may become an economically harmful and politically counterproductive instrument. First, it tries to offset the negative impact of other taxes or cost-increasing fees and restrictions which should be eliminated to the benefit of all economic agents. Second, it creates uncertainty among the investors, because everybody fears that, sooner or later, unique benefits will be withdrawn or reduced. In this light, short-term enrichment should be the "correct" business answer, just the opposite to what the economic policy would expect from foreign capital. Third, a fraction of domestic companies establishing joint ventures with foreign firms enjoys considerable tax preferences against the majority of firms and may build up highly undesirable monopoly positions by restricting competition on a traditionally monopolistically organized domestic market. Fourth, short-term financial considerations of the partners (not least the host country companies) disregard the efficiency, competition and structural requirements of production and focus on speculative financial transfers (as it really happened in 1989, where several hundreds of small, mostly one-man companies were created in order to avoid higher Hungarian taxation). And fifth, dispreferred status of domestic capital and entrepreneurs is the best way of creating an influential lobby and overall socio-psychological atmosphere that may become increasingly hostile to prospective foreign investments.

The adequate policy is not necessarily the cutting of available benefits. Evidently, in some cases, tax holidays could be connected to well-defined performance criteria (exports, technological development, employment, reinvestment of profits, etc.). In some areas characterized by excess demand (shortage situations) and/or monopolistic pattern, the granting of tax allowances could also be reconsidered. Large tax allowances or tax holidays can be replaced by new cost-saving possibilities (accelerated depreciation, generous loss-carry-forward provisions) compensating for higher but internationally still competitive taxes. Previously granted tax holidays should, however, remain in force, considering the importance of confidence building in the present stage of attracting FDI. It would, however, be absolutely erroneous if the regulatory overview were limited to such "technical" issues. The fundamental point is that domestic and foreign capital should get the same liberal treatment. It is essentially not the foreign capital the possibilities of which should be restricted, but it is the domestic capital whose chances should considerably be enhanced. A sound, well-functioning and efficient network of domestic enterprises is a key factor of also attracting international capital.

An additional controversial area is the fitting of FDI into the structural policy of the host government. To be sure, it is relatively easy to determine those sectors and activities in which foreign participation should be ruled out. Most countries apply some prohibitions or severe restrictions in so-called "national security-sensitive" areas. At the same time, it is much more difficult to prepare a list of preferred sectors. Such an approach that certainly has deep roots in the still surviving mentality and lobby interests originated in the centrally planned systems tends to divert scarce resources into sectors with less than optimal efficiency, deprives other prospective activities of vital inputs and acts against the creation of a "homogeneous" economic environment, which is the main conditions of attracting FDI.

Some of the success stories of the last years and additional ventures in the process of negotiation would hardly fit into this structuralist approach. The Chicago-based Schwinn Bicycle Company, with a 51 percent majority investment improved the quality of previously largely uncompetitive Hungarian bicycles in one year so much that they are now ready to be exported to the West. Various deals in the structurally weak Hungarian steel industry are another example: foreign capital may find it profitable to invest in this sector for different reasons (technology, capacity utilization, some efficiently managed parts of the factories, etc.) that would hardly be considered in a centrally conceived structuralist approach.

4.2 Adverse Impacts on the Balance of Payments?

In the last three decades, the impact on the balance of payments of FDI has been heatedly discussed. However, no unequivocal proof has been found to demonstrate its adverse effects. Although the currently still modest amount of FDI in Central and Eastern European countries is realistically unlikely to give serious concerns to this problem, the issue has already been taken up in some countries and by some political groups. It may become a major problem in the future as FDI is supposed to increase substantially. Therefore, some fundamental points have to be made here.

First, the contribution of FDI to the general performance of the host economy cannot be measured exclusively in its direct impact on the balance-of-payments situation. It is obvious that some CMEA countries have to face the consequences of serious indebtedness. Debt servicing requires huge resource transfers in the coming years. Higher amounts of direct capital inflows could provide a modest direct contribution to compensate for imbalances. However, its indirect impact, i.e. the rapidly increasing export performance of the economy, should be given special emphasis. Second, increasing capital inflow may be accompanied by a higher level of capital outflow in the form of profit remittances and other transfers. Any intervention in this process might be extremely risky and confidence destructing. Third, export-import-balance of joint ventures cannot be considered as a true picture of foreign trade and trade balance implications caused by FDI. At present, the amount of foreign trade conducted by mixed companies is a very modest if not negligible part of the total trade of all Central and Eastern European countries in convertible currencies. In consequence, this trade cannot be blamed for the overall trade performance of any country.

Recent Hungarian calculations based on data provided by 98 joint ventures for 1988 demonstrate that their overall trade in convertible currency was in slight surplus (*Benedek, 1989*). Export-import balances should not be assessed on a yearly basis. Particularly investments in new activities require substantial initial imports that, however, will be covered by rapidly increasing exports in the subsequent years. The Levi Strauss company set up in Hungary required an initial import of US $2 million to equip its blue jeans factory in 1988 without meaningful exports in the same year. However, already in 1989, sales started to expand rapidly, while no more larger additional imports were necessary.

In evaluating the net foreign trade effect, import substituting activities of joint ventures should also be taken into account. Also this hard-currency saving activity should be given the same treatment as granted to export generating business. More importantly, a number of joint ventures produce goods for other companies that export them as an input of their own products. Last but not least, also the general multiplier effect of FDI is to be considered: its impact on the management, training, marketing, entrepreneurial values, mentality and on other hardly quantifiable but highly important factors of international competitiveness.

4.3 Potential Markets: Industrialized World, USSR or Both?

Cooperation with foreign direct capital has to be adjusted to the rapidly and lastingly changing international economic environment. A major market reorientation of the Central (and partly Eastern) European economies from the CMEA to Western Europe, and first of all to the EC seems very likely. At the same time, at least theoretically, reformed bilateralism in the CMEA may create additional markets for foreign investors. Intra-CMEA trade in convertible currency, to be initiated in 1991, eliminates a major obstacle to export joint venture products to neighboring countries. To be sure, a long expected vast market is opening up, and most small countries have certainly a number of comparative advantages in this market. However, rapid gains are seriously discounted by liquidity problems and political and economic disturbances in the region, mostly in the Soviet Union. Moreover, the structural captivity of the huge shortage market and strategic issues of unilateral (economic) dependence should also be considered in the process of harmonizing national economic interests with those of potential foreign investors.

4.4 Is Growing Dependence on FDI Dangerous?

In the last months, although to different extent, as part of the election campaign, political claims were expressed in most countries of the region concerning the desirable size and role of foreign capital. Beyond ideological reasons and built-in reflexes based on the closed, autarchic past of the economy, some inadequate economic steps are also to be blamed for these voices. Intransparent and highly controversial "spontaneous" privatization affairs between and among mostly domestic companies, a list containing 5O Hungarian companies to be offered to potential international investors during 1989 without previous agreement of the companies themselves, or some apparently cheap buy-outs and buy-out attempts of well-known Hungarian firms were among the factors supporting a tougher approach to foreign capital. Similar and sometimes openly hostile attitudes became manifest in some other countries as well.

The newly elected Governments in Central and Eastern Europe will consistently work on improving the political climate for FDI, as an important factor of the "basket of comparative advantages" of a capital-importing country. Realism should prevail in assessing the (potential) activities of FDI.

First, the share of foreign-owned property is about 1 percent of Hungary's capital stock (before 1945 it was about 9 percent and in the Austro-Hungarian Monarchy even much higher), and much less in all other countries.

Second, even large scale and immediate privatization which does not seem likely both for legal, financial and institutional reasons, would affect a marginal share of the total capital stock (about US $4O billion in Hungary alone).

Third, nobody should be surprised that capital owners in general, and foreign investors in particular, reveal more interest in buying efficient and profitable companies than firms with outdated machinery and large masses of unskilled labor. At the same time, it is remarkable, how diversified the attention of FDI is concerning investment possibilities. Looking at current production and potential gains from a different angle, foreign investors often times presume interesting investment chances in sectors, production lines or companies "written off" by the authorities.

Fourth, the price of the acquisition of a company or part of it is extremely difficult to assess. To be sure, the recent Hungarian practice, that is the lack of adequate pricing and the survival of monopolistic alliances and businesses "behind the curtain", did not help create transparency and confidence. More importantly, the financial terms of a deal cannot be determined without taking into account the general economic, infrastructural, and social environment of the company to be sold. The same machinery, building, manpower, and capital stock usually have a higher value in an efficiently functioning, highly developed environment than in conditions characterized by infrastructural bottlenecks, social and political uncertainties and organizational and management problems. Central and Eastern European companies cannot be detached from the environment they are located in, even if the available stock of physical and human capital could be sold at a much higher price if it were in Japan, the United States or Switzerland (For an international comparative survey see: *Eun-Janakiraman, 1990*). This point once again turns the main attention to the rapid development of the general environment attracting FDI. The more and the sooner these conditions can be improved, the higher price can be claimed for the capital stock in general in the Central and Eastern European countries.

5. Prospects and Tasks Ahead
5.1 Growing Interest in Central and Eastern Europe

As a result of the dramatic political changes and of economic reforms aiming at establishing market economies in Central and Eastern Europe, international direct capital started to rethink its strategy for the nineties and consider investments in these countries as a real alternative to activities in other parts of the world. The rapidly rising investment flows experienced after 1989 can be considered as a prelude to massive capital inflows that may follow in the next years. According to a recent survey based on investment plans of 128 large multinational companies, all with sales or assets exceeding US $1 billion, nearly two-thirds of the responding firms are planning investments and 42% are already investing in the region. Their total investment is expected to amount to more than US $3 billion, and is likely to attract a number of other companies that are still hesitating (*Scott 1990; The Financial Times, September 20, 1990*).

Central and Eastern Europe's attraction as a location for FDI is based on low labor costs, high level of education and training of the labor force, availability of energy and raw materials (mostly in the Soviet Union), industrial inputs available as a result of earlier industrialization, prospective growth of the domestic market and improved access to international markets as a result of lower tariff and non-tariff barriers to trade.

5.2 Differentiated Approaches
5.2.1 Location Choices

As in most other areas, the European CMEA countries do not form a homogeneous bloc concerning FDI. Their economic structure, comparative advantages, sociopolitical environment, geographic location, economic openness, and regulatory frameworks are all rather different from each other.

The Soviet Union possesses huge natural resources and a potentially vast market. However, economic and infrastructural problems seem to raise substantial barriers to the massive inflow of FDI. At present, the territory of the former German Democratic Republic and Hungary are considered as the relatively best locations for potential investments, followed by Czechoslovakia and Poland.

The main advantages of the Eastern part of Germany consist in its political and economic reunification with West Germany and the likely rapid transition to a free-market economy with the adoption of the West German economic and legal system, accompanied by the stability guarantee of the strong German mark and the Bundesbank's overall policy. Still, both West German and foreign capital seem to be more reluctant than expected in starting major investment projects there. At present, activities focus on improving infrastructure, retraining, and housing that are all substantial preconditions of efficient investments. But the investment boom is also delayed by a number of other factors. First, with the exception of Romania, the former GDR economy and society appears to be the least prepared for market economy changes, and its population had the least direct (production and technological) contact with the developed world. Second, sudden transformation may involve still unforeseen opposition to total economic (and ideological) buyout. Property transformation also has some unsettled questions. Third, wage and labor contracts always compared to West German patterns may substantially increase the costs of investment and "outcompete" the country as a potential investment location. Fourth, desolate infrastructure and unprecedented pollution may add to the comparative disadvantages.

Last but not least, in various sectors, companies located in West Germany have built up sufficient capacities to deliver the required products from the West German production sites and have no reason for establishing new capacities in that part of the country.

The Hungarian advantages are partly rooted in the two decades of step-by-step, sometimes controversial, but mentality-transforming and society-educating reform process that has brought the Hungarian economy nearest to the Western market economies. The institutional and legal framework of a functioning market economy is in a more advanced stage than in any other country of the region (from the network of commercial banks through the incipient stock market to the privatization process). Another part of the advantages are the rich experiences with joint ventures during almost two decades, but particularly in the last five years. A third element is the still small but rapidly growing, innovative, flexible and hard-working private sector that represents at least 15 percent of GDP. As a fourth element, the essential infrastructure of joint ventures can be mentioned. Compared with other Central and Eastern European countries, Hungary not only has the largest number of functioning joint ventures but it also succeeded in attracting a wide range of services supporting the activity of foreign capital (American, West German, and British financial institutions, training centers, accounting firms, law companies, and transportation agencies set up dozens of offices). Among Hungary's disadvantages can be mentioned its stagnating growth, high level of indebtedness, narrow domestic market, and more recently growing uncertainties about the future of CMEA trade and occasionally controversial government declarations.

Czechoslovakia has long industrial traditions and its geographical location in Europe is excellent. However, the establishment of the favorable legal, institutional and economic framework needs a longer period than did spectacular political changes.

Poland's longer-term outlook may improve once the ambitious economic reform package introduced in January 1990 starts to produce its positive impacts. For the moment, however, first stabilization successes still were not able to essentially increase the inflow of foreign direct capital. Confidence building generally takes a longer time. Moreover, the impacts of German reunification and developments in the Soviet Union are hardly to be assessed at the moment. On the one hand, they can divert badly needed capital from Poland, but, on the other hand, also substantially increase the country's strategic importance between its Western and Eastern neighbor.

5.2.2 Behavior of Potential Investors

Turning to the international scene, relative shortage of investment capital cannot be excluded and international competition for international investments will certainly become keener. Central European countries, particularly Czechoslovakia and Hungary, may be well placed in this competition if their (and the region's) political and economic stability can be maintained. Additional impetus may originate from the shift of the center of investment capital to Western Europe (*Julius, 1990*), the favorable impacts of the deregulated Western European market and the increasing multinationalization of medium- and small-sized companies that have played a leading role in East-West joint ventures.

Central (and to a much less extent Eastern) Europe may also become a favorite place for transnational investments. This development predicts a double competition: competition among the respective host countries in order to get the best deals, and competition among potential investors in order to get the best locations.

Regarding growing Western competition in investing in this part of Europe, the Federal Republic of Germany (with the overwhelming majority of newly-founded joint ventures and takeovers in the former GDR and with well-established subsidiaries in Hungary and Poland), smaller European countries, such as Austria, Sweden or Switzerland, and the United States seem to take the lead. Japan and other Far Eastern countries also became more active in recent months. Major EC members, with the exception of the FR of Germany, are still in a "wait-and-see-position".

It has to be stressed that there are considerable differences among the various potential investor countries both in their basic philosophy of assessing the chances and risks of the region and in their actual investment decisions. West Germany, Austria, and Switzerland are overwhelmingly represented by small- and medium-size ventures. Some US multinational companies - after a rather long period of hesitation and slow reaction - decided to strengthen their Central European commitment, concentrating on Hungary (GE, Ford, GM) and the Eastern part of Germany (GM). Simultaneously, it is repeatedly emphasized that their natural location would be the Soviet Union. Japanese companies - as other Far Eastern investors - are collecting basic information and undertake a number of business trips but their effective commitment still remained limited (Hungary being a partial exception). Most interestingly, larger EC countries (with the exception of the Federal Republic) are among the least interested in investing in this part of Europe. Although some French companies recently changed their mind - probably not for economic but for political reasons - when they made the first substantial investments in the former GDR, mainly motivated by the desire to prevent total West German domination there. West German appeals to other potential investors and probably also East German priorities of balancing the unprecedented selling-out process may have contributed to this change in the traditional French position (*The Financial Times, July 17, 1990*).

At the same time, British views are still dominated by emphasizing the political and economic risks of investing in Central and Eastern Europe, the narrowness of the virtual market and better investment possibilities elsewhere. It is a widespread and self-comforting view that, in risky markets, the latecomer's advantages are likely to be larger than benefits to be earned by pioneer status (*The Economist, June 16, 1990*).

The different behavior of various foreign capitals is adequately reflected in the available Hungarian and Polish data. Comparing the share of the individual OECD countries in the commodity trade with and direct capital imports by the two countries, some discrepancies are striking (*Table 3*). While the EC is by far the leading OECD trading partner for both countries, in direct capital imports of Poland and Hungary it is substantially underrepresented. This is primarily due to the very modest commitment of France and the United Kingdom (and in the case of Hungary also that of Italy). At the same time, EFTA countries have a higher share in direct capital imports by Poland and Hungary than in their total OECD trade.

Beyond these similarities, there are also essential differences in comparing the pattern of trade and capital flows in Hungary and Poland. First, although West Germany is the unquestionable leading trade partner of both countries, it is only second to Austria as capital exporter to Hungary. While the Polish joint ventures reveal a strong concentration on West Germany, including West Berlin (41 percent of the ventures and 30 percent of the foreign registered capital), Hungary shows a more balanced geographic distribution measured in terms of capital and the number of ventures. Second, and at least for the time being, non-European capital (US and Japan) has clearly preferred Hungary to Poland. Third, although both countries' trade and capital flows are characterized by an above-average share of neighboring OECD economies, Hungary could rely on Austria and Switzerland more than Poland could on Sweden.

5.3 Main Tasks Ahead
5.3.1 Tasks of the Host Countries

The main tasks of the capital importing Central (and Eastern) European countries can be summarized in six main points:

- If and where necessary, investment codes and rules shall be made internationally competitive and general and unclear statements (targets, instruments and conditions of preferential treatment) unambiguously specified. Foreign and national capital have to be given the same possibilities. Ageing capital stock, budget considerations and direct or indirect contribution to hard currency export revenues are strong arguments in favor of accelerating and opening up privatization processes to potential foreign investors, even if, in some cases, the process may require direct government control. (As a first example, Hungary published the first

package of 2O companies to be sold in open bid, and announced that further lists containing
about 8O more companies will follow within a year.)

- Adequate stability-oriented macroeconomic policies should be followed in order to increase
  the "absorption capacity" of the economy. This includes the creation of market economic
  conditions (market clearing prices, wages, exchange rates) and the strengthening of the
  entrepreneurial (private) sector.

- Taking into account that FDI is generally positively related to dynamic growth, growth-
  oriented policies should be preferred if they are not jeopardizing the stability of the
  economy. However, expanding markets can not only be found in the host country but also in
  the markets of the host countries' main trading partners - if a world market oriented
  economic policy is implemented.

- Special attention shall be given to the infrastructural development that is a major incentive to
  attract foreign direct capital and to use it efficiently.

- The economic and political stability and transparency of the capital importing country has to
  be maintained and strengthened.

- Democratic systems are generally preferred by international capital to dictatorial states, as
  long as democracy is stable and predictable. The establishment of the new political system
  must not be accompanied by uncertainties or disruptions in macro- and microeconomic
  decision-making processes that would significantly increase the risk factor of investments
  and lead to decreasing interest in the individual potential host countries and also in the
  region as a whole. While capital imports will predominate, competitive and efficient national
  companies should be encouraged to invest abroad.

5.3.2 Western Contribution

- Improved and predictable terms of market access should be created for Central and Eastern
  European goods (lifting of quota restrictions, GSP not dependent on yearly renewals,
  association treaty with Brussels with later opportunity of joining the EC as a full member).

- Clear rules of origin have to be established for products to be produced by foreign - mostly
  American and Asian - companies interested in reaching the Western European market
  through their Central (Eastern) European subsidiaries.

- COCOM rules negatively affecting both strategic decisions of potential investors and the development of the telecommunication sector as a major factor of successful competition for foreign investments should be eliminated or substantially eased.

- Western Governments should extend investment insurance against political risks to companies expanding in this part of Europe.

- Investment agencies, financial funds and other institutions supporting foreign investments and also channelling available local capital into joint businesses should be set up.

- Large multinational companies should enhance their commitment in reforming Central (and Eastern) European countries by incorporating their newly founded subsidiaries in the region into their worldwide production and distribution network and consider the emerging pan-European dimension of resource, production and market possibilities in their strategic business decisions (first steps have already been taken by Siemens, Ford, General Motors, and Maxwell.

- Adjustment to the emerging new realities in Europe requires that old mentality patterns on Communism, expropriation, "iron curtain" and "East bloc" be abandoned.

- In the same context, generalizations concerning the political, economic and social situation of different Central and Eastern European countries should be avoided. They may hurt the position of the relatively most market-oriented economies and may decrease the interest of foreign capital in potential new locations in the region (*The Financial Times, May 2, 1990*).

5.4 The Political Scope

A qualitatively higher level of cooperation with international direct capital, and the forging of strategic alliances possesses outstanding political and economic importance. Politically, it can become one of the main pillars on which long-term stability in Europe can be based. This means not only support for young democracies in Central (and perhaps Eastern) Europe but also the establishment of a more balanced power structure in this part of the world. Replacing the former unilateral orientation and structural dependence of the reforming small countries by a new but not less unilateral orientation would certainly not contribute to long-term stability and balanced power relations. The potential host countries are vitally interested in forging strong economic contacts with all major (and smaller) national economies and multinational companies. In this light, American, Japanese, French and British companies are likely to be particularly welcomed in order to counterbalance the certainly strong German economic influence. (The desirability of such a development has been expressed several times in official German declarations.) Economically, FDI is expected to play an important role in shaping the main development (modernization) path reforming Central and Eastern European countries are starting on or just have started on after having reached the political point of no return.

References

BENEDEK, T. (1989), A vegyesvallalatok hatasa a hazai devizamerlegre (The Impact of Joint Ventures on the Hungarian Balance in Convertible Currency), Kozgazdasagi Szemle, 12.

EUN, C. S. and S. JANAKIRAMAN (1990), International Ownership Structure and the Firm Value, The World Bank (manuscript).

Foreign Trade Research Institute (1990), Foreign Investments in Poland. Regulations, Experience and Prospects, Warsaw.

INOTAI, A. (1989), A mukodotoke a vilaggazdasagban (Direct Capital in the World Economy), Kossuth and Kozgazdasagi es Jogi Kiado, Budapest.

JULIUS, D. (1990), Global Companies and Public Policy: The Growing Challenge of Foreign Direct Investment, Royal Institute of International Affairs, Pinter Publishers.

MISALA, J. (1990), Current Joint Venture Law and Its Impact on the Polish Economy (manuscript).

NAVROCKI, I. (1989) Kapital zagraniczny w polskiej gospodarce w latach 1976-1989 (Foreign Capital in the Polish Economy in the Years 1976 to 1989), Handel Zagraniczny, 4-5.

SCOTT, N. (1990), Foreign Direct Investment, Joint Ventures in Particular Among the Pentagonal Countries, Paper presented on the occasion of the Conference: Cooperation in the Adriatic-Danube Region, Vienna, October 14-16, 1990 (manuscript).

Table 1: Basic Data on Joint Ventures in Central and Eastern Europe and the USSR

	Number of Joint Ventures	Foreign Registered Capital	Average Foreign Capital	Major Joint Ventures Per Venture('000$)	Major Countries of Origin
Bulgaria 1989	35	NA	NA		
CSFR July 1990	120	30	250		FRG, France Austria
GDR June 1990	600	NA	NA		FRG
Hungary Sept. 1990	2000	1000	500	GM, GE Ford Suzuki	Austria, FRG Switz., USA Japan
Poland March 1990	1145	187	163	Kvaerner Interdell	FRG Sweden
Romania 1989	5	NA	NA		
USSR March 1990	1500	3140	NA		FRG, Italy Austria USA, UK
Total Sept. 1990	5405	6500	NA		

Note: Figures are estimates based on data available from the United Nations Economic Commission for Europe and national statistics and press releases. Their comparability is limited by the different periods they cover.

Table 2: Foreign Investment Legislation in Central and Eastern European Countries
(as of October 30, 1990)

	Bulg	Czech	GDR*	Hung	Pol	Rom	USSR
Legislation:							
first	1980	1985	1990	1972	1976	1972	1987
effective	1989	1990	1990	1988	1988	1990	1990
Foreign participation	no limit	100%	20-49%	100%	100%	100%	100%
Corporate tax rate (%)	30-50	40	no regime	40	40	30	30
Tax holiday in priorized areas (yrs)	5****	2	NA	5-10	3-6	no	3
Tax reduction in priorized areas (in percent of effective tax rates)	–	–	NA	40-60	–	–	–
Tax on dividends	10-15	25	NA	no	30	10	20
Repatriation of profit							
only after profits in hard currency	yes	yes	yes	no	no	no	no
other profits (conversion share)				free	15%	8%	free
Customs free imports to venture	yes	yes	yes	yes	yes**	yes	yes
Approval:							
number of institutions***	more	more	more	2	1	more	more
feasibility study	no	no	yes	no	yes	yes	yes
required		yes	yes		yes	yes	yes
- only if foreign equity is higher than (%)	49%			50%			

* until July 1, 1990
** in the first three years
*** including consulting institutions (if approval is provided by one ministry or agency)
**** only for high-tech activities established in customs-free areas

Source: National Legislations of the European CMEA Countries, press releases.

Table 3: Hungarian and Polish Foreign Trade and FDI Patterns
(share in trade with and FDI from the OECD, in percent)

	Hungary (1988)			Poland (1989)		
	trade a	FDI capital	number of firms	trade a	FDI capital	number of firms
OECD total b	100.0	100.0	100.0	100.0	100.0	100.0
EC	56.9	32.7	37.4	69.9	53.6 c	65.0 d
EFTA	26.3	44.8	49.5	16.6	16.7 e	20.1 d
non-Eur. OECD	10.4	18.6	11.7	10.1	6.4 f	9.7 d
FR of Germany	29.5	15.1	19.6	34.6	26.7	42.1
Italy	8.8	1.1	3.6	8.1	9.3	4.2
France	4.8	1.8	1.3	6.3	2.0	4.4
United Kingdom	4.3	1.4	3.6	6.9	2.8	4.4
Netherlands	3.6	4.5	4.0	5.6	8.2	4.3
Austria	15.2	25.1	28.5	5.8	5.1	6.6
Switzerland	5.5	9.0	11.1	2.2	1.8	2.6
Sweden	3.1	2.2	4.5	4.4	9.8	9.1
United States	6.2	11.8	5.8	6.5	5.3	6.5
Japan	2.9	6.8	4.5	2.7	-	0.1
Multinationals	-	-	-	-	9.0	4.1

a Exports + imports

b About 95 to 97 percent of total FDI originates from OECD countries. (However, in Hungary, two large Korean ventures changed the geographical distribution of registered foreign capital substantially in 1989.)

c Excluding Greece, Ireland, Luxemburg, Portugal and Spain, all countries with no or negligible direct investment in Poland.

d Excluding investments by multinationals.

e Excluding Finland, Iceland and Norway, from which only Finland had limited investment activity in Poland.

f Excluding Australia, Japan and New Zealand, from which only Japan was registered as investor in one case.

Sources: OECD Statistics of Foreign Trade (Serie A); Hungarian Chamber of Commerce: Joint Ventures in Hungary with Foreign Participation (Register), Budapest, 1989; Sadowska-Cieslak, E., Uwagi na temat obowiazujacego ustawodawstwa dotyczacego dzialalnosci kapitalu zagranicznego w gospodarce Polskiej (Remarks Concerning Law Aspects of Activity of Ventures with Foreign Capital in the Polish Economy), Instytut Koniunkturi Cen Handlu Zagranicznego (Foreign Trade Research Institute), Warszawa 1990 (manuscript).

COMMENTS: MULTINATIONAL CORPORATIONS IN THE EASTERN EUROPEAN ECONOMIC TRANSITION

Peter Murrell

1. Multinational Activity in Eastern Europe up to the Present

The most important single fact to be noted in discussing the present role of multinational corporations in Eastern Europe (in which I include the Soviet Union) is the insignificance of the activities of these corporations. Full acceptance of multinational activity has come only very recently in this region, of course. For example, the possibility of 100% ownership by foreign companies appeared only in the year of revolutions, 1989, and even then not by every country. Despite this possibility, there is enough equivocation in present legislation and ambivalence of attitude amongst Eastern European politicians that it might be many years before the officials of Western corporations come to believe that Eastern Europe welcomes and protects their investments as much as does, for example, Turkey, Portugal, or Greece.

The past negative attitudes toward foreign domestic investment imply that Eastern Europe is decades behind its potential economic rivals in securing the benefits from what is surely one of the most potent productive forces in the modern world -- the multinational corporation. To see how far Eastern Europe lags, it is best not to focus on how small is the level of foreign direct investment in Eastern Europe, for it is indeed insignificant. Rather, it is much more pertinent to remark upon the vast significance of the activities of multinational corporations in the European capitalist peers of Eastern Europe. Thus, according to the figures of *Dunning and Cantwell (1987)*, multinational corporations employed 21% of the manufacturing labor force in Greece in 1977, 26% in Austria in 1981, 35% in Ireland in 1981, and 13% in Portugal in 1978. (There is no doubt that these percentages will have risen since that time.) Hence, if the Eastern European economies are to catch up with their potential rivals, there would have to be a massive injection of foreign investment and a massive reallocation of the labor force.

Yet, these massive changes will not happen quickly. Present developments in the Soviet Union evidence this point quite clearly. (*See, for example, PlanEcon Reports VI.17 and V.10.*) Foreign domestic investment in the Soviet Union became possible in April 1987, in the form of participation in joint ventures. Given the previous isolation of the Soviet economy and the consequent potential for new investment opportunities, one might predict that there would be a flood of investments into this vast economic region. However, that potential is apparently outweighed by the tremendous uncertainties in the present political and economic climate. Thus, although interest was high -- measured by the fact that over 1500 joint ventures were registered within the first three years of operation of the joint-venture legislation -- activity is low. It is estimated that only 15% of these joint ventures are operational. Their total yearly sales currently amount to less than one dollar per Soviet citizen. Moreover, these joint ventures are focused on a rather narrow set of activities, in two senses. First, the sectoral interests of foreign partners are mainly in the area of services, while there is little activity in manufacturing. Second, the location of activity is highly skewed toward Moscow, which has received nearly half of the joint ventures. Evidently, these joint ventures are contributing little to the establishment of a decentralized manufacturing base, which is the necessary condition for foreign direct investment to reverse the effects of 60 years of planned autarky.

The foreign capital stock that does exist in Eastern Europe has, up to now, been installed as the result of joint venture-activity. This observation is crucial both in gaining an understanding of the effects of past foreign direct investment on future economic performance and in understanding why joint-venture legislation is not sufficient in the present context. Joint-venture operations lead to a very different structure of activity than in operations conducted under conditions of complete foreign ownership (*Murrell, 1982*). When a foreign company cannot completely control an overseas activity in which it participates, that company is much less willing to undertake certain types of operations. For example, companies often insist upon complete control of activities if they are to transfer the technology for making new products or to put at risk a reputation for quality that is embodied in their trademarks. Hence, compared to wholly foreign-owned subsidiaries, joint ventures are less likely to function in sectors in which new products are important and in areas where the use of brand names is crucial. This simple fact can be seen by comparing the structure of foreign direct investment in two countries that are similar in many respects -- Turkey and Yugoslavia -- but which have differed in their past attitude toward foreign direct investment. In Turkey, 100% ownership was allowed, while, until recently, foreign direct investment in Yugoslavia had to take place within joint ventures.

The following table shows the cross-sectoral structure of foreign direct investment in the two countries. The sectors are listed in the table roughly in the inverse order of the importance of new product technology and quality reputation in the activities of the sector (*Murrell 1990, Chapter IV*). Yugoslavia, which did not allow complete foreign ownership, has a much higher concentration of foreign direct investment in activities in which raw materials processing is most important and less in the sectors in which new products and quality are most important. Of course, this latter group of sectors is exactly the one in which the performance of the Eastern European economies has been poor relative to their capitalist peers (*Murrell 1990*).

Table A1: The Structure of Foreign Direct Investment in Manufacturing in Yugoslavia and Turkey

Sector:	Proportion of Foreign Domestic Investment in	
	in Yugoslavia	in Turkey
Basic metals	0.310	0.211
Chemicals	0.263	0.159
Wood, paper	0.046	0.054
Rubber	0.063	0.036
Food processing	0.058	0.160
Metal products	0.052	0.077
Transport equipment	0.184	0.202
Electrical machinery	0.025	0.102

Note: The data in the table is taken from Cory (1985) and OECD (1983). The figures for Yugoslavia are for 1980 and for Turkey in 1982. The data on the service sector and on manufacturing sectors not strictly comparable in the two data sources are not reported and are excluded from the totals on which the proportions are based. Hence, the proportions in each column sum to unity.

Hence the stock of foreign direct investment that has been inherited from the old economic regimes, and any accumulating now under joint venture arrangements, will not be relevant in addressing the most significant areas of failure evidenced by the Eastern European economies in the past.

Is the level of multinational activity likely to change dramatically in Eastern Europe in the near future? Of course, some small Eastern European country might be the fortunate beneficiary of a relatively large amount of multinational activity. For example, as *Andras Inotai (this volume)* shows, the situation might be somewhat hopeful for Hungary. But there is every reason to believe that Hungary's location, past economic history, and promise of tranquil politics make it special, rather than typical of Eastern Europe. The present flow of foreign direct investment into other countries in the region is certainly less than into Hungary. Moreover, the laws now being passed in Eastern Europe still evidence a large degree of ambivalence towards foreign corporations. For example, the relevant Polish legislation allows case-specific government intervention that can impede the setting up of the operations of a foreign company. Reflecting the old fears of capitalist monopolies, the laws presently awaiting the approval of the Soviet parliament restrict a foreign company to majority ownership in only one enterprise (*Moscow News, October 14, 1990*). In addition, the general economic instability of the region argues for great caution on the part of any potential foreign investor. Thus, only radical changes in the incentives facing multinational corporations are likely to change the foreign direct investment picture soon. I return to the subject of such incentives in section 4 of this paper, where I make some normative comments on policy relevant to the present situation.

2. The Effect of the Past Absence of Multinationals

The almost total absence of multinational corporation activity in Eastern Europe in the past has had notable effects on the nature and level of economic activity in that region of the world. First, there has been a significant effect on the level of trade. Modern economic theory *(for example, Helpman and Krugman 1985)* focuses on internalization of trade as the central characteristic of the operations of multinational corporations. Hence, transactions that would otherwise be too costly can occur when there are multinational corporations. Theory, then, predicts that countries shunning multinationals will have lower levels of trade. In a recent paper *(Murrell, 1989)*, I have shown that this effect is verified both for capitalist and Eastern European countries in the 1970-80 time period. Indeed, within a standard gravity model, a variable measuring multinational activity can explain all the differences in levels of trade between Eastern and Western Europe that cannot be explained by the usual measures of country size -- population and gross domestic product.

Perhaps more important than levels of trade, the absence of multinationals has led to a peculiar structure of international trade for the socialist countries. The need for internal organization (rather than arm's length transactions) varies greatly across sectors. That variation is evidenced in the cross-sectoral importance of the activities of multinational corporations. For example, *Blomstrom, Kravis, and Lipsey (1988)* find that nearly fifty percent of the exports of electrical machinery of less-developed countries is due to the operations of U.S., Japanese, and Swedish companies. (Such patterns of activity are, of course, also reflected in the table above, in Turkey and Yugoslavia.) The corresponding figure for metal products is only eight percent. Given this fact, it is not surprising that, when one compares the pattern of trade of the Eastern European countries with that of comparable capitalist countries, the former specialize in simple semi-processed materials and have a large comparative disadvantage in higher-quality high value-added products *(Murrell, 1990)*. Moreover, the high-technology imports of Eastern European countries are much less significant than those of capitalist countries, even though Eastern Europe has had well known difficulties in developing its own technologies. The absence of cross-border internal organization -- multinational corporations -- means that the socialist countries have simply been unable to absorb new products as fast as those countries that embrace foreign direct investment.

The above implies that the Eastern European countries lost two sources of technology because they refused to countenance the internal operations of multinational corporations. First, there was the technology embodied in new goods, which often cannot be easily exchanged on the market because of the uncertain value of new products. (Presently 75% of R&D activity in Western countries is directed at creating new products, as opposed to new processes). Second, there was the direct transfer of technology occurring within organizations. Three-quarters of direct technology transfer by U.S. corporations is deemed to flow to multinational corporation affiliates, rather than at arm's-length to licensees *(Vernon 1980, p. 737). Mansfield et al. (1982, p. 36)* estimate that it takes six years to transfer a technology overseas to a multinational corporation subsidiary in a developed economy, but that the lag is thirteen years if licensing is the method of transfer. Moreover, there are likely to be spillover effects into domestically-owned industry from the presence of multinational corporations. *Blomstrom and Wolff (1989)* emphasize the effects of competition on domestic firms, the spread of labor trained by the multinational corporation, and the impact of the multinational corporations on the practices of their domestic suppliers. They show that these factors can help to explain differences in rates of productivity change across Mexican industries. All these facts underscore the conclusions of *Brada (1980)* and *Murrell (1990)* who emphasize the constraints on East-West technology transfer imposed by the absence of the operations of the multinational corporations.

3. The Spillover Effects from the Presence of Multinational Corporations

The discussion in the previous paragraphs leads directly to the most important issue in thinking about appropriate policy toward multinationals during the Eastern European transition. As emphasized in the first section of this paper, the prevailing attitude in Eastern Europe (and to be fair, in many other countries) toward multinational corporations is somewhat negative. There seems to be a suspicion in most Eastern European countries that capitalist corporations must be monitored very closely and restricted in their operations, or otherwise exploitation will occur -- to use a favorite term inherited from the old regimes. Here, I would like to argue that, in fact, the opposite might well be the case. It is likely that the multinational corporations will contribute more to the development of the Eastern Europe economies than these corporations are able to extract from the region. Because of the very nature of multinational corporations and the spheres of the economy in which they tend to be important, there are likely to be large positive spillover benefits for most Eastern European countries from foreign direct investment. In order to make this argument, I simply list the spillover benefits that are likely to occur from the operations of multinational corporations and show how these benefits directly address the problems that will be particularly important in Eastern Europe in the years of transition.

a. Technological spillovers can occur in myriad ways -- for example, through the three routes emphasized by *Blomstrom and Wolff (1989)* and discussed above and through the copying and imitation of products and processes that are inadequately covered by patents. Given the technological lag between Eastern Europe and the rest of the world in many sectors of activity, these spillover benefits are likely to be very significant in the earliest years of reform.

b. More important perhaps than the high-technology which is often the obsession of economic policy, there are the elements of business and organizational culture that are so intrinsic in the operations of modern capitalism, but which are missing from the operations of the Eastern European enterprises. Thus, the operations of multinationals are bound to spread modern techniques of accounting, Western business practices, the use of international standards in the manufacture of products, and simple ideas about organization (e.g., franchising operations). Here, it must be emphasized that these basic elements of modern business culture will inevitably spread from the operations of Western corporations to the rest of the economy because they are not the types of ideas that are protected by patents or by secrecy. It is only the previous isolation of Eastern Europe that has stopped the spread of such ideas in the past. Moreover, these ideas often cannot be spread by textbooks or by the counsel of consultants. They are ideas that often can only be transmitted by practice and personal contact -- learning by doing. Therefore, the participation of multinational corporations is absolutely essential for the quick diffusion of such ideas within Eastern European countries.

c.   When the quality of a product can vary greatly as a result of variations in the manufacturing process, it is often in the interest of companies to gain a reputation for quality. As I have argued elsewhere (*Murrell, 1982*), until foreign companies have clearly established their reputations, there will be a tendency for buyers to use country-of-origin as a signal of quality. This tendency has been important in Eastern Europe in the past where individual company trademarks have been little used. Needless to say, the quality reputations of the Eastern European countries are not high. Hence, anything that changes customers' perceptions of quality might have enormous significance in increasing the selling price of a country's products. Sales of products made using the technology of multinationals might do exactly this. To the extent that such sales change foreign customers' perceptions of a country's products, they provide a beneficial externality for the country in question.

d. It is an unavoidable fact that economic activities are highly dependent upon the processes of politics. Even if an economic activity cannot gain much from the solicitousness of politicians, it might lose much from the enmity of the body politic. Hence, multinational corporation activity -- indeed private sector activity in general -- requires political support that protects it and defends it from political encroachment. This support could be most reliably generated by the workers and managers of the foreign-owned enterprises that are operating in an economy and the suppliers and customers of these companies. Hence, there is an inevitable political-economy externality in the setting up of a multinational enterprise during the early stages of the Eastern European reforms. The creation of such an enterprise will be instrumental in creating the political conditions favorable for multinationals.

e. The presence of multinational corporations tends to be greater in industries that pollute less per unit of value-added. (The reason for this is simply that multinationals operate in industries where transaction costs are high -- where organizational and technological skills are at a premium. For natural reasons, these industries are ones where value-added is high and raw materials processing is less important. Raw materials processing industries are the high-polluting ones.) Hence, the addition of substantial multinational production capability might well be a significant second-best anti-pollution policy for a nation suffering the after-effects of the laxness that the communist regimes showed on matters of environment policy.

4. Conclusion: What Policy for Multinationals in Eastern Europe?

The three preceding sections constitute a single strand of reasoning that proceeds in three steps. Once the threads of this argument are clearly seen, there inevitably follows a simple conclusion concerning the nature of the appropriate Eastern European policy toward multinationals. The first step in the argument is to recognize the drastic limits that have been placed in the past on the operations of multinational corporations in Eastern Europe. Second, the absence of multinationals (compared to their important role in capitalist economies) is one of the most important factors explaining the relatively poor economic performance of the Eastern European economies over the past two decades. Third, in the activities of multinational corporations, there are a very large number of beneficial externalities that will be crucial in changing the Eastern European landscape.

The conclusion that stems from this argument is straightforward and contains the only major disagreement between this paper and the one by *Andras Inotai (1991)* contained in this volume. A passive policy towards multinationals is not sufficient in the present situation. Instead, the Eastern European countries must undertake a very active effort to encourage foreign direct investment activities. If such encouragement requires tax concessions and subsidies, then what is necessary must be done. Inevitably, such policies will involve unequal treatment between domestic and foreign enterprises, favoring the latter. This must be accepted because it is either this choice or stagnation. For the Eastern European countries must acknowledge that policies favoring multinational corporations are the inevitable consequence of their past economic mistakes, especially the retreat into autarky that was such an essential part of their planned past.

References

BLOMSTROM, M. and WOLFF, E. (1989), Multinational Corporations and Productivity Convergence in Mexico, NBER Working Paper, #3141, Cambridge, Mass.

BLOMSTROM, M.; KRAVIS, I.B. and LIPSEY R. E., (1988) Multinational Firms and Manufactured Exports from Developing Countries, NBER Working Paper, Cambridge Mass..

BRADA, J. C. (1980), Industry Structure and East-West Technology Transfer: A Case Study of the Pharmaceutical Industry, ACES Bulletin, Vol. 22(1), 31-59.

CORY, P. F. (1985), Industrial Cooperation, Joint Ventures, and the MNE in Yugoslavia, in: RUGMAN, A., ed., New Theories of the Multinational Enterprise, New York: St. Martin's.

DUNNING, J. and CANTWELL, J. (1987), IRM Directory of Statistics of International Investment and Production, Basingstoke: MacMillan.

HELPMAN, E. and KRUGMAN, P. R. (1985), Market Structure and Foreign Trade: Increasing Returns, Imperfect Competition, and the International Economy, Cambridge, MA: The MIT Press.

INOTAI, A. (1991), Foreign direct Investment in Reforming CMEA Countries: Facts, Lessons, and Perspectives, this volume.

MANSFIELD, E.; ROMEO, A.; SCHWARTZ, M.; TEECE, D.; WAGNER, S.; and BRACH, P. (1982), Technology Transfer, Productivity, and Economic Policy, New York: Norton.

MURRELL, P. (1982), Product Quality, Market Signaling and the Development of East-West Trade, Economic Inquiry, Vol. 20(4), 589-603.

MURRELL, P. (1989), The Effect of (the Absence of) Multinational Corporations on the Level of Eastern European Trade, University of Maryland, Working Paper.

MURRELL, P. (1990), The Nature of Socialist Economies: Lessons From Eastern European Foreign Trade, Princeton: Princeton University Press.

OECD (1983), Foreign Investment in Turkey, Paris: OECD.

VERNON, R. (1980), The Multinationalization of U.S. Business: Some Basic Policy Implications, in Special Study on Economic Change, Volume 9 - The International Economy: U.S. Role in a World Market, Washington, D.C.: U.S. Government Printing Office.

GERMAN MULTINATIONALS IN EUROPE:
PATTERNS AND PERSPECTIVES

Günter Heiduk and Ulrike W. Hodges

1. Introduction

Rising levels of interdependence both economically and politically among the world's nations have especially since World War II characterized worldwide economic developments. This continuous interdependence is reflected in the phenomenon of multinational enterprises (MNEs) which have come to be one of the most significant integrated strategies for firms to internationalize. This internationalization process has intensified in the 1970s and 1980s when Japanese firms joined the ranks of international investors.[1] German firms have responded to this challenge and reinforced FDI in traditional areas of strength.[2]

When analyzing German MNEs today, we have to take into consideration

(i) the long-term development of FDI:
On its own, the increase of German FDI seems rather impressive: it increased by 17.95 Billion DM in the 60s; in the 70s, it grew by 53.24 Billion DM and between the years 1980 and 1989 it increased by as much as 111.59 Billion DM (*Table 1*). Compared to other leading industrial nations, however, the stock of German FDI is, on the whole, relatively modest. While in terms of exports Germany has since the 1960s numbered among the three leading exporting nations, she only ranks fourth as far as FDI is concerned (*Table 2*). And although the flows of German FDI increase steadily year by year, the amount will not be sufficiently high to close the gap between her and the three leading "World Investors" in the foreseeable future. Even France had higher FDI flows in 1988 than Germany (*Table 3*).

There obviously exists in Germany a close correlation between exports and direct investment, as is apparent by the fact that out of the ten most important countries for German FDI, nine also belong to the most important purchasers of German exports (*Table 4*).

Table 1: Stock of German FDI by Regions, 1952-1989, in Billion DM

	Total	Industrial Countries				LDCs (incl. OPEC)	Eastern Countries
		Total	EC	USA	Japan		
1952-55	0.42	-	-	-	-	-	-
1960	3.16	-	-	-	-	-	-
1965	8.32	-	-	-	-	-	-
1970	21.11	-	-	-	-	-	-
1976	43.10	34.49	18.01	5.32	0.47	8.61	0.01
1980	74.35	61.54	30.03	15.54	0.98	12.73	0.09
1984	125.87	104.78	43.72	35.76	1.76	21.05	0.05
1988	165.83	147.73	65.69	49.33	3.50	16.80	0.30
1989	185.94	161.62	78.26	53.17	3.77	17.71	0.39

Source: Bundesverband der Deutschen Industrie; Bundesminister für Wirtschaft (6/1990); Bundesanzeiger

Table 2: Stock of FDI by Major Countries of Origin and Exports in Billion US-$, 1987

	Stock of FDI	Exports
USA	308,794	252,894
Great Britain	161,600	131,242
Japan	77,022	231,332
Germany	65,348	294,165

Source: Bundesminister für Wirtschaft (6/1990)

Table 3: Flows of FDI by Major Countries of Origin, 1988, in Billion US-$

1.	Japan	34,210
2.	Great Britain	26,877
3.	USA	17,534
4.	France	12,751
5.	Germany	10,393

Source: Bundesminister für Wirtschaft (6/1990)

Table 4: Rank 1 - 1O of Host Countries of German FDI and Import Countries of German Goods, 1988, in Billion DM

Stock of German FDI			Import of German Goods		
1	USA	49.3	1	France	71.3
2	France	13.2	2	Great Britain	52.9
3	Switzerland	11.3	3	Italy	51.7
4	Netherlands	11.0	4	Netherlands	49.2
5	Great Britain	9.4	5	USA	45.7
6a	Luxemburg	7.7	6	Belgium/Lux	42.1
6b	Belgium	7.5	7	Switzerland	34.4
7	Spain	7.4	8	Austria	31.9
8	Italy	6.6	9	Spain	17.3
9	Brazil	6.4	10	Sweden	16.6
1O	Austria (1986)	5.2			

Source: Bundesverband der Deutschen Industrie, (1990); Statistisches Bundesamt (1989)

(ii) the development of returns and investment:
Investment activity is highly dependent on the development of profits. Between 1979 and 1982 the annual profits before tax of German firms fell from 139.8 Billion DM to 123.9 Billion DM (*Table 5*).

**Table 5: Annual Profits before Tax, Gross Investment
of German Firms, 1980-89, in Bill. DM**

	1980	1981	1982	1983	1984	1985	1986	1987	1988	1989
Profit Before Tax	132.0	125.5	123.9	142.5	147.8	157.9	166.5	172.0	188.9	208.5
Gross Invest- ment	138.5	-	104.5	112.0	131.1	132.1	119.0	177.0	195.8	211.0

Source: Deutsche Bundesbank (various issues), Monatsberichte

A gradual recovery with relatively modest growth rates has taken place since 1983. It was above all domestic production capacity that was enlarged by investment activity. Growing export demand was largely responsible for at least a part of domestic investment. This demand did in fact lead to an increase in foreign turnover which as part of total turnover grew from 24.1% in 1978 to 30.1 % in 1987. Quite obviously, growing exports also induce foreign investment. The share of foreign investment by German manufacturing firms as part of total investment rose from 8% (1982) to 13% (1989). Again, it is clear from these developments that export orientation has been and still is a dominant feature in the internationalization strategy of German firms. Multinationalization via FDI has not yet reached a comparable importance.

(iii) changes in the political-economic environment:
It is to be expected that in the unified Germany there are attractive opportunities to invest in the former GDR. To give only one example: Mercedes-Benz AG, member of the Daimler-Benz group, is going to invest DM 1 Billion to modernize an East German truck plant and turn it into one of the world's biggest and largest truck production plants. By mid-199Os, the production capacity will be expanded to 4O,OOO trucks per year. There is some reason to believe that in the future German FDI will at least increase in East European countries since GDR contacts in Eastern Europe could well put German firms at a competitive advantage in relation to those of other Western countries. There are already some foreign firms taking

shares in those West German companies that have good market prospects in the former GDR as well as in Eastern Europe on the whole. Contract- or capital-based ties to West German companies could well be a compromise solution to conflicts arising from internationalization strategies planned for the longer term and necessary short-term decisions. It could well be that the opening of Eastern Europe will cause a new wave of multinationalization which in turn could lead to an increase in the growth of German FDI.

2. German Multinational Enterprises: A Macro-Economic View

The period of reconstructing the German economy was supported by a relatively high export-orientation. From the mid-60s onwards conditions in the international economic framework began to change in such a way that the international competitive position of Germany's economy was expected to deteriorate. But neither the two oil crises, nor the revaluation of the German Mark, nor increased competition from new suppliers from other countries, nor the lack of progress towards EC-integration ("Eurosclerosis"), nor indeed the pressure from increasing costs at home have had in any way a detrimental effect on Germany's economic position as a nation strong in exports. The share of exports as part of GNP has increased in the past 20 years by approximately 10 percentage points (*Table 6*).

The fact that since the early 1970s growth rates of German FDI have stagnated and that they have lately even been on the decline is further proof of the assertion that exports are the driving force behind the internationalization of the German economy. It seems that the role of FDI is seen by German firms as that of a supportive instrument in internationalization strategy. The same may also be said for the varied forms of international company cooperation, though only studies of an empirical nature with special reference to specific industries and regions exist in this regard (*see section 6*).

Table 6: Indicators of Internationalization of the German Economy

	Growth Rate of Exports	Exp. GNP	Growth Rate of German FDI
1955	–	20.0	–
1960	12.1	22.0	51.7
1965	9.2	20.0	21.4
1970	12.2	18.7	20.5
1975	15.5	21.5	14.8
1980	6.6	23.6	15.0
1985	9.3	29.1	17.3 (1980-84)
1989	7.2	28.4	9.5

Note: The growth rate indicates the average of the preceding five year period.
Source: Deutsche Bundesbank (various issues), Monatsberichte

Analyses about the motivation for internationalization have further corroborated this overall pattern.

German firms aim at exploiting in full their capacities through the expansion of sales to foreign markets. Since traditionally the domestic demand has been relatively small, it has been crucial to German economic growth to secure and extend already existing markets as well as to secure and control marketing in the host country (*Kayser and Schwarting, 1981*). That is to say, German MNEs are directed towards taking advantage of the market potential in the host country, as shown most recently by their concentration on the EC market. This is generally done by market expansion (export), diversification (FDI) and/or integration (new alliances).

Among the motivations for German firms to multinationalize, we traditionally find marketing as the most important reason. That is, firms investing abroad expect to participate in the growth of a particular market. Since the first phase of multinationalization of German enterprises, this motive has been a dominant feature, and we find this fact reflected in the way in which location is chosen for German-owned branches. These are industrialized nations with rapidly expanding markets. Among these, since the early 1980s, we find increasing concentration on the EC and the US market (*Table 1*). With reference to the EC, the increase of German FDI reflects not only the market-oriented motivation of German FDI, but also the relatively low barriers to EC capital movements as well as, since 1987, the individual entrepreneurs' considerations in regard to the economic union to come in 1992. Nevertheless, the USA is still the most important country for German FDI. In addition to wishing to secure the USA as an export market, there are no doubt other reasons as well - like, for example, the revaluation of the German Mark - why German FDI has advanced in the USA.

3. Regional Orientation of German FDI

The most important, and certainly least surprising fact about regional orientation of German FDI, is its concentration on industrialized nations. This tendency can be explained by the fact that, generally speaking, one of the main motivations for FDI is the expansion of existing or the establishment of new markets as well as the securing of one's market share in the international market. These intentions can most successfully be pursued in nations that are characterized by rapid growth of the individual markets, i.e., the industrialized nations, since size and development of the markets are crucial to the decision of the locations of FDI.

Among the industrialized nations the EC has been the most important target region for German MNEs. Like those of France, the United Kingdom and the United States, German MNEs have increasingly concentrated on the EC. This concentration on the EC market has been most apparent for German and US FDI. While between 1960 and 1970, the share of German FDI directed towards EC nations increased from 14 percent to 31 percent, the share of US FDI directed towards the EC out of the total US FDI almost doubled in this period from 8 percent to 15 percent in 1970.

While remaining fairly stable throughout the 1970s, the share of German FDI directed towards the EC out of the total German FDI increased more rapidly than that of any other nation, from less than a third (32%) in 1982 to 42% in 1989. In contrast, the growth rates of German FDI flows into the USA have since about 1985 decreased slightly (*Graph 1*).

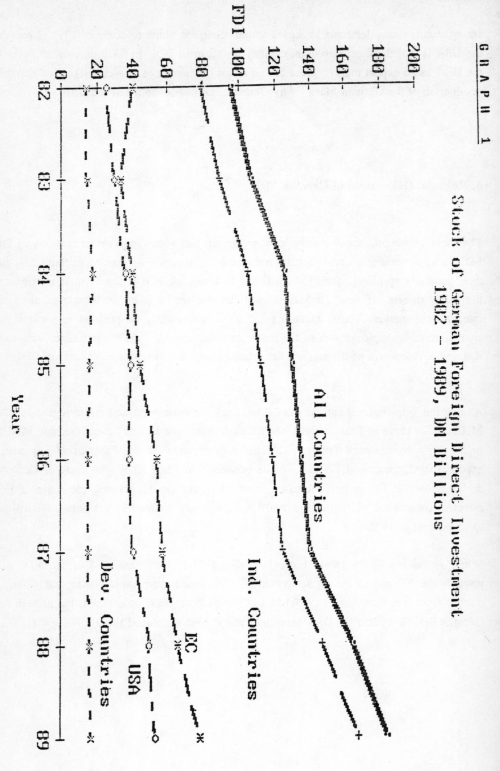

GRAPH 1

Stock of German Foreign Direct Investment
1982 - 1989, DM Billions

Source: Bundesverband der Deutschen Industrie e.V., Deutsche Direktinvestitionen im Ausland. Cologne: 1990

Table 7: Stock of German Foreign Direct Investment in the European Community, 1976-89, in Billion DM

	1976		1980		1985		1988		1989	
	DM	%	DM	%	DM	%	DM	%	DM	%
All	18,010	100.0	30,036	100.0	43,722	100.0	65,691	100.0	78,259	100.0
Belgium[1]	2,465	13.7	2,933	9.8	4,333	9.9	7,540	11.5	9,378	12.0
Denmark	365	2.0	667	2.2	712	1.6	902	1.4	937	1.2
France	4,468	24.8	8,253	27.5	9,516	21.8	13,152	20.0	15,830	20.2
Greece	277	1.5	446	1.5	571	1.3	637	1.0	690	0.9
Great Britain	1,268	7.0	3,063	10.2	5,123	11.7	9,432	14.4	13,893	17.8
Ireland	179	1.0	406	1.4	511	1.2	662	1.0	1,699	2.2
Italy	1,002	5.6	2,002	6.7	4,746	10.9	6,608	10.1	7,078	9.0
Luxembourg	2,121	11.8	4,874	16.2	6,953	15.9	7,695	11.7	7,695	9.8
Netherlands	3,870	21.5	4,711	15.7	7,113	16.3	10,992	16.7	12,657	16.2
Portugal	310	1.7	273	0.9	418	1.0	693	1.1	786	1.0
Spain	1,685	9.4	2,408	8.0	3,726	8.5	7,378	11.2	8,614	11.0

Note: 1 The FDI directed toward Luxembourg in 1989 is included in FDI for Belgium and not listed separately.

Source: Statistisches Beiheft zu den Monatsberichten der Deutschen Bundesbank, Series 3, various years, cited in Bundesverband der Deutschen Industrie e.V., Deutsche Direktinvestition im Ausland, (Cologne, 1990).

Within the EC the most important recipients of German FDI have traditionally been France, the United Kingdom and the Netherlands: in 1989, these countries had accumulated 20 percent, 18 percent and 16 percent of German FDI stock, respectively, amounting to more than 50 percent of German FDI. Great Britain and Spain were able to increase their share in EC-FDI of German firms visibly (*Table 7*).

It will surely not be possible for German MNEs to shun the general trend towards increased foreign investment. The M&A boom having its origin in the USA and Great Britain is now being "answered" by German MNEs with an increased number of foreign purchases. This has meant that the cross-border balance vis-a-vis these two countries has been reversed (*Graph 2*).

GRAPH 2

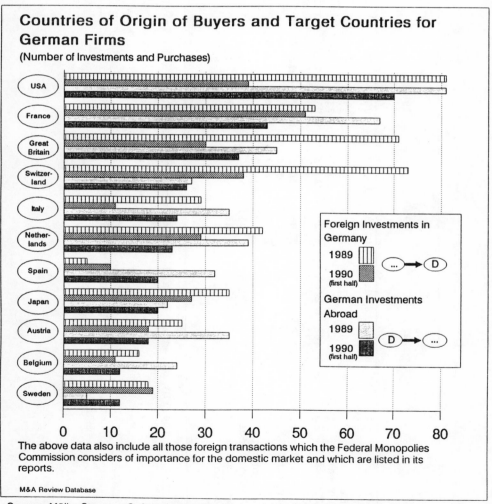

Source: Müller-Stewens, G. (1990), ed., M&A Review, 5 (1990/5), Duisburg University

4. German FDI by Industries

Until the mid-80s the major part of German FDI flowed into the manufacturing industry of other countries (*Table 8*). In 1988, however, this sector had its share in the stock of German FDI reduced to only 34.5%. With 44.4% the service sector is the most important target branch for German FDI, though a large part of the firms invested in holding companies could well be listed as belonging to the manufacturing sector. In the manufacturing industry the four largest export branches correspond to the four most important parent or target branches of German FDI.

Table 8: Stock of German FDI by Industries in the Host Countries, 1976 - 1988 in Percent

	1976	1980	1984	1988
Manufacturing industries	42.9	39.5	38.6	34.5
- Chemical industry	13.7	12.2	12.3	11.3
- vehicle industry	6.2	7.0	6.5	5.9
- Electrical engineering	6.4	5.3	6.9	6.1
- Mechanical engineering	4.7	4.3	3.8	3.2
Services	33.3	36.6	37.3	44.4
- Holding companies	19.0	19.7	19.2	26.8
- Banking	5.1	7.4	6.0	7.0
- Insurance	1.5	1.8	2.1	2.4
Trade	18.3	18.8	17.7	18.0
Others	5.5	5.1	6.4	3.1

Source: See Table 1

Table 9: Investment Abroad by Leading Export Industries

	Share of Exports in Total Exports in %, 1989	Share of FDI in Total Stock of German FDI of Manufacturing Industry in %, 1988
Chemical industry	10.1	33.0
Vehicle industry	18.0	17.3
Electrical engineering	8.6	15.3
Mechanical engineering	19.0	8.9

Source: See Table 1; Statistisches Jahrbuch 1990

5. Case Studies: Daimler Benz and BASF
5.1 Globalization Strategies

In order to illustrate our findings at the company level, let us compare some aspects of the internationalization of Daimler Benz and BASF. These German firms ranked first and sixth among the German enterprises in terms of turnover in 1989. Although they are giants among German enterprises, if we put these firms in an international perspective, they are of only moderate significance, ranking fourth and eighteenth among European enterprises and thirteenth and 31st among the biggest global enterprises in 1989, respectively.

A closer look at these two firms reveals some very different globalization strategies, with each firm pursuing different goals. Let us illustrate these differences in internationalization strategy by comparing the development of the international turnover, investments abroad and employees abroad for these two firms.

Daimler Benz

The Daimler Benz firm started out in the automobile industry by merely manufacturing cars and trucks. Especially during the last decade, however, this firm has evolved into an integrated technology firm. This was achieved not only through in-house technological developments and intensive R&D, but mainly through extensive takeovers in the aerospace and electrical

Table 10: Daimler Benz Concern: Turnover by Region, 1980 - 1989, in Million DM

	1980	1981	1982	1983	1984	1985	1986	1987	1988	1989
Germany only (%)	13,855 (44.6)	13,577 (37.0)	13,316 (34.2)	15,177 (37.9)	14,682 (33.7)	18,709 (35.7)	27,838 (42.5)	28,064 (41.6)	29,094 (39.6)	29,562 (39.7)
Europe including Germany (%)	19,821 (63.8)	20,595 (56.2)	21,131 (54.3)	22,896 (57.2)	23,132 (53.2)	29,658 (56.6)	43,054 (65.7)	44,619 (66.13)	48,155 (65.5)	50,989 (66.7)
North America (%)	3,089 (9.9)	5,313 (14.5)	6,931 (17.8)	8,452 (21.1)	11,328 (26.0)	12,776 (24.4)	13,030 (19.9)	12,135 (18.0)	11,817 (16.1)	13,032 (17.1)
Latin America (%)	3,099 (10.0)	3,323 (9.1)	2,635 (6.8)	1,847 (4.6)	2,471 (5.7)	3,044 (5.8)	2,621 (4.0)	3,610 (5.4)	4,899 (6.7)	3,790 (5.0)
Africa, Asia, & Australia (%)	5,045 (16.2)	7,430 (20.3)	8,208 (21.1)	6,810 (17.0)	6,574 (15.1)	6,931 (13.2)	6,793 (10.4)	7,111 (10.5)	8,624 (11.7)	8,581 (11.2)
Total Turnover	31,054	36,661	38,905	40,005	43,505	52,409	65,498	67,475	73,495	76,392

Note: Figures in parentheses indicate percentage of total annual turnover.

Source: Daimler Benz, Geschaeftsbericht, various issues.

engineering sectors, so that, for example, in 1984 the two groups of MTU and Dornier (both aerospace and engine sectors) were consolidated under the Daimler Benz firm, followed by AEG (mainly electrical engineering, tools and applicances) in 1985. This M&A strategy consistently pursued by Daimler Benz has turned a car manufacturer into an internationally competitive technology firm. Along with this takeover strategy, Daimler Benz has continued to expand its branches throughout the world, though concentrating on the European nations.

As can be seen in *Graph 3*, the turnover achieved outside Germany out of the total turnover increased from 55.4 percent in 1980 to 66.1 percent in 1984, before dropping again to 61 percent in 1989, as a consequence of the national takeovers. Similarly, the European share (including West Germany) out of the total turnover increased during the same period (1980-89) from 63.8 percent to 66.7 percent (*Table 10*). This concentration on Europe is, as was discussed earlier, a reflection of German firms preparing for an integrated European market. In the case of Daimler Benz, this is achieved by intensifying sales of cars, particularly in Italy, France, Spain and the United Kingdom. Another, even stronger indicator for the degree to which a firm is involved internationally is the investments abroad: In the case of Daimler Benz, we observe an increasing share of investments abroad out of total investments since the end of the economic slowdown in the early 1980s, as shown in *Table 11*.

Table 11: Daimler Benz Group: Share of Investments Abroad Out of Total Investments[*], 1980 - 89, in Million DM

Year	Total	Change (%) over the previous year	Abroad	Change (%) over the previous year	Share of Total (%)
1980	2,057	--	394	--	19.2
1981	3,033	+47.5	800	+103.1	26.4
1982	3,427	+13.0	423	− 47.1	12.3
1983	3,464	+ 1.1	417	− 1.4	12.0
1984	3,374	− 2.6	1,208	+189.7	35.8
1985	4,014	+19.0	1,261	+ 4.4	31.4
1986	5,385	+34.2	1,494	+ 18.5	27.7
1987	3,834	−28.8	442	− 70.4	11.5
1988	6,628	+72.9	590	+ 33.5	8.9
1989	7,242	+ 9.3	783	+ 32.7	10.8

[*] Investments in financial assets are not included, since they are not divided by nations.
Source: Daimler Benz (various issues), Geschäftsbericht

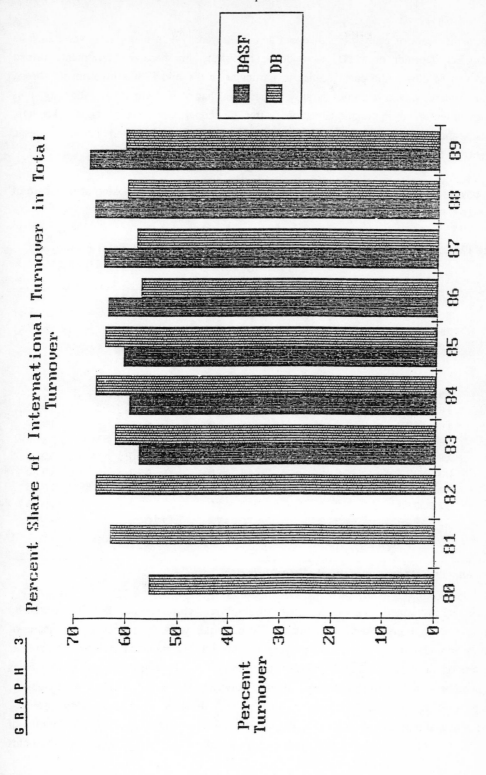

GRAPH 3 Percent Share of International Turnover in Total Turnover

BASF
DB

Percent Turnover

70 — 60 — 50 — 40 — 30 — 20 — 10 — 0

80 81 82 83 84 85 86 87 88 89

Source: compiled from Daimler Benz, Geschäftsjahr, various issues; and BASF, Geschäftsjahr, various issues.

Aside from the years of economic slowdown and those years when major takeovers, such as those of AEG, Dornier or MTU, were done (1987-88), the share of investments abroad continued to rise during the past decade. In particular in the mid-1980s investments abroad continued to increase at a rate considerably higher than that of investments in Germany, thus indicating an enforced multinationalization. After the conclusion of the above takeovers, investments abroad appear to increase again at a rate slightly higher than that of domestic investments in 1989.

The underlying trend towards internationalization is also evident when looking at the share of employees out of the total employees at Daimler Benz (*Table 12*).

Table 12: Daimler Benz Firm: Share of Employees Abroad Out of Total Employees, 1980-89

Year	Total Emplo- yees	Change (%) over the previous year	Abroad	Change (%) over the previous year	Share of Total(%)
1980	183,392	--	37,069	--	20.2
1981	188,039	+ 2.5	38,943	+ 5.1	20.7
1982	185,687	- 1.0	36,569	- 6.5	19.7
1983	184,877	- 0.4	33,604	- 8.8	18.2
1984	199,872	+ 8.1	41,829	+24.5	20.9
1985	231,077	+15.6	44,425	+ 6.2	19.2
1986	319,965	+38.5	62,427	+40.5	19.5
1987	326,288	+ 2.0	63,630	+ 1.9	19.5
1988	338,749	+ 3.8	70,472	+10.8	20.8
1989	368,226	+ 8.7	70,027	- 0.6	19.0

Source: Daimler Benz (various issues), Geschäftsbericht.

Other than the investments abroad, the share of employees abroad is not directly affected by the Daimler Benz transactions in Germany. Even in the years of takeover, the share of employees abroad out of the total employees remained fairly stable at around 20 percent. Among one of the most spectacular international transactions between the two industrial firms of the past few months was the strategic alliance between Daimler Benz AG and Mitsubishi, involving joint research, information exchanges and possibly joint production projects. Opening a new dimension of international competitiveness in technology, the possibilities of joint ventures and technological exchange between the "allies" are being explored in the fields of electronics, services and aerospace. However, cooperation has so far not extended beyond the "getting-to-know-one-another" phase. Aside from Daimler Benz and Mitsubishi, we find such tendencies towards concentration repeatedly in the automobile industry: for instance, between Renault and Volvo as well as General Motors and Saab, which also entered partnerships this year.

The economic consideration behind these developments is the intention to stabilize or achieve a leading position among the international competitors first of all by holding the leading edge in technology and know-how and secondly by sharing the risk with the partner.

BASF

Differing sharply from the strategy of Daimler Benz, the BASF firm, a chemical firm, reveals a far more consistent internationalization pattern: Throughout the 1980s, it continuously reduced its domestic share of turnover, from 42.2 percent in 1983 to 31.9 percent in 1989, while increasingly investing abroad (*Graph 3*).

Contrary to expectations, however, the turnover share achieved in the EC nations out of the total turnover declined from 60.7 percent in 1983 to only 56.8 percent in 1989 (*Table 13*). Instead, BASF heavily invested in the United States to secure and expand the important US market for BASF export products, with the turnover share of the US market increasing from 15.3 percent in 1983 to 22.1 percent in 1989. This concentration on the North American market can be explained by the ideology underlying the BASF globalization strategy: Unlike, for instance, the Daimler Benz firm, BASF does not pursue strategic alliances, but concentrates on the demand for its products. It still subscribes to the "traditional" way of multinationalization where market conditions are the determining factor for investing abroad.

In this sense we need to consider the BASF firm representative not only for a large German firm, since it also represents a globalization strategy very similar to that of German medium-sized firms. These, too, (as was discussed earlier) continue to rely on exports as the most important form of economic involvement abroad. This strategy of following the demand for a certain set of products also becomes obvious when we look at the categories of products BASF is making, as shown in *Table 14*.

Table 13: BASF Group: Turnover by Region, 1980 – 1989, in Million DM

	1980	1981	1982	1983	1984	1985	1986	1987	1988	1989
Germany only (%)	12,962 (46.7)	13,840 (43.6)	14,294 (44.0)	14,869 (42.4)	16,344 (40.5)	17,396 (39.2)	14,568 (36.0)	14,476 (35.0)	14,539 (33.2)	15,211 (31.9)
All EC Countries (%)	17,611 (63.5)	19,370 (61.0)	20,103 (61.9)	21,300 (60.7)	23,810 (59.0)	25,834 (58.2)	23,901 (59.1)	24,001 (59.7)	25,348 (57.8)	27,065 (56.8)
Non-EC Western European (%)	2,491 (9.0)	2,585 (8.1)	2,515 (7.7)	2,683 (7.6)	3,101 (7.7)	3,795 (8.3)	2,117 (5.2)	2,075 (5.2)	2,202 (5.0)	2,306 (4.9)
Eastern Europe (%)	948 (3.4)	879 (2.7)	956 (2.9)	943 (2.7)	1,090 (2.7)	1,138 (2.6)	1,003 (2.5)	959 (2.4)	1,056 (2.4)	1,175 (2.5)
North America (%)	3,078 (11.1)	4,120 (13.0)	4,112 (12.7)	5,364 (15.3)	6,555 (16.2)	7,782 (17.5)	8,231 (20.3)	7,910 (19.7)	9,137 (20.8)	10,478 (22.1)
Latin America (%)	1,385 (5.0)	1,794 (5.6)	1,902 (5.9)	1,682 (4.8)	2,064 (5.1)	2,152 (4.9)	1,866 (4.6)	1,848 (4.6)	2,025 (4.6)	2,427 (5.1)
Africa & West Asia (%)	829 (3.0)	1,129 (3.6)	964 (3.0)	1,033 (2.9)	1,193 (3.0)	1,166 (2.6)	1,065 (2.6)	947 (2.4)	1,016 (2.3)	1,173 (2.5)
South & East Asia, Australia (%)	1,389 (5.0)	1,889 (6.0)	1,934 (5.9)	2,106 (6.0)	2,587 (6.4)	2,600 (5.9)	2,288 (5.7)	2,498 (6.2)	3,081 (7.0)	2,993 (6.3)
Total Turnover	27,731	31,766	32,486	35,111	40,400	44,377	40,471	40,238	43,868	47,617

Note: Figures in parentheses indicate percentage of total annual turnover.

Source: BASF, (various issues), Geschäftsbericht.

Table 14: BASF Group: Turnover by Product Category, 1980 - 1989, in Million DM

Product Category	1980	1981	1982	1983	1984	1985	1986	1987	1988	1989
Raw Materials & Energy (%)	6,124 (22.1)	6,976 (22.0)	7,101 (21.9)	7,240 (20.6)	8,159 (20.2)	8,990 (20.3)	6,280 (15.5)	5,738 (14.3)	5,672 (12.9)	5,752 (12.1)
Chemicals (%)	5,240 (18.9)	6,525 (20.5)	6,449 (19.9)	7,109 (20.3)	8,304 (20.6)	8,204 (18.5)	8,251 (20.4)	8,237 (20.5)	9,036 (20.6)	9,729 (20.4)
Products for Agriculture (%)	4,668 (16.8)	5,235 (16.5)	5,149 (15.9)	5,447 (15.5)	6,411 (15.9)	6,593 (14.9)	5,208 (12.9)	4,915 (12.2)	4,782 (10.9)	5,104 (10.7)
Synthetic Fibres (%)	4,649 (16.8)	4,758 (15.0)	4,693 (14.5)	5,310 (15.1)	6,340 (15.7)	6,686 (15.1)	6,291 (15.6)	6,689 (16.6)	7,996 (18.2)	8,645 (18.2)
Dyes and Refined Products (%)	3,879 (14.0)	4,424 (13.9)	4,633 (14.3)	5,139 (14.6)	5,706 (14.1)	6,709 (15.1)	6,350 (15.7)	6,527 (16.2)	7,657 (17.5)	8,711 (18.3)
Consumer Products (%)	3,171 (11.4)	3,848 (12.1)	4,461 (13.7)	4,816 (13.7)	5,480 (13.6)	7,195 (16.2)	8,091 (20.0)	8,131 (20.2)	8,726 (19.9)	9,676 (20.3)
Total Turnover	27,731	31,766	32,486	35,111	40,400	44,377	40,471	40,238	43,868	47,617

Note: Figures in parentheses indicate percentage of total annual output.

Source: BASF (various issues), Geschäftsbericht.

Throughout the past decade, the range of product categories has not changed significantly and in most cases the share of turnover in one product category out of the total turnover remained stable. This is not to say that there was no technological progress; on the contrary, BASF has maintained its international competitiveness by refining its products and diversifying within the individual products. Nevertheless, we do not find a change in industries as is the case with Daimler Benz.

The continuity and stability in the BASF internationalization strategy is also evident from the investments made abroad. Although affected by the economic slowdown in the early 1980s, the share of investments abroad remained fairly high between 46 and 33 percent (*Table 15*).

Table 15: BASF Group: Share of Investments Abroad out of Total Investments, 1980-89, in Million DM

Year	Total	Change (%) over the previous year	Abroad	Change (%) over the previous year	Share of Total (%)
1980	1,841	--	607	--	33.0
1981	2,059	+11.8	704	+16.0	34.2
1982	2,003	- 2.7	575	-18.4	28.7
1983	1,630	-18.6	411	-18.6	25.2
1984	2,051	+25.8	NA	NA	NA
1985	2,794	+36.2	1,272	NA	45.5
1986	2,657	- 4.9	885	-30.5	33.3
1987	2,758	+ 3.8	872	- 1.5	32.0
1988	3,495	+26.7	1,620	+83.1	46.4
1989	3,956	+13.2	1,760	+ 8.6	44.5

NA = not available

Source: BASF (various issues), Geschäftsbericht

However, whenever the firm reduced its investments, those made abroad, as was the case with Daimler Benz, were reduced far more strongly than those at home, in order to reduce the risk of international involvement.

Turning to our third indicator for internationalization, let us look at the share of employees abroad (*Table 16*). This share increased consistently after the economic slowdown had been absorbed, with an enforced increase in 1985, when the involvement with the US market was intensified.

Table 16: BASF Group: Share of Employees Abroad Out of Total Employees, 1980-89

Year	Total	Change (%) over the previous year	Abroad	Change (%) over the previous year	Share of Total(%)
1980	116,518	--	29,145	--	25.0
1981	116,646	+ 0.1	28,811	- 1.1	24.7
1982	115,868	- 0.7	28,315	- 1.8	24.4
1983	114,128	- 1.5	28,035	- 1.0	24.6
1984	115,816	+ 1.5	28,524	+ 1.7	24.6
1985	130,173	+12.4	41,658	+46.1	32.0
1986	131,468	+ 1.0	42,017	+ 0.9	32.0
1987	133,759	+ 1.7	44,207	+ 5.2	33.1
1988	134,834	+ 0.8	46,150	+ 4.4	34.2
1989	136,990	+ 1.6	47,826	+ 3.6	34.9

Source: BASF (various issues), Geschäftsbericht

Aside from this exception, the increase in employees quite closely followed the overall expansion of personnel, with increased changes since the intensified engagement in the US market in the mid-1980s.

With such a globalization strategy, of course, BASF is not representative for MNEs employing new forms of internationalization, but it reflects a consistent strategy that has proven successful despite the new development among MNEs in Germany.

5.2. Correlation between German FDI and International Turnover of DB and BASF

As an interesting way of putting the globalization strategies of these two German firms in perspective to the overall German involvement abroad, let us compare international with the German FDI in the world. As can be seen from *Graph 4*, the two firms observed are representative of the general trend of German FDI.

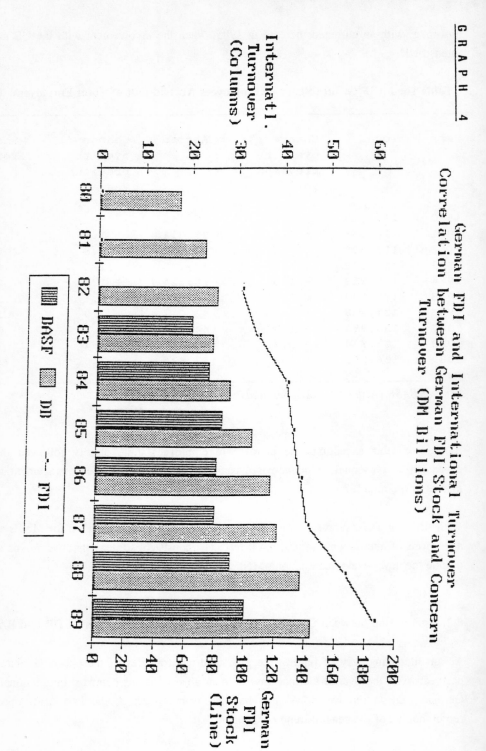

GRAPH 4

German FDI and International Turnover
Correlation between German FDI Stock and Concern
Turnover (DM Billions)

Source: compiled from Bundesverband der Deutschen Industrie e.V., Deutsche Direktinvestitionen
im Ausland (Cologne, 1990); Daimler Benz, Geschäftsjahr, various issues; and BASF,
Geschäftsjahr, various issues.

It should be noted here that the turnover of DB does include AEG, MTU and Dornier from the time they were consolidated under DB. This explains most of the spectacular turnover increase that we find for Daimler Benz since 1986.

The BASF international turnover is the one that follows the overall development of German FDI most closely, reflecting the consistency of its rather traditional globalization strategy.

6. Internationalization of the Ruhr Region

In a recent empirical study (*Rath, 1990*), we listed the development and current state of foreign economic activity by companies in the Ruhr Region. Although this study covered merely one region, the Ruhr Region is one of the most important economic and industrial centers in Germany. In this study of 803 firms located in the Ruhr Region, which covered the chemical industry as well as electrical and mechanical engineering, we found that of the 367 companies which responded, 81.5 percent are active abroad. Although export is the dominant form of internationalization (81.2 percent), at least 22.6 percent of the companies had engaged in FDI, while as many as 30.2 percent had concluded cooperation agreements without capital participation (*Heiduk, 1989*).

The regional orientation of these foreign activities reflects the national figure with a concentration on the industrial nations. The form of internationalization most frequently found in all the countries and regions involved is a combined use of exports and cooperative agreements, though it should be noted that in Eastern Europe and the developing countries this combination is of more importance than in the industrial or newly industrializing nations.

There is a significant correlation between the size of a company and its foreign involvement. Small and medium-sized companies (SMCs) are in most cases far less active in foreign countries, and their activities are often limited to export and largely restricted to industrial countries. When comparing this internationally, we need to point out, however, that German SMCs are relatively more active abroad than those of other industrialized nations.

It becomes obvious that the higher a firm's share of exports, the more other forms of internationalization are also being used. Cooperative agreements without capital participation are realized already after an export activity of 0 - 5 years, while 100%-owned subsidiaries are founded after 6 - 10 years of foreign economic activity. It takes up to 11 - 15 years of economic involvement abroad, however, before firms enter joint ventures.

Motive analysis shows that securing and opening up foreign markets is the dominant motive for internationalizing. This is also confirmed by the kinds of goods produced within a given cooperative project. Supplying local markets with goods from a cooperative project is considered more important than supplying third-country markets or the German market. In addition to the above marketing motives it is furthermore the use of (non-technological) knowledge and ability of the local partner in the country of cooperation and a commercial utilization/application in a foreign country of one's own technologies which are considered of importance in concluding foreign cooperative agreement agreements. The international utilization/application of any other (non-technological) knowledge and ability by Ruhr Region companies proved to be a relatively insignificant point in the motive analysis. To make use of the foreign partner's technological know-how is of importance only to the small and medium-sized business sector.

Similarly, to think that foreign cooperative agreements are founded as a defensive reaction to existing or prospective limitations of trade and restrictive investment policies, is, on the whole, of little significance. However, for SMCs and for companies which have concluded cooperative agreements outside industrial countries, new forms of company cooperation do serve as a way of getting around trade and investment restrictions. Viewed as a whole, though, the motive structure for all three company case studies does not differ significantly. However, it should be noted that there is no definite proof of a connection between the motives for cooperation and the regional orientation of a company's foreign involvement.

7. Perspectives

At this point in time, it is more than difficult to venture a conclusion. What we attempted to present here was merely a sketch of the status quo of German MNEs. The phase of a European economy with restrictive effects of political and economic borders is coming to an end, with Germany being at the center of events in various respects:

(i) The German economy has recovered from the slowdown of the mid-1980s; the companies, i.e. the MNEs more than others, have accumulated high liquidity. From an economic standpoint this fact alone puts them in a fairly strong position among international competitors. They have gained bargaining power.

(ii) Moreover, and possibly more important in the long run, Germany today is at the center of rapid, fundamental political change, having to strike a balance between East and West. This, of course, effects the behavior of many MNEs. The political changes in East European countries have together with the initiative EC 1992 brought about an economic "renaissance" of Europe. In economic terms, Germany will play a leading role in European integration. A visible sign of this development is the well over 6OO German-Polish Joint Ventures which constitute over 4O% of all the Joint Ventures Poland has licensed.

(iii) Investment in what was formerly the GDR is increasing rapidly. In the short term this could lead to the impression that German firms are starting to miss out on internationalization.

What may be the possible consequences of this new situation:

(i) With reunification the potential of new German MNEs has been enlarged.

(ii) The economic reconstruction of the East German Region will strengthen the export orientation of the German economy, especially to the East.

(iii) The new possibilities to invest in East European countries, especially Poland and Hungary, will be a key to the multinationalization of medium-sized German firms.

(iv) Cross-border transactions will grow at a high rate. On the one hand, German firms with contacts to the Eastern markets are attractive targets for foreign MNEs. On the other hand, high liquidity as well as the coming of EC 1992 will create favorable preconditions for increased M&A activity within the EC.

(v) Seen as a whole, however, the typical picture of the multinationalization by German firms being essentially export-led will not change, at least not in the medium term.

(vi) It is to be hoped that the increased multinationalization of firms is a visible sign for a rapid integration on a political level as well.

Endnotes

[1] See on the internationalization process *Chandler (1989), Porter et al. (1989), Ohmae (1990a)* and - emphasizing the EC perspective - *Welfens (1990a, 1990b)*.

[2] On German FDI and the role of German MNCs see e.g. *Michalski (1970), Holthus (1974), Krägenau (1975; 1982), J..hl (1985), Schulz (1978), Olle (1984), Gilroy and Broll (1987) and Wilkens and Hackenbruch (1989)*. For a comparative study see *Negandhi and Baliga (1979)*.

References

AKTIENGESELLSCHAFT (1989), Fusionskontrolle bei Auslandszusammenschlüssen: §§ 24, 98 GWB: 'MAN/Sulzer', 11, 403-6.

BALZER, A. and LEMMER, R. (1990), Mythos der Stärke: Im Handstreich übernehmen Großkonzerne ganze Branchen, Wirtschaftswoche, Vol. 24 (1990/6), 40-47.

BASF AKTIENGESELLSCHAFT (1980-89), Geschäftsberichte (annual shareholder reports of BASF AKTIENGESELLSCHAFT), Ludwigshafen.

BETRIEBSTECHNIK (1989), Marketingstrategie für den EG-Binnenmarkt prüfen. Systematische Planung mindert unternehmerische Risiken, Betriebstechnik, 8, 12.

BUNDESANZEIGER (May 15, 1990), Runderlaß Außenwirtschaft No. 8/90.

BUNDESMINISTER FÜR WIRTSCHAFT (6/1990), Entwicklungstendenzen von Direktinvestitionen, BMWI Dokumentation No. 306.

BUNDESVERBAND DER DEUTSCHEN INDUSTRIE (1990), Deutsche Direktinvestitionen im Ausland, Dokumentation.

BUNDESVERBAND DER DEUTSCHEN INDUSTRIE E.V. (1990), Deutsche Direktinvestitionen im Ausland. Struktur und Entwicklung 1976 bis 1989 und Vergleich mit ausländischen Direktinvestitionen in der Bundesrepublik Deutschland, Cologne: Bundesverband der Deutschen Industrie.

CHANDLER, A.D. (1989), Die Entwicklung des zeitgenössischen Wettbewerbs, in: PORTER, M., ed., Globaler Wettbewerb, Munich: Gabler.

DAIMLER BENZ (various issues), Geschäftsberichte (annual shareholder reports of DAIMLER BENZ AG).

DEUTSCHE BUNDESBANK (various issues), Monatsberichte.

DEUTSCHE BUNDESBANK (1990), Die Kapitalverflechtung der Unternehmen mit dem Ausland nach Ländern und Wirtschaftszweigen, 1982 bis 1988, Beilage zu Statistische Beihefte zu den Monatsberichten der Deutschen Bundesbank, Serie 3, Zahlungsbilanzstatistik, No. 4, April 1990.

DEUTSCHE BUNDESBANK (1990), Die Zahlungsbilanz der Bundesrepublik Deutschland mit dem Ausland 1978 bis 1989, Beilage zu Statistische Beihefte zu den Monatsberichten der Deutschen Bundesbank, Serie 3, Zahlungsbilanzstatistik, 7, July 1990.

DIE PRESSE (1990), Frankreichs Firmen drängen ins Ausland. Akquisitionen in der EG und in den USA, Die Presse, July 1990.

DUNNING, J.H. (1985), ed., Multinational Enterprises: Economic Structure and International Competitiveness, New York: John Wiley & Sons.

EMCH, U. (1989), Wie wirken Unternehmenszusammenschlüsse auf die Produktion, IO Management Zeitschrift, No. 9, 68, 91-4.

FORTUNE (1990), The Global 500. The World's Biggest Industrial Corporations, July 30, 1990.

FRANKFURTER ALLGEMEINE ZEITUNG (1990), Drastische Zunahme der Joint Ventures in Osteuropa, Frankfurter Allgmeine Zeitung, July 25, 1990.

GILROY, M.B. and BROLL, U. (1987), German Multinationals, Diskussionsbeiträge des Sonderforschungsbereichs 178 "Internationalisierung der Wirtschaft", University of Constance, Serie II, 19, March 1987.

HANDELSBLATT (1990), 134, July 16, 1990.

HANDELSBLATT (1990), 144, July 30, 1990.

HEIDUK, G. (1989), Internationalization Strategies of German Firms: The Case of Three Industries in The Ruhr Region, paper presented at the Annual Meeting of the Euro-Asia Management Studies Association "International Business and the Management of Change", Nagoya, December 6 - 8, 1989.

HOLTHUS, M. (1974), ed., Die Deutschen Multinationalen Unternehmen, Frankfurt: Athenäum.

JACKSON, T. (1989), Is Fusion Feasible? An Assessment of the Methodology and Policy Implications, Energy Policy, Vol. 4, 407-412.

JUHL, P. (1985), The Federal Republic of Germany, in: DUNNING, J.H., ed., Multinational Enterprises: Economic Structure and International Competitiveness, New York, 1985: John Wiley & Sons.

KAYSER, G. and SCHWARTING, U. (1981), Foreign Investment as a Form of Enterprise Strategy: On the Results of a Survey, Intereconomics, November/December 1981, 295-99.

KRÄGENAU, H. (1975), Internationale Direktinvestitionen 1950-1973. Vergleichende Untersuchung und statistische Materialien, Veröffentlichungen des HWWA-Institut für Wirtschaftsforschung, Hamburg: Verlag Weltarchiv.

KRÄGENAU, H. (1982), Internationale Direktinvestitionen. Ergänzungsband 1982, Veröffentlichungen des HWWA-Institut für Wirtschaftsforschung, Hamburg: Verlag Weltarchiv.

MICHALSKI, W. (1970), Export- und Wirtschaftswachstum, Veröffentlichungen des HWWA-Institut für Wirtschaftsforschung, Hamburg: Verlag Weltarchiv.

MÜLLER-STEWENS, G. (various issues), M&A Report. Beteiligungsstrategien. Mergers & Acquisitions, Strategische Partnerschaften, Allianzen, Joint-Ventures, Duisburg (University of Duisburg Press).

NEGANDHI, A. and BALIGA, B.R. (1979), Quest for Survival and Growth. A Comparative Study of American, European and Japanese Multinationals, Frankfurt: Athenäum.

OECD (1987), Recent Trends in International Direct Investment, Paris.

OLLE, W. (1984), Internationalisierungsstrategien in der deutschen Automobilindustrie, FSA-Print, 4, Berlin 1984.

OHMAE, K. (1990), The Borderless World, Power and Strategy in the Interlinked Economy, New York: Harper Business.

PORTER, M. ET AL. (1989), Das strukturelle Gefüge internationaler Koalitionen, in: PORTER, M., ed., Globaler Wettbewerb, Munich: Gabler.

RATH, H. (1990), Neue Formen der internationalen Unternehmenskooperation. Eine empirische Untersuchung unter besonderer Berücksichtigung ausgesuchter Industriezweige des Ruhrgebiets, Duisburger Volkswirtschaftliche Schriften, 8, Hamburg: S + W Steuer- und Wirtschaftsverlag.

SCHMIDT, E. (1970), Wandlungen und Tendenzen in der Unternehmensführung internationaler Konzerne, Zeitschrift für Organisation, Vol. 3, 93-96.

SCHULZ, U. (1978), Deutsche Direktinvestitionen im Ausland. Struktur, Bestimmungsgründe und Wirkungen auf die Wirtschaft der Bundesrepublik Deutschland, Schriftenreihe der Hochschule für Wirtschaft, 8, Bremen, 1978.

STATISTISCHES BUNDESAMT (1989), Statistisches Jahrbuch.

STUTTGARTER ZEITUNG (1990), Schwierigkeiten mit der Steuerharmonisierung: Vorbehalte der Hochsteuerländer; Bonn und die EG-Kommission isoliert, Stuttgarter Zeitung, July 24, 1990.

THE ECONOMIST (1990), A Tokyo-Stuttgart Axis?, The Economist, March 10, 1990.

WELFENS, P.J.J. (1990a), Privatization, M&As and Inter-Firm Cooperation in the EC: Improved Prospects for Innovation?, paper presented at the Biennial Meeting of the International J.A. Schumpeter Society "Entrepreneurship, Technical Innovation, and Economic Growth: International Perspectives", Airlie House, Virginia, June 3-5, 1990.

WELFENS, P.J.J. (1990b), Internationalisierung von Wirtschaft und Wirtschaftspolitik, Heidelberg: Springer.

WILKENS, H. and HACKENBRUCH, M. (1989), Direktinvestitionen als Element der weltwirtschaftlichen Verflechtung der Wirtschaft der Bundesrepublik Deutschland, Aussenwirtschaft, Vol. 43, 505-48

WIRTSCHAFTSWOCHE (1990), Konjunktur Inland: Investitionen, Wirtschaftswoche, 28, 12, July 5, 1990.

COMMENTS ON: GERMAN MULTINATIONALS IN EUROPE: PATTERNS AND PERSPECTIVES

Anthony Wallace

Dr. Heiduk has given us a very illuminating and useful paper. It provides excellent empirical support to impressions many of us have held about trends in foreign direct investment by the larger German firms. In my comments on his work, I will be speaking for myself and not for my company.

I would like to take the opportunity presented by this forum to look at Dr. Heiduk's subject from the other end, i.e., from the point of view of U.S. firms interested in establishing a presence in Germany and other EC member states. I do not expect Dr. Heiduk to defend the policies of the Federal Republic with regard to foreign investment in the FRG, but I would be interested in what trends he perceives in this area. This is of vital interest to U.S. firms because many have concluded that, in order to share fully in the expected benefits of the post-1992 single European market, equity joint ventures with European firms will be indispensable.

My questions for Dr. Heiduk are as follows:

1. In the paper, you talk about the strategic advantage which German companies have in entering Eastern European markets. You see a role for German firms as intermediaries for U.S. and Japanese firms interested in doing business there. Could you expand on this? What forms could this intermediation take? Do you see increased scope for joint ventures between U.S. and German firms designed to enter Eastern European market?

2. German companies have greatly increased foreign direct investment activities in other EC countries and, to a lesser extent, in the U.S. Many have achieved true global status as a result of these activities. Some U.S. firms have been frustrated in their attempts to follow a similar strategy in Germany or elsewhere in Continental Europe. There is a certain asymmetry. German firms have a relatively easy time acquiring shares in U.S. firms while some U.S. firms have encountered great difficulty in implementing joint ventures in the FRG involving more than token equity participation. The nature of share ownership in Germany (e.g., large blocks of shares are held by banks and do not come on the market) can make large purchases

difficult. Do you see any policy changes in tJhe offing which might change this situation and bring it more into balance?

3. The GDR, soon to become part of reunified Germany, is viewed by many U.S. firms as FRG turf and off limits for U.S. suppliers. Without a German subsidiary, they believe, U.S. companies will not be able to participate in the vast commercial opportunities presented by the economic reconstruction of the GDR. Where do you think U.S. firms have gained this impression? Is the East in effect off limits to foreign companies?

4. I would appreciate any thoughts might wish to share with us on the recent announcement of a strategic alliance between Daimler Benz and Mitsubishi. This is a striking example of the "triad philosophy" espoused by Kenichi Ohmae and others. U.S. and European firms are, of course, vitally interested in how this alliance might be implemented. It is certainly a bold departure from the more conservative international activities of many German firms. Thank you for giving me the opportunity to participate in the discussion.

THE EFFECTS OF INTEGRATION ON THE STRUCTURE OF MULTINATIONAL CORPORATION ACTIVITY IN THE EC

John Cantwell[1]

1. Introduction

EC industries may be affected in two major ways by the adjustments which multinational corporations (MNCs) make to their operations in response to regional economic integration. Firstly, there is the impact made by "new entrants", i.e. MNCs based outside the EC which establish new production outlets in EC countries to maintain and improve upon their position in Community markets. Secondly, there is the reorganization of existing MNC activity within the EC, associated with a rationalization of the European networks of MNCs. This paper examines these two issues, with particular reference to the impact of the first phase of integration in the EC on the technological strengths of different MNCs and national industries.

Over the past 30 years, there have been two bursts of new entry into EC production by non-EC MNCs. The first was the substantial growth in investment by US MNCs in the years after 1957, which became known as the "American challenge" (*Servan-Schreiber, 1967*). The reduction of tariff barriers between member states and the formation of a common external tariff encouraged US firms to locate import-substituting investments within the EC. This process was strongly reinforced by the growth of European markets.

The completion of the internal market or EC 1992 sparked off a new burst in inward investment - this time from Japanese companies. This wave of new investment is viewed by many as the "Japanese Challenge". Like US firms in the 1950s and 1960s, Japanese companies today are internationalizing from a position of technological and organizational strength. They are attracted to EC production in part since this is where a number of their major rivals are based; in part due to the opportunities opening up through the completion of the single internal market; and in part because of fears surrounding the possibility of a "Fortress Europe" emerging after 1992. The scale and composition of Japanese MNC involvement in the EC is considered in section 2.

The impact of Japanese inward investment, like that of US inward investment before it, will vary across sectors. It will depend upon the technological position of indigenous industry (*Cantwell, 1987; 1989*). As with the previous wave of US MNC activity, the economic impact is most likely to be beneficial where local firms are technologically strong. There may be some benefits where local industry is weak or declining badly. Adverse "Trojan horse" effects are most likely where indigenous companies are moderately advantaged, but lagging behind the technological frontier.

When inward investment is directed to a location which is itself a center for innovation in the industry concerned, MNCs are more likely to invest in important local research and development facilities. They aim to gain access to a new source of technological capability allied to their own existing achievements, but in doing so they contribute to the strength and diversity of local research. Moreover, their direct local presence tends to stimulate indigenous competitors to increase their own innovation, as the extent of technological competition rises. This has been the experience of US inward investment in several European countries; and the results have been well documented (see, for example *Dunning, 1958; Cantwell, 1989*).

In the case where local industry is ailing, MNCs are unlikely to invest in fundamental research capabilities, but they may still have a positive role to play. Apart from the direct employment effects of the investments of MNCs themselves, through entering into joint ventures and contractual arrangements with these efficient newcomers, local firms may enjoy at least a partial revitalization. However, where indigenous firms are moderately strong but have depended on a protected local market, the entry of the most highly internationally competitive MNCs from outside is likely to damage their position. The new entrants remain more likely to invest in assembly-based rather than research-related activity, and their ability to capture market shares from indigenous producers may have the effect of reducing and downgrading the scale of local research.

For the same reasons, in any industry there may be a difference in the impact of non-EC MNC investment across member states. Those which have the strongest or weakest technological positions are more liable to wish to promote Japanese investment, while those in between tend to favor a cautious policy in an attempt to restrict or reduce the speed of new entry. The impact of the expansion of EC production by Japanese firms is discussed in section 3.

A related issue is the reorganization of MNC activity within the EC. The trend towards a rationalization of MNC networks in Europe goes back to the late 1960s, when the Ford Motor Company after acquiring 100% ownership of all its EC subsidiaries began to rationalize its European operations (as, for example, described in *Dicken, 1986*). A major motive of such rationalization was to take advantage of scale and scope economies by increasing the degree of specialization of production in each plant whether *horizontally* (certain products or parts of the product range being confined to production in a single location) or *vertically* (the separation of intermediate products and final assembly). This type of rationalization is likely to be given a further major impetus by the completion of the single internal market, especially in sectors which until now have been dominated by regulated national markets. The trends in the horizontal and vertical rationalization of activity by US MNCs in the EC since 1957 are discussed in section 4, while section 5 considers the determinants of such corporate rationalization in an integrated region.

In addition, and connected with the argument concerning the differential impact of new inward investment, it has been hypothesized that economic integration may lead to the locational polarization of assembly-based and research-related production. Fundamental research and development is liable to become more concentrated in the main centers of innovation. This is due to a tendency for the technologically strongest MNCs expanding the R&D facilities they control or have access to in the main centers for research in their sectors. The incentive to do so depends upon the locational specificity of technological activity (*Lundvall, 1988*), which operates in accordance with local scientific traditions and business requirements. Complementary avenues of technological development in different countries can then be integrated within the MNC. A crucial motive for increasing the technological and allied activity carried out in key locations in this way is the increasing interrelatedness between formerly separate technologies. This requires a greater degree of technological diversification on the part of MNCs, and an international network of research-related activity provides one of the means of accomplishing this.

One aspect of this reorganization of MNC activity within the EC is that technological competition may be increased. However, another is that cooperation through cross-licensing arrangements and technological joint ventures is likely to be increased at the same time. The rationalization of MNC networks is therefore associated not only with greater competition but also with a growth of strategic alliances between firms.

The industry wide impact of the reorganization of MNC activity in Europe is the subject of section 6. A final section 7 looks somewhat more into the future, going beyond the current competition and restructuring of production by EC, Japanese and US firms in member states in preparation for 1992. It examines whether there may be a third wave of investment into the EC following the Japanese entry, mounted by MNCs from the newly industrialized countries (NICs).

2. The Technological and Organizational Advantages of Japanese Firms as a Determinant of their Involvement in Europe

The relative technological and organizational strengths of Japanese firms vis-à-vis their European (and US) rivals are amongst the principal determinants of both the extent and the sectoral composition of Japanese MNC involvement in the EC. The strong technological performance of Japanese firms has served as a platform for a sustained expansion of exports and more recently international production. The transition from exports towards international production has come about in part because the trading success of Japanese industry has led to an appreciation of the yen and trade restrictions abroad, both of which have increased the locational advantages of producing in the EC rather than in Japan.

Since Japanese companies are at a relatively early stage in their multinational growth (by comparison with US or UK MNCs), their technological success has been an important driving force of the expansion of both their exports and international production. Japanese firms enjoy their greatest technological strengths in the electrical equipment and motor vehicles sectors. As a result, the comparative advantage of Japan as a country and the comparative advantage of Japanese firms in total international economic activity (indigenous firm exports plus international production) are both concentrated in these same sectors (*Cantwell, 1989*). This contrasts with the position for the US and the UK, in which the greater maturity of internationalization has meant that exports and international production have become more substitutable for one another, rather than being strictly complementary.

It is therefore not surprising that the growth of Japanese owned manufacturing production in the US since the 1970s and in Europe since the early 1980s has been concentrated in the electrical equipment and motor vehicle industries (*Dunning and Cantwell, 1991*). However, as this has been associated with an increasing technological prowess on the part of Japanese companies in these sectors, it has been accompanied by a continuing growth of exports rather than a substitution for them. The improving ownership advantages of Japanese firms have enabled them to increase their international market shares whether by exports or international production.

Some evidence on this is presented in Tables 1 and 2. Although Japanese firms had started to shift from exports towards production especially in the US during the period, there was no decline in Japan's relative trading performance in electrical equipment or motor vehicles between the early 1970s and early 1980s. In Table 1 revealed comparative advantage is estimated in the form of an index that varies around unity, which is defined as follows. If X_{ij}

represents the value of exports in industry i from country j in a given period, then the revealed comparative advantage in any industry i of country j is given by:

$$RCA_{ij} = (X_{ij}/\Sigma_j X_{ij})/(\Sigma_i X_{ij}/\Sigma_i \Sigma_j X_{ij})$$

This index is thus based on the relative export shares across industries of the country in question. *Table 1* shows that in these terms Japan improved her comparative position in international markets for both electrical equipment and motor vehicles between 1974 and 1982. This was a period in which Japan's share of world exports of manufactures rose significantly, but her share in the two sectors in which her firms were strongest rose fastest of all. Exports continued to grow alongside international production. It was in the areas of chemicals, shipbuilding and textiles that the Japanese export position slipped back.

Table 1:
The Revealed Comparative Advantage of Japan in Exports of Manufactures, 1974 - 82

		1974	1982
1.	Food Products	0.09	0.08
2.	Chemicals	0.72	0.47
3.	Metals	1.82	1.50
4.	Mechanical engineering	0.87	1.07
5.	Electrical equipment	1.28	2.01
6.	Motor vehicles	1.69	2.26
7.	Other transport equipment	2.75	1.40
8.	Textiles	0.97	0.62
9.	Rubber products	0.96	1.01
10.	Non-metallic mineral products	0.83	0.88
11.	Coal & petroleum products	0.06	0.03
12.	Other manufacturing	0.90	0.86

Source: Cantwell (1989). For definitions see text.

Further support for the view that the growth of exports and international production have been complementary, each associated with the underlying technological strengths of Japanese firms in recent years, can be found in Table 2. In this case revealed comparative advantage is defined in a different way, in relation to trade as a whole. Denoting the value of imports in industry i into country j by M_{ij}, then revealed comparative advantage is given by:

$$RCA_{ij} = 2 \; [(X_{ij}-M_{ij})/\Sigma_j(X_{ij}+M_{ij})]/[\Sigma_i(X_{ij}+M_{ij})/\Sigma_i\Sigma_j(X_{ij}+M_{ij})]$$

This relies on the country's net export position in relation to its total trade (*UNIDO, 1986*), and it varies around zero rather than unity.[2] Once again, it is clear from *Table 2* that Japanese net exports of electrical equipment and motor vehicles were positive and improved their relative standing between the early 1970s and early 1980s. It may be necessary to qualify this argument today, since the expansion of international production by Japanese manufacturing firms has been greater in the 1980s than it was in the 1970s, and so a clearer substitution away from exports may now have begun. It has only been in the 1980s that a serious extension of Japanese owned foreign affiliate production in electrical equipment and motor vehicles has begun in Europe. However, the general impression remains that until now the rise of Japanese company production in the EC and the US is primarily a matter of an increase in their market share due to their ownership advantages, rather than a replacement of exports from Japan. This is so even if the existence of trade barriers is a reason for capturing market shares through local production rather than a still greater increase in exports.

Table 2:
The Revealed Comparative Advantage of Japan in
Trade in Selected Manufactures, 1970 - 83

	1970-72	1981-83
Office Machinery	0.18	1.04
Electrical power machinery	1.08	1.72
Electrical distribution equipment	1.99	2.46
Telecommunications apparatus	4.93	3.71
Domestic electrical equipment	1.26	1.87
Medical electrical equipment	0.19	0.69
Other electrical equipment	0.69	1.36
Motor vehicles	1.80	3.07

Source: UNIDO (1986). For definitions see text.

It is also worth mentioning that the ownership advantages of Japanese MNCs in the electrical and vehicle sectors are not purely of a technological kind. It has been argued that Japanese firms are stronger than their European and US competitors in their organizational capabilities, and that much of their present success depends upon their ability to organize contractual networks encompassing a range of small producers (*Ozawa, 1991*). If this is so then it may mean that Japanese participation in Europe in the sectors concerned will increase more markedly in the 1990s. This is because one of the locational advantages of producing in the EC which is expected to follow from the completion of the internal market is the greater facility for organizing more complex contractual networks.

Allied to this, Japanese firms may be relied upon to initiate the establishment of strategic alliances between European producers for similar reasons. Local firms may favor Japanese partners for their skills in making subcontracting arrangements work. However, a cautionary note should be sounded since it may be even more difficult to transfer organizational capability from Japan to Europe than it is to transfer technological capability. It is not yet clear that Japanese firms will be able to reestablish the sophisticated contractual networks they have in Japan to their production outlets in the EC.

3. The Likely Effects of Japanese Inward Direct Investment Post 1992

As argued in the introduction to this paper, the effect on European firms of the growth of Japanese inward direct investment encouraged (amongst other things) by the opportunities opening up post-1992 will vary across sectors. The extent to which Japanese owned affiliate production in the EC spreads across a wider rather than a narrower range of sectors depends in turn upon the extent of the overall participation of Japanese MNCs in European industry. It is possible to distinguish (*Dunning and Cantwell, 1991*) between a "low penetration scenario" in which Japanese involvement remains concentrated in the electrical equipment and motor vehicle sectors, and a "high penetration scenario" in which Japanese MNCs in most manufacturing industries set up operations within the EC.

The rate of growth of Japanese international production in the EC will be greater to the extent that the ownership advantages of Japanese firms are sustained and enhanced; their establishment of organizational networks in Europe meet with success; the value of the yen continues its longer term appreciation against European currencies; import restrictions are imposed by the EC on Japanese goods; local content requirements and other restrictions on EC operations do not prove to be prohibitive; and Japanese MNCs become more involved in strategic alliances with European partners.

It seems plausible to suggest that the impact of Japanese MNCs on the working of European industry will be more favorable as the overall extent of their involvement rises. This is not only because sophisticated types of local production and complex organizational contractual networks are more likely to be established. It is also because in the sectors in which Japanese firms are strongest of all European firms are not terribly well placed to respond. In electrical equipment European firms are generally weaker than their Japanese and US counterparts, while in motor vehicles European strength is patchy. As is clear from the experience of the earlier wave of US MNC investment in Europe, a process of helpful interaction between local and foreign firms is at its greatest in areas in which they are mutually advantaged (*Cantwell, 1989*). There may be more such cases as the scale of Japanese investment rises.

Japanese firms may be able to play a positive role in stimulating a beneficial reorganization of European industry in the rubber products and non-metallic mineral products sectors. In these cases both Japanese and EC firms have had a position of technological advantage. It may be possible to increase the share of research related production carried out in the EC, rather as happened with US MNC entry in chemicals and pharmaceuticals. The prospects are perhaps even brighter now in that the completion of the internal market encourages the growth of research related activity in the main European centers of innovation. This is of course somewhat counterbalanced by the likelihood that research will shift away from other European locations which were previously more sheltered.

Such reorganization of productive activity within the EC can be relatively easily accommodated to the extent that the increase in regional disparities in the sectors concerned tend to offset one another. To this extent it would represent an extension of the division of labor within the integrated region, and this may be seen as a benefit of integration. The problems created are those of structural adjustment. However, if a rise in regional disparities becomes reinforcing across sectors then national governments are more likely to attempt to intervene with countervailing measures to prevent the erosion of local technological capability.

The wide variation in national responses to increasing Japanese participation in EC motor vehicle production is already an illustration of this. The German response has been positive helped by the fact that the German motor vehicle firms are also technologically advantaged, and amongst component producers Bosch has proved itself technologically dynamic. Their presence increases the chance that Japanese producers may introduce research related activity in Europe, encouraging a beneficial interaction with the most capable indigenous firms.

The British response has also been favorable, in part due to the perceived organizational, managerial and industrial relations skills of Japanese firms. At the same time the British motor vehicle industry has been steadily declining. The major motor vehicle producer is weak, and even if component firms have their strengths, it is hoped that local industry will be revitalized through entering into joint ventures and contractual agreements with Japanese MNCs. Whether fundamental research capacity can be restored remains doubtful, but by linking up with the research strengths of Japanese companies a new role may still be forged.

By contrast, the French and Italian motor vehicle firms are moderately advantaged in their technological activities, but their market shares have still depended upon local protection. This helps to explain the lack of enthusiasm for Japanese investment by French and Italian officials. The position of indigenous firms may be weakened by a growth of Japanese production in the EC, and the focus of European research activity may be shifted away from France and Italy.

4. The Reorganization of MNC Activity Within Europe

One of the main affects of regional economic integration is to bring about a reorganization of the location and ownership of economic activity. In response to the first phase of integration in the EC, non EC, and particularly US MNCs took the lead. The best known example of this was in the motor vehicle sector. In this case a vertical division of labor across national European boundaries has been organized by US MNCs, in which research and the production of components have been geographically separated from final assembly. The motor vehicle industry has also witnessed an increased intra-industry horizontal specialization in the EC, with certain models being produced in just one country for the entire EC market.

However, it is useful to try and discern the significance of regional economic integration in its specific effect upon the international integration of MNC activity. After all, it has become widely accepted that MNCs have been rationalizing their operations throughout the world since at least the early 1970s, and not just in the EC. Some data on the international integration of the networks of US MNCs since 1957 allow us to assess the quantitative significance of regional integration in the EC for corporate rationalization.

Two hypotheses are tested using this data. The first is that the horizontal and vertical international integration of US foreign affiliates located in the EC have both been rising. Secondly, this corporate rationalization has proceeded faster within the EC than elsewhere, and affiliates here have become more closely integrated with other EC firms and markets than with firms and markets outside the EC. In addition, the relative importance of horizontal as against vertical integration for US MNCs in the EC is examined, as is the geographical composition of linkages within the EC.

The international linkages of foreign owned affiliates can be measured by the value of their export sales. These are to be distinguished from local sales within the country in which they are located, which represent the local market oriented (or import substituting) element of their production. The data on US foreign affiliate exports also enable us to make a loose distinction between the international horizontal and international vertical integration of US owned firms.

The extent of international horizontal specialization is roughly given by the value of export sales to unaffiliated firms or individuals, while international vertical integration can be measured by the value of export sales to other affiliates which are part of the same MNC or the parent company itself.

It is certainly clear that where the firm is internationally vertically integrated there must be intra-firm flows of exports accordingly. However, the idea of international horizontal specialization needs some clarification. Firstly, the firm may be supplying quite different products from each of its affiliates located in various countries. Its pattern of geographical specialization may therefore correspond to an inter-industry rather than an intra-industry division of labor within the firm. Strictly speaking, it is thus only horizontal integration to the extent that the firm's industry is very broadly defined. Secondly, it is possible that some of the output associated with international horizontal specialization is included in intra-firm exports, where it is simply sold on through a local affiliate to a distributor (or where the local affiliate is just a trading branch) without further processing. Unfortunately, such sales are usually recorded both under the export sales of one set of affiliates and under the local sales of another.

Accepting the measures proposed as proxies for international horizontal and vertical specialization, it is possible to begin by examining the trends in the integration of the worldwide networks of US MNCs. This provides a point of comparison for the course followed by their affiliates within the EC since 1957. *Table 3* shows that the international integration of US MNCs increased between 1957 and 1987, as reflected in the growing share in total sales of affiliate exports, switching away from their own local markets. However, while there was a steady increase in integration between networks of affiliates themselves (as shown by a steady rise in affiliate exports to third countries until at least the mid-1980s), integration between affiliates and the home country, the USA, fluctuated much more erratically.

It seems that the sharp drop in the integration of US owned affiliates with the US economy from 1977 to 1982, and the stabilization of the integration between affiliate networks in the 1980s was essentially due to the reorganization of the oil industry. In the wake of the formation of the OPEC cartel and the further oil price rise of 1979-80, US oil firms switched to sources of supply closer to home. There was no such decline in international integration in manufacturing, as can be seen from *Table 4*. There was a steady rise in integration between affiliates and both the USA and third countries, with two consequences. Firstly, integration in

Table 3:
The Geographical Distribution of the Sales of All
US Majority Owned Foreign Affiliates, 1957 -1987 (%)

	1957	1966	1977	1982	1987
Local Sales	72.6	75.1	61.8	65.5	66.1
Total Exports	27.4	24.9	38.2	34.5	33.9
to third countries	17.5	18.5	19.8	24.0	23.1
to USA	9.9	6.4	18.5	10.5	10.7

Source: US Department of Commerce, US Business Investment in Foreign Countries, 1960;
Survey of Current Business, August 1975; US Direct Investment Abroad, 1977; US Direct
Investment Abroad: 1982; unpublished data for 1987.

Table 4:
The Geographical Distribution of the Sales of US Majority
Owned Foreign Affiliates in Manufacturing, 1957 - 1987 (%)

	1957	1966	1977	1982	1987
Local Sales	84.1	81.4	69.2	66.1	61.4
Total Exports	15.9	18.6	30.8	33.9	38.6
to third countries	9.9	13.0	21.7	24.2	26.2
to USA	6.0	5.7	9.1	9.7	12.4

Source: As for Table 3.

Table 5:
The Geographical Distribution of the Sales of US
Majority Owned Affiliates Located in the Original
EC 6 Countries, 1957 -1987 (%)

	1957	1966	1977	1982	1987
Local Sales	86.9	77.7	72.5	66.0	63.4
Total Exports	13.1	22.3	27.5	34.0	36.6
to third countries	12.7	20.8	25.4	31.6	33.6
to USA	0.4	1.5	2.1	2.4	3.0

Source: As for Table 3.

Table 6:
The Geographical Distribution of the Sales of US
Majority Owned Affiliates in Manufacturing, Located in the Original
EC 6 Countries, 1957 -1987 (%)

	1957	1966	1977	1982	1987
Local Sales	85.0	73.3	61.7	54.3	53.5
Total Exports	15.0	26.7	38.3	45.7	46.5
to third countries	14.1	24.9	36.0	43.4	N.A.
to USA	0.8	1.8	2.3	2.2	N.A.

N.A. = Not Available.
Source: As for Table 3.

MNCs in manufacturing rose much faster; the share of affiliate export sales more than doubled from 15.9% to 38.6%, while overall they rose by only about a quarter, from 27% to 33.9%. Secondly, the level of international integration in manufacturing had reached the same point as in other sectors by 1982, and gone well beyond it by 1987, despite the greater historical export links of resource based affiliates.

Table 5 shows that US owned affiliates located in the EC have been involved in a much stronger trend towards international integration from a lower starting point (which largely reflects the greater significance of manufacturing investments in Europe). The share of affiliate exports in sales increased from 13.1% to 36.6% between 1957 and 1987, while the share of exports to third countries rose from 12.7% to 33.6%. However, the linkage with the USA is weaker than for affiliates elsewhere. For this group of affiliates located in the original six countries of the EC the increase in international integration in manufacturing considered separately is even more remarkable. In this case, the share of exports increased from 15.0% of affiliate sales in 1957 to 45.7% in 1982; and exports to third countries rose from 14.1% to 43.4% over the same period. The details of this systematic increase in the integration of manufacturing affiliates located in the EC are set out in *Table 6*, and it can be seen that if anything the trend has become stronger over time.

Turning now to the distinction between horizontal and vertical integration, in the worldwide networks of US MNCs international horizontal integration recorded a more sustained increase between the mid-1960s and the early 1980s than did international vertical integration - although the latter has recovered in the 1980s. As shown in *Table 7*, unaffiliated exports rose from 9.1% of affiliate sales in 1966 to 16.5% in 1982, before falling back to 12.8% in 1987, while intra-firm exports increased from 17.0% to just 18.0% over 1966-82, but rose to 21.1 in 1987. Affiliated exports to third countries actually fell from 12.1% to 9.3% from 1966-82, and affiliated exports to the USA declined sharply between 1977 and 1982 due largely to the reorganization of oil companies. By 1982, as a result of these changes, international horizontal and vertical integration were roughly of the same importance, accounting for 16.5% and 18.0% of the sales of US MNC affiliates respectively. However, by 1987 international vertical integration had recovered its more important position.

Table 7:
The Geographical Distribution of Sales and the Structure
of Exports of US Majority Owned Foreign Affiliates,
1966 - 1987 (%)

	1966*	1970*	1977	1982	1987
Local Sales	73.9	70.5	61.8	65.5	66.1
Total exports	26.1	29.5	38.2	34.5	33.9
to third countries	20.1	23.0	19.8	24.0	23.1
to USA	6.0	6.6	18.5	10.5	10.7
Unaffiliated exports	9.1	11.3	11.8	16.5	12.8
to third countries	8.0	10.2	9.9	14.7	11.0
to USA	1.2	1.1	1.9	1.8	1.8
Affiliated exports	17.0	18.2	26.4	18.0	21.1
to third countries	12.1	12.8	9.8	9.3	12.1
to USA	4.8	5.4	16.6	8.7	8.9

* The figures for 1966 and 1970 relate to a survey of 298 US TNCs, whose foreign affiliate sales accounted for 72.5% of all such sales in 1966. This explains the discrepancy between the shares shown in this table and those given in Table 3 for the year 1966.

Source: US Department of Commerce, Survey of Current Business, January 1973; US Direct Investment Abroad, 1977; US Direct Investment Abroad: 1982; unpublished data for 1987.

Table 8:
The Geographical Distribution of Sales and the Structure
of Exports of US Majority Owned Foreign Affiliates in Manufacturing,
1966 - 1987 (%)

	1966*	1970*	1977	1982	1987
Local Sales	77.2	74.4	69.2	66.1	61.4
Total exports	22.8	25.6	30.8	33.9	38.6
to third countries	16.2	18.0	21.7	24.2	26.2
to USA	6.7	7.6	9.1	9.7	12.4
Unaffiliated exports	8.9	9.2	10.9	11.4	10.4
to third countries	7.8	8.2	9.2	10.1	8.8
to USA	1.1	1.0	1.7	1.3	1.6
Affiliated exports	14.0	16.4	19.9	22.5	28.3
to third countries	8.4	9.8	12.5	14.1	17.4
to USA	5.6	6.6	7.4	8.3	10.9

* The figures for 1966 and 1970 relate to a survey of 298 US TNCs, whose foreign affiliate sales in manufacturing accounted for 81.9% of all such sales in 1966. This explains the discrepancy between the shares shown in this table and those in Table 4 for the year 1966.
Source: As for Table 7.

The same does not hold for manufacturing considered separately, as is apparent from Table 8. In manufacturing by 1982 international vertical integration was roughly twice as important as horizontal integration, in 1987 nearly three times as important, and it had risen at a faster rate throughout the period since the 1960s. Unaffiliated exports rose only moderately, from 8.9% of the value of affiliate sales in 1966, to 10.4% in 1987. By comparison, affiliated exports rose more markedly, from 14.0% to 28.3% during the same period.

Table 9:
The Geographical Distribution of Sales and the Structure
of Exports of US Majority Owned Affiliates Located in
the EC, 1977 - 1987 (%)

	1977	1982	1987
Local sales	68.9	67.0	65.7
Total exports	31.1	33.0	34.3
to third countries	27.7	29.3	30.4
to USA	3.4	3.7	3.9
Unaffiliated exports	12.4	15.4	12.5
to third countries	11.9	14.5	11.7
to USA	0.5	0.9	0.8
Affiliated exports	18.7	17.6	21.8
to third countries	15.8	14.8	18.7
to USA	2.9	2.8	3.1

Source: US Department of Commerce, Direct Investment Abroad, 1977, Washington DC, April 1981; US Direct Investment Abroad: 1982 Benchmark Survey Data, Washington DC, December 1985; unpublished data for 1987.

Table 10:
The Geographical Distribution of Sales and the Structure
of Exports of US Majority Owned Affiliates in Manufacturing,
Located in the EC, 1977 - 1987 (%)

	1977	1982	1987
Local sales	61.4	58.1	57.3
Total exports	38.6	41.9	42.7
to third countries	36.3	39.4	N.A.
to USA	2.3	2.5	N.A.
Unaffiliated exports to third countries	15.0	15.8	N.A.
Affiliated exports to third countries	21.3	23.6	N.A.

N.A. = Not Available
Source: As for Table 9.

In general, US owned affiliates located in the EC have a similar distribution of international horizontal and vertical integration as applies to all affiliates. *Table 9* shows that in 1982 and 1987 both unaffiliated and affiliated exports accounted for a similar proportion of sales for affiliates in the EC as for those in the world as a whole (in Table 7). What is more, the share of affiliated exports from an EC location also declined between 1977 and 1982, suggesting a drop in international vertical integration, before rising again between 1982 and 1987. It is worth noting, though, that as shown from a comparison with Table 5 there was a much greater increase in international integration from 1977 to 1987 amongst affiliates located in the original EC six than those located in countries joining subsequently. Exports of affiliates located in the UK, for example, were responsible for about 31% of their sales in both 1977 and 1982. This may be explained partly by a lag in the effect of regional integration on corporate integration in new member states, given that as observed above the trend towards rationalization seems to have become greater in the EC six over time. It may also be attributable to a strong immediate adjustment in the aftermath of EC entry; UK located affiliate exports rose substantially from 20.1% of sales in 1966 to 31.1% in 1977, which may have corresponded to an initial overreaction to EC entry.

In manufacturing, the international horizontal and vertical integration of EC located affiliates are both higher than for affiliates located elsewhere. Integration with third countries as measured by the share of exports in affiliate sales is about half as high again as for all affiliates (comparing *Tables 10 and 8*), but integration with the USA is much lower. In this case it is not possible to disaggregate affiliate exports to the USA into horizontal and vertical components, but since they are comparatively small this is not a serious deficiency. The unaffiliated exports of US affiliates in EC manufacturing sent to third countries took 15.8% of sales in 1982, and intra-firm exports accounted for a further 23.6%. The greater significance of vertical integration for MNC operations in manufacturing in the EC corresponds to the worldwide position depicted in *Table 8*.

Given that the increase in international integration has been greater for affiliates located in the EC than elsewhere, the question that remains is the extent to which this has been due to rationalization within the EC. *Table 11* shows that such intra-EC integration has been high and rising. Over a fifth (21.1%) of US owned affiliate sales in 1982 represented cross-border linkages within the EC. As was the case for affiliates outside the EC, international horizontal integration rose faster than vertical between 1977 and 1982; unaffiliated intra - EC exports increased from 5.1% to 9.2% of affiliate sales from an EC location.

Table 11:
The Intra-EC Export Share of Sales of US Majority Owned Affiliates
Located in the EC, 1977 - 1982 (%)

	1977	1982
Total intra-EC exports	15.6	21.1
Unaffiliated intra-EC exports	5.1	9.2
Affiliated intra-EC exports	10.5	11.9

Source: As for Table 9.

Table 12:
The Intra-EC Export Share of Sales of US Majority Owned Affiliates
in Manufacturing Located in the EC, 1977 - 1982 (%)

	1977	1982
Total intra-EC exports	21.8	28.0
Unaffiliated intra-EC exports	6.8	8.8
Affiliated intra-EC exports	15.0	19.2

Source: As for Table 9.

In the case of manufacturing, intra-EC horizontal integration was at about the same level as for all affiliates, but intra-EC vertical integration was considerably higher. Total intra-EC exports stood at well over a quarter (28.0%) of affiliate sales in manufacturing in 1982, as can be seen from *Table 12*. The intra-firm component of intra-EC affiliate exports alone accounted for nearly a fifth (19.2%) of sales in manufacturing in 1982. The greater significance of vertical as against horizontal integration in manufacturing once again follows the general pattern of rationalization in the worldwide networks of US MNCs.

Returning to the hypotheses mentioned at the start of this section, it has now been demonstrated that the horizontal and vertical integration of US affiliates located in the EC have both been rising, and rising faster than for affiliates located elsewhere. It can now also be shown that EC located affiliates have become more closely integrated with other EC firms and markets than with firms and markets outside the EC. *Table 13* shows that between 1977 and 1982 the significance of both horizontally and vertically integrated linkages outside the EC diminished. The total non-EC third country exports of US owned affiliates located in the EC fell from 12.1% to 8.2% of sales, which represented a drop of about a third in the share of affiliate sales.

Table 13:
The Non-EC Third Country Export Share of Sales of US Majority Owned Affiliates Located in the EC, 1977 - 1982 (%)

	1977	1982
Total non-EC, non-US exports	12.1	8.3
Unaffiliated non-EC, non-US exports	6.8	5.3
Affiliated non-EC, non-US exports	5.3	2.9

Source: As for Table 9.

Table 14:
The Non-EC Third Country Export Share of Sales of US Majority Owned Affiliates in Manufacturing, Located in the EC, 1977 - 1982 (%)

	1977	1982
Total non-EC, non-US exports	14.5	11.4
Unaffiliated non-EC, non-US exports	8.2	7.0
Affiliated non-EC, non-US exports	6.3	4.4

Source: As for Table 9.

A similar pattern can also be observed for the external linkages of manufacturing affiliates. In their case, as can be seen from *Table 14*, the share of non-EC third country exports declined from 14.5% of sales in 1977 to 11.4% in 1982. It is also notable that for international ties outside the region, vertical integration was weaker than horizontal integration, the reverse of the general picture for US MNC affiliates in manufacturing. This is further evidence of the weakness of inter-regional as opposed to intra-regional rationalization for affiliates located in the EC, as a certain level of unaffiliated third country exports will arise even where affiliates operate entirely independently of one another, but the same is not true of intra-firm trade.

The effects of an increasing intra-regional integration combined with a falling inter-regional integration of the EC networks of US MNCs are shown in *Table 15*. The share of intra-EC exports in total third country affiliate exports rose substantially between 1977 and 1982, to reach extremely high levels. Overall, it increased from somewhat over a half (56.1%) to nearly three quarters (71.9%). The intra-EC element is especially important in international vertical integration. Intra-firm intra-EC exports accounted for no less than 80.1% of all affiliated exports destined for third countries in 1982. It can be concluded that the shift towards the integration of corporate activity within the EC has been at the expense not only of the traditional import-substituting role of EC located affiliates (as witnessed by the decline in the share of their local sales), but also of integration with the rest of the world outside the EC region.

This applies as much in manufacturing as in other sectors, as is clear from *Table 16*. As has already been remarked upon, in manufacturing intra-EC rationalization is relatively more developed in vertical as opposed to horizontal cross-border integration. Of affiliated exports sent to third countries by US owned affiliates located in the EC 81.4% were sold to other affiliates located elsewhere in the EC. The shift away from inter-regional and towards intra-regional integration between 1977 and 1982 has not been quite so pronounced in manufacturing as in other sectors. However, a comparison of *Tables 16 and 15* reveals that this is largely due to the fact that the rationalization of US MNC operations in manufacturing within the EC had already reached a relatively greater significance by 1977.

Table 15:
The Intra-EC Share of Exports to Third Countries of US
Majority Owned Affiliates Located in the EC, 1977-82 (%)

	1977	1982
Total exports to third countries	56.1	71.9
Unaffiliated exports to third countries	42.7	63.5
Affiliated exports to third countries	66.3	80.1

Source: As for Table 9.

Table 16:
The Intra-EC Share of Manufacturing Exports to Third Countries of US
Majority Owned Affiliates Located in the EC, 1977-82 (%)

	1977	1982
Total exports to third countries	59.9	71.0
Unaffiliated exports to third countries	45.1	55.5
Affiliated exports to third countries	70.4	81.4

Source: As for Table 9.

Table 17:
Purchasing Country Shares of the Intra-EC Unaffiliated Exports of US Majority Owned
Affiliates Located in the EC in 1977 (%)

Local Producing Country	Belg/Lux	Den/Ire	France	Germany	Italy	Neth	UK	EC
Belgium & Lux.	2.6	3.2	20.7	26.1	9.7	27.7	10.0	100
Denmark & Ireland	4.1	3.6	10.7	27.4	8.1	6.1	40.1	100
France	14.1	3.8	N.A.	37.0	19.8	11.6	13.6	100
Germany	14.3	8.7	27.7	N.A.	17.3	21.0	11.0	100
Italy	7.0	2.8	34.9	30.1	N.A.	7.3	17.7	100
Netherlands	16.2	3.7	15.4	38.4	11.8	N.A.	14.5	100
UK	9.1	19.3	14.6	28.2	12.3	16.5	N.A.	100
Total EC	10.3	7.4	17.7	26.4	12.5	15.1	10.6	100

N.A. = Not Applicable.

Source: US Department of Commerce, Direct Investment Abroad, 1977,
Washington DC, April 1981.

Table 18:
Purchasing Country Shares of the Intra-EC Affiliated Exports of US Majority Owned
Affiliates Located in the EC in 1977 (%)

Local Producing Country	Purchasing Country							
	Belg/Lux	Den/Ire	France	Germany	Italy	Neth	UK	EC
Belgium & Lux.	1.7	1.3	14.9	38.3	7.1	12.7	23.8	100
Denmark & Ireland	9.2	0.5	14.6	18.6	5.7	9.2	42.2	100
France	12.4	2.3	N.A.	37.9	16.9	11.0	19.5	100
Germany	17.6	3.9	23.6	N.A.	13.4	14.5	27.0	100
Italy	8.7	1.8	37.3	28.7	N.A.	7.1	16.1	100
Netherlands	18.4	2.2	17.0	36.0	7.9	N.A.	18.4	100
UK	9.2	14.8	12.2	23.2	30.2	10.4	N.A.	100
Total EC	11.9	5.4	15.0	23.9	15.7	10.4	17.7	100

N.A. = Not Applicable.

Source: As for Table 17.

Having shown that the rationalization of MNC activity has been given an impetus by the regional integration of the EC, and the extent of vertical integration within US MNC networks has especially increased, the detailed geographical composition of these cross-border linkages can now be examined.

It is possible to view these linkages either from the perspective of the immediate host country in which the affiliate is located (the local producing country) or from the perspective of the third country to which the exports of affiliates located elsewhere in the EC are sent (the purchasing country). Table 17 takes the former producing country perspective in the case of horizontal or unaffiliated product market specialization. For each EC producing country, it shows the geographical distribution of unaffiliated exports to other EC countries by US MNC affiliates in 1977.

Table 17 thus indicates the relative importance of EC countries as markets for the horizontally specialized activities of US owned affiliates located in a particular part of the EC. It is perhaps not surprising that overall Germany has been the most important market (with 26.4% of unaffiliated exports in 1977), followed by France (17.7%). What may be more interesting is that the Netherlands was the third largest market for unaffiliated exports (accounting for

15.1% overall), well ahead of Italy (12.5%), which in turn was clearly a larger purchaser than the UK (10.6%). The overall importance of UK markets was little different from Belgium and Luxembourg, which received 10.3% of unaffiliated intra-EC exports in 1977. The UK was a more important market for affiliates located in Ireland and Italy, but of much less significance for those based in Germany or Belgium. It is also notable that affiliates located in Germany, France or Italy are especially geared to serving the markets of the other two countries.

The same perspective is applied to the intra-EC vertical integration of US MNCs in *Table 18*. In the case of vertical linkages the UK is a much more significant location for US MNC networks. Overall, UK located affiliates purchased 17.7% of intra-EC affiliated exports, second only to those based in Germany, which received 23.9% in 1977.

While for international horizontal specialization there are strong three-way ties between Germany, France and Italy, networks of vertical integration seem to extend to cover four countries, namely Germany, France, Italy and the UK. However, the connections between the first three are still especially strong. UK located affiliates appear to be particularly prone to supply affiliated enterprises in Italy. Similarly strong linkages run from Italy to France, from France to Germany, and from Germany to the UK, suggesting that a completed circle of exchange dominates the vertical integration of US MNC networks in the EC.

Table 19:
Producing Country Shares of the Intra-EC Unaffiliated Exports
of US Majority Owned Affiliates Located in the EC
in 1977 (%)

Local Producing Country	Purchasing Country							
	Belg/Lux	Den/Ire	France	Germany	Italy	Neth	UK	EC
Belgium & Lux.	6.4	10.9	29.2	24.8	19.4	45.9	23.7	25.0
Denmark & Ire.	0.8	1.0	1.3	2.2	1.4	0.8	8.0	2.1
France	13.3	5.1	N.A.	13.7	15.4	7.5	12.5	9.7
Germany	22.8	19.2	25.6	N.A.	22.6	22.9	17.1	16.4
Italy	2.6	1.4	7.5	4.3	N.A.	1.8	6.4	3.8
Netherlands	37.0	11.7	20.5	34.4	22.3	N.A.	32.3	23.6
UK	17.1	50.7	16.0	20.7	19.0	21.1	N.A.	19.4
Total EC	100.0	100.0	100.0	100.0	100.0	100.0	100.0	100.0

N.A. = Not Applicable.
Source: As for Table 17.

Table 20:
Producing Country Shares of the Intra-EC Affiliated Exports
of US Majority Owned Affiliates Located in the EC
in 1977 (%)

Local Producing Country	Purchasing Country							
	Belg/Lux	Den/Ire	France	Germany	Italy	Neth	UK	EC
Belgium & Lux.	2.2	3.8	15.4	24.7	7.0	18.9	20.6	15.4
Denmark & Ire.	1.7	0.2	2.2	1.7	0.8	1.9	5.2	2.2
France	17.7	7.1	N.A.	26.9	18.3	18.0	18.6	17.0
Germany	37.6	18.2	40.3	N.A.	21.8	35.6	38.9	25.5
Italy	2.3	1.1	7.7	3.7	N.A.	2.1	2.8	3.1
Netherlands	20.6	5.4	15.2	20.1	6.8	N.A.	13.8	13.4
UK	18.0	64.1	19.2	22.9	45.4	23.5	N.A.	23.5
Total EC	100.0	100.0	100.0	100.0	100.0	100.0	100.0	100.0

N.A. = Not Applicable.
Source: As for Table 17.

The same data are examined from a purchasing country perspective in Tables 19 and 20. Considering the pattern of horizontal specialization, *Table 19* shows that overall US affiliates located in Belgium, the Netherlands or Luxembourg account for almost half of intra-EC unaffiliated exports. This very high proportion helps to qualify any idea that integration has been achieved primarily between the largest countries. Affiliates based in Italy provided only 3.8% of intra-EC unaffiliated exports in 1977. This geographical structure is largely a consequence of the market size of countries. Affiliates located in Belgium or the Netherlands are clearly more likely to be oriented towards serving the markets of other larger EC countries at an earlier stage. They may have had an internationally integrated role from the beginning, whereas affiliates in France, Germany, Italy or the UK were initially oriented principally to their own local markets. The relative importance of the three-way linkage between France, Germany and Italy can again be observed.

The larger countries play a much greater role as the source of exports related to vertical intra-firm linkages, as depicted in *Table 20*. Germany (with 25.5% of intra-EC affiliated exports in total) and the UK (with 23.5%) are the leading local producing countries, and France is third (with 17.0%). Italy remains comparatively unimportant as a source of integrated linkages, and its firms like its markets are substantial net recipients of intra-EC affiliate exports. However, as already suggested Italian located affiliates receive a high proportion of their intra-firm imports from the UK (45.4% of those received from other EC countries); UK located affiliates receive most (38.9%) from Germany; German located affiliates take the greatest proportion (26.9%) from France; and French located affiliates purchase a relatively high share (7.7%) from Italy, but still most of all (40.3%) from Germany.

The balance between exports and imports in the international linkages of rationalized US corporate groups in the EC in 1977 is set out in Tables 21 and 22. *Table 21* relates to the horizontal specialization of US MNC networks within the EC. It confirms that Italy received over three times as many unaffiliated imports from affiliates located elsewhere in the Community as Italian based affiliates sent to other countries. France and Germany were also net importers, while the UK, Belgium and the Netherlands were net exporters to other markets. The geographical pattern of US intra-firm trade in the EC was broadly similar in this respect, as is shown in *Table 22*. However, in the case of vertically integrated linkages all countries were closer to trade balance except Italy, and France and Germany were net exporters. The main reason for Italy not being closer to balance was the substantial intra-firm imports which local affiliates received from the UK, which were over 14 times the level of exports going in the opposite direction.

Table 21:
**The Ratio of Unaffiliated Exports Sent from the Producing Country
to Unaffiliated Exports Received from the Purchasing Country in the
Horizontal Intra-EC Linkages of US Majority Owned Affiliates in 1977**

Local Producing Country	Purchasing Country							
	Belg/Lux	Den/Ire	France	Germany	Italy	Neth	UK	EC
Belgium & Lux.	1.00	9.38	3.75	2.78	9.08	1.81	1.42	2.42
Denmark & Ire.	0.11	1.00	0.60	0.41	1.60	0.15	0.23	0.29
France	0.27	1.67	N.A.	0.79	1.46	0.31	0.47	0.55
Germany	0.36	2.46	1.26	N.A.	2.48	0.38	0.33	0.62
Italy	0.11	0.63	0.69	0.40	N.A.	0.10	0.28	0.30
Netherlands	0.55	6.75	3.21	2.63	10.04	N.A.	1.07	1.56
UK	0.71	4.43	2.14	3.02	3.54	0.93	N.A.	1.83
Total EC	0.41	3.51	1.82	1.61	3.30	0.64	0.55	1.00

N.A. = Not Applicable.
Source: As for Table 17.

Table 22:
The Ratio of Affiliated Exports Sent from the Producing Country to Affiliated Exports Received from the Purchasing Country in the Vertical Intra-EC Linkages of US Majority Owned Affiliates in 1977

Local Producing Country	Purchasing Country							
	Belg/Lux	Den/Ire	France	Germany	Italy	Neth	UK	EC
Belgium & Lux.	1.00	1.03	1.09	1.31	4.06	0.80	1.71	1.29
Denmark & Ire.	0.98	1.00	0.84	1.07	2.18	0.68	0.27	0.40
France	0.92	1.19	N.A.	1.07	2.50	0.82	1.15	1.13
Germany	0.76	0.94	0.94	N.A.	3.84	0.77	1.26	1.07
Italy	0.25	0.46	0.40	0.26	N.A.	0.21	0.07	0.20
Netherlands	1.25	1.46	1.22	1.30	4.86	N.A.	1.00	1.28
UK	0.59	3.75	0.87	0.79	14.27	1.00	N.A.	1.32
Total EC	0.78	2.47	0.88	0.94	5.08	0.78	0.75	1.00

N.A. = Not Applicable.
Source: As for Table 17.

Table 23:
The Intra-Firm Share of the Intra-EC Exports of US Majority Owned Affiliates Located in the EC in 1977 (%)

Local Producing Country	Purchasing Country							
	Belg/Lux	Den/Ire	France	Germany	Italy	Neth	UK	EC
Belgium & Lux.	44.6	34.8	47.7	65.0	48.2	36.8	75.1	55.9
Denmark & Ire.	83.0	22.2	73.8	59.0	61.5	76.5	69.4	68.3
France	75.9	67.9	N.A.	78.6	75.4	77.3	83.7	78.2
Germany	79.6	59.0	73.2	N.A.	71.3	68.9	88.7	76.2
Netherlands	57.0	41.0	56.4	52.3	43.8	N.A.	59.8	53.8
Italy	67.5	52.4	64.2	61.5	N.A.	61.8	60.4	62.6
UK	71.5	65.7	67.6	67.4	86.0	61.3	N.A.	71.4
Total EC	70.4	60.2	63.5	65.1	72.0	58.6	77.6	67.3

N.A. = Not Applicable.
Source: As for Table 17.

It can be noted from Table 11 above that in 1977 the intra-firm element of the intra-EC exports of US owned affiliates amounted to about two thirds. Although this fell back by 1982, in manufacturing it held up at over two thirds, as is clear from Table 12. More details of the relative significance of vertical as against horizontal integration amongst US MNCs in the EC in 1977 are to be found in *Table 23*. This shows that relative to the role of horizontal specialization, it has been affiliates located in the UK that have been most tied in to vertically integrated MNC networks in the EC region, both as producers and purchasers. French and German located affiliates tended to produce for vertically integrated chains, but French and German markets were also served more often from affiliates in other EC locations. Belgian located affiliates seem to have had a particularly important assembly role, making up components sent from affiliates in France, Germany and the UK, and often processing them for markets in other EC countries. Especially in the smaller EC countries, affiliates have thereby combined vertical and horizontal rationalization as part of a regional MNC strategy. In Italy US owned affiliates have been heavily involved in vertical processing, with intermediate products arriving especially from the UK, but making final products directed primarily at local markets.

5. The Determinants of MNC Rationalization in the EC

While there was a general trend towards the closer cross-border integration of MNC activity in the EC from the 1960s, firms in some sectors continued to serve only segmented markets because of non-tariff barriers. It is precisely those industries which are most likely to be affected by the more recent Mark II integration. Examples include the pharmaceutical and many service sectors which have been highly regulated and/or subject to national procurement policies or cross border controls.

Even allowing for deregulation and the elimination of non-tariff barriers, it is clear that the extent of corporate integration achieved by MNCs in the EC will continue to vary across industries. Some industries are more prone to MNC rationalization than others, and in any given industry so called global (or regional) strategies are more likely to be successful in certain periods than others (*Baden-Fuller and Stopford, 1989*). In some cases the gains to be made from international integration are more than balanced by the requirements of national responsiveness to differentiated markets (*Doz, 1986*), and this may help to explain why amongst the very largest industrial firms those that chose to remain domestic have performed well in the recent past (*Cantwell and Sanna Randaccio, 1989*).

It is possible to identify the broad characteristics of industries in which MNCs are especially prone to integrate their operations given the opportunity of the increasing ease of cross-border transactions within a region. The types of firms which are more likely to adopt a strategy of

Table 24:
Industry Characteristics which Promote Corporate Integration

1. Economies of scale, where minimum efficient scale exceeds size of individual national markets.
2. Economies of experience, which may be   (i) location specific; (ii) firm specific.
3. Economies of location.
4. Product differentiation by customer sets and product types, but not by country.
5. Research intensive production.
6. Distribution channel concentration, with limited local servicing requirements.
7. Financial and taxation arrangements differ between countries.
8. Few direct sales to government controlled agencies, or deregulation and competitive official procurement policies.
9. Strong growth of technological opportunities, differentiated by country.
10. Transport costs of intermediate products lower than final products; and transport and communication costs a low proportion of total value added.

Source: Adapted from Doz (1986).

corporate rationalization can also be distinguished. This combination of the conditions under which production is organized in each industry, and the competitive position of firms within their industry, determines whether MNCs are liable to gain an advantage relative to other firms through the reorganization of their operations in response to regional integration.

The industry characteristics which tend to promote the integration of MNC operations in free trade areas are summarized in *Table 24*. There is an incentive to concentrate activity in fewer locations, and to increase the degree of specialization in each location, where economies of scale are important. This becomes especially forceful where the minimum efficient scale of production exceeds the size of individual national markets. As examples, economies of scale are known to be particularly significant in the production of motor vehicles, petrochemicals, television tubes, electrical generators, and agricultural machinery (*Doz, 1986*).

The existence of scale economies typically leads to a vertical rather than a horizontal reorganization, though it may generate horizontal integration where the firm is itself a producer of intermediate products or capital goods. This is because economies of scale are generally conducive to specialization by processes rather than by products. Indeed, economies of scale in distribution or servicing may well reduce any propensity towards horizontal specialization in product provision. Alternatively, in this case, integrated MNCs may subcontract sales and servicing arrangements to independent local agents.

Economies of experience also have the effect of promoting the integration of affiliate operations. These economies represent the cumulative benefits of learning by doing and learning by using as production grows over time. The result is a steady fall in the costs to the firm of producing a given output in a plant of a given size as it improves its efficiency with experience. Such economies may be either location specific or firm specific. Where they are location specific they are more likely to lead to MNC rationalization, as there is an incentive to specialize by both products and processes according to which centers provide the most conducive environments for each type of activity. Production of each kind can then be allowed to grow most rapidly where the potential for improvements in productivity or product quality in the process or product concerned is at its greatest.

Firm specific economies of experience do not necessarily engender corporate integration, since they suggest that similar types of plant can be set up in a variety of countries, each gaining from a wider international corporate learning process. Indeed, they may even inhibit product specialization if the learning effect depends upon a flexible product variety. However, to the extent that learning is cumulative and is only transferred to new locations at some cost, an incentive is created for process or vertical specialization. Under these conditions the potential gains from learning by doing and using can be obtained and exploited most effectively. Economies of experience are likely to be significant in sectors which are capital intensive, or in which the rate of product innovation is high.

Corporate rationalization in an integrated region may also be driven by cross-country variations in the relative cost of different inputs, or in their availability. This provides locational economies from vertical integration, where separate processes use particular inputs especially heavily. A branch of production can be sited where the input it uses intensively can be acquired at low cost or (as in the case of skilled or scientific and technical labor) is more readily available, is of a higher quality, and offers a wider variety of contributions. It is possible that these economies of location work in tandem with one another, with for example the production of sophisticated component parts established in the more advanced regions of Northern Italy or Central and Northern Europe (where technical resources are available), and assembly carried out in parts of Southern Europe where labor and other costs are lower. The scope for integration to take advantage of economies of location is highest in industries which encompass the widest variety of types of production. The motor vehicle and electrical sectors are again cases in point.

Industries in which there is substantial product differentiation may work to the advantage or disadvantage of a MNC strategy of integration. Where differentiation is of a national kind, integration is strongly discouraged. Where, though, a similar pattern of differentiation prevails across countries, whether by customer sets or income groups or by product types, then horizontal integration and product specialization is facilitated. Each plant can be designated to serve a particular (EC) market segment, or to manufacture a particular part of the product range. The food industry provides examples of both national and European customer group differentiation. National differentiation prevails in sauces and biscuits, in which integration is liable to fail, while differentiated customer sets or products types running across EC countries can be identified in the markets for coffee and cereals, in which integrated EC strategies are feasible. Drink offers an illustration of a sector in which integration may be becoming more attractive, as national tastes seem to be converging within Europe over time. The professional and scientific instruments sector provides further examples (photographic equipment, watches and clocks, medical equipment and optical devices) in which horizontal specialization with a European marketing strategy may well be an option.

There are likely to be gains from corporate integration in industries in which production is research intensive. The more research intensive areas of production can be locationally separated from others, and concentrated in the most appropriate centers. While allowing for the continuation of local initiatives, an overall regional organization of the development, use and exchange of technology is likely to pay dividends.

It is sometimes suggested that the motives for integration created by high levels of research are linked to the earlier consideration of economies of scale, as large plants may be able to employ more efficient technology, and technological development may increase the minimum efficient scale of production. However, recent technological developments have on balance pointed in the reverse direction, towards smaller though more specialized plants, with a diminishing role for the traditional scale economies associated with mass production. The type of integration promoted is therefore of a very different kind from that which is inspired by the creation of large scale plants. There is no reason why production should become geographically more concentrated. Indeed, there may instead be reasons why it should become more widely dispersed in terms of the benefits of diversity of related learning activities, and an ability to respond in a more flexible way to changes in the firm's environment.

Moreover, the integrated MNC in this context is more liable to focus on core business areas which are central to its strategic advantage and which are closely allied to its main research strengths. Secondary activities which were previously encompassed in large scale plants can now be hived off to other smaller firms under contractual arrangements. This form of research related specialization is therefore supportive of the organization of strategic alliances between MNCs with complementary technological development, and a system of subcontracting with other firms. This would not arise so readily if the essential motive were the increased sale of production operations within the MNC.

The pharmaceuticals sector offers an example of research intensive production, on which grounds MNCs in this field stand to gain from a closer integration of their EC networks. It is also, though, a sector in which there are various other countervailing factors which must be taken into account. While the switching of certain types of research related activity towards a strong center such as Germany may appear attractive, the MNCs which do so must themselves begin with substantial innovative capability to be able to sustain their position against their strong indigenous German competitors, and to win away from them a body of local scientific personnel. In addition, the integration of the EC operations of MNCs in this industry requires progress over deregulation and more open government procurement policies. Under these conditions, a shift towards greater corporate integration is likely.

For strategies of horizontal specialization to be successful requires distribution channels to be concentrated and local servicing needs to be limited. This may be achieved either where MNCs have their own distribution networks, or where they require agreements with a relatively small number of independent distributive agents. The implication is that in some sectors integration may be geographically restricted to certain parts of the EC. In food products, for example, integration may arise between affiliates in Northern and Central Europe, but exclude operations in Southern Europe where distribution channels need to be more dispersed.

In sectors in which distribution is organized independently from manufacturing, MNC integration in the relevant industry can only be achieved easily where permanent distribution channels are in place. In sectors such as aircraft or construction a nationally responsive local presence may be more important than the greater efficiency which would derive from an international coordination of operations.

The ease of access to capital and the potential for transfer pricing may be further reasons for MNCs to integrate their operations in sectors in which financial and taxation arrangements differ between countries. These are general motives which may follow from either a vertical or a horizontal form of integration, as they do not depend on the structure of production or marketing links across countries. However, the scope for transfer pricing and profit switching is greater in the case of vertical linkages with intermediate product trade, especially in manufacturing sectors in which the distribution network is independent. Financial considerations of this kind are more likely to be important in sectors in which MNCs carry out a wide range of activity (in which, for example, one sphere is heavily taxed and another subsidized by governments), or in sectors in which international acquisitions have become intensive. However, they are unlikely to be the most significant factor leading to MNC integration, but rather more a side effect of it.

By comparison, the role of government within an industry is known to be a crucial determinant of the extent of MNC integration. This goes beyond the cross-sectoral variation in non-tariff barriers and regulations which have already been suggested as a key constraint under Mark I integration which is being relaxed in the Mark II phase. Irrespective of deregulation and more competitive official procurement policies, where government controlled agencies remain important customers local affiliates may well still require to be seen to be nationally responsive to their demands. This is liable to remain a major consideration in defense related sectors, such as aircraft or the provision of components for military equipment. In such cases there is a political element which need not enter into the calculations of firms in more purely commercial sectors (at least not in an industrialized region such as the EC). In other sectors not completely dominated by government controlled customers, such as computers or civilian aircraft, certain MNCs may be able to benefit from the integration of their operations under free trade arrangements.

Integration may also be favored by MNCs in sectors in which technological opportunities are rising rapidly. This may be allied to a high research intensity of production as commented upon earlier, though there are sectors in which despite high R & D expenditures the productivity of research is low due to the drying up of technological opportunities (here again, this applies in defense related industries). Aside from the locational separation of research oriented and other production already discussed, the specialization of research related production itself is encouraged where process development is nationally differentiated. The incentive is stronger the faster is the growth of technological opportunities in the industry, so creating greater potential gains from diverse experience. This can be thought of in a similar way to the increased learning capacity deriving from corporate integration in the case of economies of experience. This factor may help to promote integration in sectors such as microelectronics and biotechnology.

The final influence indicated in *Table 24* is the role of transport and communication costs, which again varies as between industries. A vertically integrated cross-country MNC structure is facilitated where the transport costs of intermediate products is low relative to the costs of moving final products; where, for example, component parts are small in bulk and light in weight. Both horizontal and vertical integration become possible where the general costs of transport and communication in the business constitute a low proportion of the total value added. It may be that these costs have been falling in most industries, in which case this may not be a significant determinant of cross-sectoral variations in MNC integration for much longer.

Having outlined the industry characteristics which promote MNC integration given the context of a broader regional economic integration, the competitive position of firms within each industry can be introduced into the argument. Even in an industry in which the general conditions are conducive to integration, only certain MNCs may be in a position to take up this option. A critical variable at the level of the individual company seems to be its market share (*Doz, 1986*). MNCs are more likely to rationalize their EC operations where they hold a higher market share. Where the relative size of firms increases the scope for integration rises as the potential for specialization widens and the regional organization of research, production and distribution becomes feasible.

Industry and firm specific characteristics can be combined on a case by case basis to examine the likelihood of MNC restructuring. *Figure 1* furnishes an illustration which combines the role of government in a sector, and the market shares of individual firms within it. This is an especially significant dimension in the context of the effects of Mark II integration in the EC, which will create changes in the extent and form of official intervention.

Figure 1

**The Role of Government and the Competitive Position of
MNCs as Joint Determinants of the Degree of Integration
of MNC Activity in the EC**

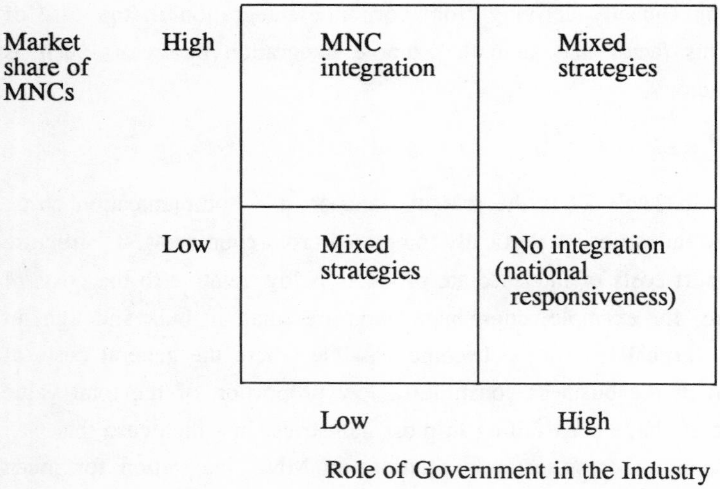

Market share of MNCs	High	MNC integration	Mixed strategies
	Low	Mixed strategies	No integration (national responsiveness)
		Low	High

Role of Government in the Industry

Source: *Adapted from Doz (1986).*

In sectors in which the government plays little direct role, whether as a regulator or a purchaser, and other industry characteristics are present which promote integration, MNCs with substantial market shares are likely to specialize their European activity in accordance with its geographical location. At the other extreme, where governments continue to play a prominent role smaller MNCs will tend to rely on a set of largely independent and nationally responsive affiliates. In other conditions more mixed strategies are likely to prevail, in which MNCs follow a strategy of partial integration but attempt to retain a degree of national responsiveness on the part of at least some affiliates.

The effect on Mark II integration is to tend to shift the diagonal which runs from bottom left to top right in Figure 1 downwards. This is the consequence of a decline in non-tariff barriers and hence in politically inspired influence, which broadens the number of sectors and firms for which integration is perceived as a desirable strategy. Thus new rationalization is likely to be induced through the completion of the internal market, especially amongst middle ranking MNCs in fields in which the extent of official intervention is around average.

The form which this corporate integration assumes is likely to depend upon the strategic interaction between companies in each sector. This of course brings in not only the firm's own market share but the wider structure of its industry. MNCs whose competitive position is weaker may be more inclined to become involved in a defensive rationalization, accompanied by attempts to preserve collusive agreements with other firms. Stronger MNCs, including those who are engaged in technological competition as well as those who hold dominant market positions, may adopt aggressive rationalization in which they attempt to establish differentiated advantage over their rivals. The essential difference is that where rationalization is of an aggressive kind MNCs make moves which are deliberately designed to be unmatchable by their competitors. This might entail, for example, the control of a significant distribution network which previously took a broader range of products, as a means towards its own European marketing strategy.

Sectors in which the role of government is low and other industry characteristics have helped to promote integration include motor vehicles, television tubes, agricultural machinery and microelectronics. Sectors in which government plays a prominent part and MNC operations have not been integrated include military aircraft, electrical power systems and telecommunications equipment. This is despite the fact that there are certain other factors which might suggest rationalization in these cases. More mixed strategies prevail in computers, transport equipment components and civilian aircraft.

Individual examples of MNC integration can be found in circumstances where industry and firm conditions were favorable. For example, in motor vehicles Ford drew on locational economies when siting assembly in Spain, where labor costs were about half those in Germany, and from where it could export to Italy and France. Even state owned companies such as Renault and Volkswagen have taken measures to rationalize their European operations (*Doz, 1986*). In the color television tube industry, Philips and Thomson - CSF have integrated their European tube and set manufacturing production. In agricultural machinery International Harvester and Massey Ferguson are known to have followed an integrated approach.

In sectors such as microelectronics and computers, in which governments take a keen interest though in principle free trade exists, the largest MNCs have become integrated while others pursue more mixed strategies. In microelectronics and semiconductors, Texas Instruments is a large integrated producer, while Philips is only partially integrated, which allows the company to enter into negotiation with individual European governments in critical areas such as the location of research facilities or the local product range for which the affiliate is responsible. Other firms such as Siemens, Plessey and GEC continue to operate as purely national companies in this field. In computers the dominant firm is IBM, which is well known for the integration of its operations. By comparison, Honeywell has integrated across a certain geographical group of European countries, while having a closer more responsive relationship with the national government in France. In the same sector ICL and Siemens operate a domestically based strategy.

In most defense-related industries no MNCs have seriously integrated their activities. In other sectors in which government controlled agencies are the major customers integration remains very much the exception rather than the rule. An example of an exception is L.M. Ericsson in the manufacture of telecommunications equipment, which has a degree of corporate integration in Europe. The company holds the largest market share of any in this sector, and its activity is more research intensive than its competitors, which explains the difference.

6. The Industrial Impact of the Reorganization of Technological and Other Activity by MNCs in the EC

One recent empirical study (*Kobrin, 1989*) has suggested that technological factors have become a more important determinant of MNC integration than plant economies of scale. It is in research intensive sectors that rationalization has developed most fully, subject of course to national regulations (which have hindered integration in the pharmaceuticals sector). The international integration of technological development within the firm has become steadily more significant (*Cantwell, 1989*). Where, as in the electrical equipment industry, MNCs have been rapidly reorganizing their European operations partly in preparation for 1992, involving mergers, capacity reductions and narrower plant specialization, research spending has been diversified and consolidated (*Barnevik, 1989*). While the leading research centers have been reinforced as a result, at the company level there has also been a geographical dispersion of research within the EC to ensure a presence in all the major locations for scientific and technological activity. With the integration of MNC operations in the EC, R & D responsibilities have become a prize to be won by each major affiliate (*Hood and Young, 1987*).

The outcome of the process of continuing rationalization of MNC operations is the emergence of a more refined division of labor within the EC, within industries as well as between them.

Research related production and assembly type activity are liable to become more clearly locationally separated and concentrated than they have been previously. Even in the earlier stage of regional integration in Europe in the 1960s and 1970s there is evidence that research activity had become more concentrated in some industries (*Cantwell, 1987*). To some extent, though, this has been complicated by the decline of industrial innovation in the UK. The British share of patents granted in the US attributable to inventions in a Western European location fell from 25 % in 1963-70 to 17% in 1978-84.

More details are set out in *Table 25*. Germany has consolidated its position as the main center for technological activity in Europe, while the UK has slipped back closer to the French level. Germany is especially important as a center for research related activity in chemicals, industrial engines and motor vehicles, and scientific instruments. The French area of specialization in technological development seems to be centered on electrical and office equipment and aircraft. The British record in innovation has been weakened in aircraft and rubber products, though it remains an important center for research activity in these cases, and in pharmaceuticals British industry plays an increasingly important role.

In addition to such intra-European adjustments with the rationalization of activity, the technological competitiveness of EC locations as a group has also shifted. Overall research related production has been growing faster in Japan, but the European nations have improved their position in chemicals and food in which they have been traditionally strong. It is arguable that the share of research related production in the EC as a whole will increase with the completion of the internal market. This is partly because rationalization of activity within the EC may increase the efficiency of local operations, and the share of the market served by the most technologically competitive MNCs. It is also because the growth of the market served by a European research center will attract the establishment of new research facilities to that location, thereby potentially increasing its share of world as well as EC markets.

Table 25:
National Shares of Western European Patenting
in the USA in Selected Industries, 1963-84 (%)

	W.Germany		U.K.		France	
	1963-70	1978-84	1963-70	1978-84	1963-70	1978-84
Food	33.3	28.3	20.1	16.4	13.9	14.9
Industrial chemicals	39.9	44.7	21.5	16.9	13.4	13.3
Agricult. chemicals	36.4	45.7	22.2	16.5	11.6	5.9
Pharmaceuticals	29.1	32.0	15.4	24.5	20.4	16.8
Metal products	32.5	41.5	28.6	16.2	14.2	13.6
Industrial engines	36.9	62.4	29.4	13.5	20.5	12.6
Electrical equipment	30.1	39.7	28.5	16.9	15.7	18.2
Office equipment	34.0	35.8	27.0	16.9	12.3	17.8
Motor vehicles	31.2	50.3	40.7	17.3	17.1	13.7
Aircraft	25.4	29.9	45.5	24.5	19.8	36.9
Rubber products	33.6	38.4	26.1	20.2	16.4	15.4
Building materials	26.1	32.2	24.8	17.2	17.1	19.6
Petroleum products	35.1	37.1	26.6	18.5	15.4	16.2
Scientific instrum.	43.0	45.1	22.1	16.2	14.2	13.7
TOTAL	35.0	41.6	25.1	16.7	13.9	14.8

Source: Compiled at the University of Reading using data on patent counts obtained through the Science Policy Research Unit at the University of Sussex. The data on patenting were originally prepared by the Office of Technology Assessment and Forecast, US Patent and Trademark Office, with the support of the Science Indicators Unit, US National Science Foundation.

It may also be that smaller firms based in such locations benefit from the removal of non-tariff barriers in the EC, widening their potential market. This may be at the expense of any less technologically competitive MNCs which had previously served various national EC markets through local production. However there is likely to be an increase in contractual arrangements and business agreements between smaller innovative firms and larger MNC partners. The rationalization of activity within the EC is not purely a matter of corporate rationalization of the operations of individual firms, but may also involve the establishment of more complex networks of subcontracting and business alliances.

The rationalization of MNC activity increasingly entails the networking of the firm's resources including the organization of technology flows between affiliates and interaction between research establishments (*Kobrin, 1989*). The growing role of these technological factors has also served to make plant economies of scale less important as a source of corporate integration, since the "modern factory" which appears to be the outcome of current technological trends relies on flexible specialization rather than large scale production. A broader but combined technological development can result from the strengthening of key research facilities as part of a reorganized international division of labor within the MNC, and through selected technological joint ventures between MNCs - while the use of much of the new technology facilitates the spread of subcontracting arrangements between MNCs and specialist suppliers. In other words, the same forces which have underpinned MNC rationalization have also contributed to local cooperative arrangements with smaller firms, and moves towards strategic alliances between MNCs themselves. It has also been argued that regional integration tends to lead to an increase in the size of the largest firms, and the rationalization of their operations may increase the extent of European-wide collusion between them (*Pelkmans, 1987*).

The combination of increasing competition engendered by economic integration, the increasing presence of foreign owned firms in the EC, and the imperatives of modern technology for enterprises to exploit the economies of scale and scope suggest that markets in the EC are not only becoming increasingly concentrated, but that foreign owned MNCs may be helping to promote such concentration. However, such evidence as has been accumulated by economists, such as *Fishwick (1982)*, from studies of market structure in the UK, France, and Germany, suggest that in the 1960s and 1970s there was no general trend toward more industrial concentration. In some sectors, e.g. the drinks industry, the share of the total sales of the three or four largest firms increased; in others, e.g. the pharmaceutical industry, it fell.

Furthermore, it is clear that while MNCs tend to favor the more highly concentrated industries, there is little evidence that their growing presence in the EC has increased such concentration. Again, in some sectors, e.g. automobiles and computers, it would seem that an increased concentration is associated with increased foreign participation; in others, e.g. soap and detergents, domestic appliances, and food products, the reverse would appear to be the case.

Other research (*Dunning and Pearce, 1985*) confirms that in most industrial sectors, the contribution of the largest three firms to the sales of the 500 largest U.S. and 500 largest non-U.S. companies listed in Fortune magazine, generally fell between 1972 and 1982.

On the other hand, it would appear that non-EC owned MNCs have engaged in more joint ventures and strategic alliances with EC firms than their EC counterparts. This has been because French, UK, German and other EC firms have been more comfortable, and found the transactions costs less, in associating with American (and lately Japanese) enterprises than with those in other parts of the EC. To this extent at least, non-EC based MNCs have responded more vigorously to the opportunities for cross-border and acquisitions and mergers encouraged by economic integration, than have EC firms - and have added to, rather than lessened, the trend towards industrial concentration in the EC as a whole.

In the case of research related production MNCs are likely to be more interested in finding new arrangements with innovative component suppliers, as well as in joint technological activity or exchanges with other firms. Turning to assembly type activity, the subcontracting of various tasks by larger MNCs has been observed alongside the rationalization of production (*Cowling and Sugden, 1987*). Assembly types of activity may also be especially drawn to locations in which specialist contractors emerge.

7. Third World MNCs in Europe

US and Japanese firms are not the only non-EC MNCs which may expect to take advantage of production in an integrated European region. Firms from other industrialized countries apart from Japan have also been making moves to ensure that they have a base within the EC. This applies to firms from other European countries such as Switzerland and Sweden, as well as to Canadian and Australian companies. Third World MNCs are also beginning to make their appearance in EC manufacturing, though as yet on a smaller scale.

Looking to the later 1990s, however, it may be that following the current wave of Japanese MNC investment in production in EC countries, there is a further wave of Third World MNC investment. This must remain rather speculative for the moment, but it does seem that the trend in the development of internationalization is now very much faster.

The mature MNCs of Britain and the US took many years in the transition from resource based production in LDCs towards manufacturing in the industrialized countries, through eventually to a greater internationalization of technological activity. Japanese MNCs have taken much less time (20 years or so) to accomplish the same transition. Third World MNCs have now embarked on the same path, and they have already established a limited amount of research related production in the US and EC (*Cantwell and Tolentino, 1990*).

As yet, these firms have expanded much further in the US than in Europe, though this also follows the Japanese pattern. The completion of the single internal market is likely to increase the attractiveness of an EC location (relative to the US) for Third World MNCs. Initially, research related production may be established in the larger EC countries, while assembly types of activity might be more dispersed, as it is possible that production for EC markets could be switched from LDCs to Portugal or Greece.

The impact of Third World MNCs would, like that of US and Japanese firms in Europe, vary across sectors. However, they may have a particular effect on the way production is managed and organized. They are not as yet at the technological frontier, but they often possess well developed organizational skills. Once again, this may entail a further reorganization of EC industries after 1992, and a renegotiation of the business alliances which are currently being set in train.

References

BADEN-FULLER, C.W.F. and STOPFORD, J.M. (1989) Globalisation Frustrated: The Case of White Goods, mimeo, University of Bath.

BALLANCE, R.H., FORSTNER, H. and MURRAY, T. (1987) Consistency Tests of Alternative Measures of Comparative Advantage, Review of Economics and Statistics, Vol. 69, No. 1, February.

BARNEVIK, P. (1989)) Restructuring European Industry against the Background of a Future Borderless Europe and Globalisation of Business.

CANTWELL, J.A. (1987) The Reorganisation of European Industries after Integration: Selected Evidence on the Role of Multinational Enterprise Activities, Journal of Common Market Studies, Vol. 26, No. 2, December; reprinted in Dunning, J.H. and Robson, P. (1988) eds., Multinationals and the European Community, Oxford; Basil Blackwell.

CANTWELL, J.A. (1989) Technological Innovatior and Multinational Corporations, Oxford; Basil Blackwell.

CANTWELL, J.A. and SANNA RANDACCIO, F. (1989) Growth and Multinationality Amongst the World's Largest Firms, University of Reading Discussion Papers in International Investment and Business Studies, No. 134, November.

CANTWELL, J.A. and TOLENTINO, P.E.E. (1990) Technological Accumulation and Third World Multinationals, University of Reading Discussion Papers in International Investment and Business Studies, No. 139, May.

COWLING, K. and SUGDEN, R. (1987) Transnational Monopoly Capitalism, Brighton; Wheatsheaf.

DICKEN, P. (1986) Global Shift, London; Harper & Row.

DOZ, Y. (1986) Strategic Management in Multinational Companies, Oxford: Pergamon Press.

DUNNING, J.H. (1958) American Investment in British Manufacturing Industry, London; Allen & Unwin.

DUNNING, J.H. and CANTWELL, J.A. (1991) Japanese Direct Investment in the EC post-1992; Some Alternative Scenarios, in: Burgenmeier, B., ed., Multinational Firms and European Integration 1992, London: Routledge.

DUNNING, J.H. and PEARCE, R.D. (1985) The World's Largest Industrial Enterprises, Farnborough: Gower.

FISHWICK, F. (1982) Multinational Companies and Economic Concentration in Europe, Aldershot: Gower.

HOOD, N. and YOUNG, S. (1987) Inward Investment and the EC: UK Evidence on Corporate Integration Strategies, Journal of Common Market Studies, Vol. 26, No. 2, December.

KOBRIN, S.J. (1989) An Empirical Analysis of the Determinants of Global Integration, mimeo, The Wharton School, University of Pennsylvania.

LUNDVALL, B.A. (1988) Innovation as an Intractive Process: From User-producer Interaction to the National System of Innovation, in: Dosi, G., Freeman, C., Nelson, R., Silverberg, G. and Soete, L.L.G., Eds., Technical Change and Economic Theory, London: Frances Pinter.

OZAWA, T. (1991) Europe 1992 and Japanese Multinationals: Transplanting a Subcontracting System in the Expanded Market", in Burgenmeier, B., ed., Multinational Firms and European Integration 1992, London: Routledge.

PELKMANS, J. (1987) The Community's Vivid Core: Integration Processes in Industrial Product Markets, in: Dunning, J.H. and Usui, M., Eds., Structural Change, Economic Interdependence and World Development, Volume 4: Economic Interdependence, London: Macmillan.

SERVAN-SCHREIBER, J.-J. (1967) Le Défi Américain , Paris: Editions Denoel.

UNIDO (1986) International Comparative Advantage in Manufacturing: Changing Profiles of Resources and Trade, Vienna: United Nations.

1   This paper derives from work originally undertaken for the UN Centre on Transnational Corporations (UNCTC), which provided financial support as part of a broader project on the implications of the completion of the single market in the EC for transnational corporation activity. The author is grateful to John Dunning for helpful comments on an earlier draft.

2   For a discussion of alternative measures of comparative advantage see *Ballance, Forstner and Murray (1987)*.

COMMENTS ON: THE EFFECTS OF INTEGRATION ON THE STRUCTURE OF MULTINATIONAL CORPORATION ACTIVITY IN THE EC

Werner Hasenberg

Professor Cantwell has written an impressive paper on the prospects of MNC activity in the European Community in anticipation of and resulting from the completion of the framework for the "internal market" in 1992.

In my view the principal contribution of the paper is in the field of industrial organization, of which I have little knowledge. Using mostly data published by the Bureau of Economic Analysis, U.S. Department of Commerce, Cantwell traces horizontal and vertical integration in Europe that accompanied and resulted from massive U.S. direct investment in Europe since the mid-1950s. The analysis is then carried forward to examine the prospects for further integration of the economy of Western Europe attributable to anticipated large Japanese direct investment as well as EC, U.S. and other large-scale investment in the post-1992 European Community.

My comments are directed mostly to the availability and use of the data employed by Professor Cantwell. Personally I would feel more comfortable if - in order to show the magnitude of the subject - actual amounts were given (as well as percentages) in most of the tables and the text in which they are analyzed. I also believe that data for later years were available (see below) when the paper was delivered in September 1990.

For instance, one may wish to note that in 1982 total sales by majority-owned foreign affiliates amounted to $730 billion ($160 billion to affiliated persons), of which EC-10 countries accounted for $302 billion ($67 billion to affiliated persons). By 1988 total sales had grown to $928 billion ($227 billion to affiliates), of which EC-10 countries accounted for $436 billion ($115 billion to affiliates).

Tables 17 through 24 in the Cantwell paper cover various ratios or shares of intra-EC exports by U.S. majority-owned affiliates for 1977. Professor Cantwell draws very interesting inferences about horizontal and vertical integration between specific sets of EC countries for 1977; could these same inferences still be drawn for 1982 or even later years? After all, the data reflect investment decisions by individual firms in specific industries in certain countries, rather than a theoretical framework. This is not to say that the horizontal and vertical relationships were necessarily different in 1982 (or later years) than in 1977, but only that one would like Cantwell's confirmation on the basis of his having tested available data for years after 1977.

Finally, in section 4 of Professor Cantwell's paper, he states that "since U.S. MNCs make consolidated reports to the U.S. Department of Commerce, it may be assumed that [such] trade between affiliates is not included." However, sales data published by the Bureau of Economic Analysis are *not* on a worldwide consolidated basis but are disaggregated in a manner that permits the distinction between affiliated and unaffiliated sales by majority-owned foreign affiliates of U.S. companies. For instance, in 1988 EC-12 affiliate sales amounted to $460 billion ($21 billion to affiliated persons); local sales were $290 billion ($18 billion to affiliates). But the portion of intercorporate sales varied significantly by country: for the Netherlands total sales were $42 billion ($15 billion to affiliates); local sales were $17 billion ($1 billion to affiliates). By contrast, for the United Kingdom total sales were $145 billion ($32 billion to affiliates); local sales were $102 billion ($8 billion to affiliates).

JAPANESE MULTINATIONALS IN EUROPE AND THE UNITED STATES: SOME COMPARISONS AND CONTRASTS*

Michelle Gittelman and John H. Dunning

1. Introduction

Ten years ago, a comparison of the foreign direct investment (fdi) activities of Japanese multinational enterprises (MNEs) in the United States and Western Europe would have appeared somewhat misdirected, if not completely irrelevant: Japan's export successes, rather than its overseas investments, were far more important indicators of Japan's growing international competitiveness. Since the late 1980s, however, trade has taken a back seat to fdi as a key indicator of Japan's increasing involvement in the world economy. The rapidity with which this shift is occurring is remarkable, even as the context against which it is taking place is undergoing unprecedented change.

At the same time as Japanese firms are increasing their share of world international production, economic boundaries are being re-drawn in Western Europe and North America to create regional rather than national markets, and entirely new market and production opportunities in Eastern Europe are opening up. Taken together, the interaction between the increasingly outward orientation of Japanese industry and the changing shape of the world's marketplace is likely to have a profound change in the location, organization and ownership of global economic activity.

While the proportion of production that Japanese manufacturing firms perform overseas is still relatively low (somewhere between 4 and 10 percent in 1988), and considerably less than their European and US counterparts, their direct presence in the United States and (increasingly) in Europe is having a disproportionately large impact on the competitive profile of a number of key industries such as computers, automobiles, and electronic componentry.

Although it is too early to predict the likely outcome of these trends, an analysis of recent developments raises a number of interesting questions and points to some possible answers. Will the competitive advantages of Japanese firms be modified now that they are increasingly exploiting these advantages from a foreign production base? To what extent will they be able to "export" their competitive, or ownership-specific, advantages which owe much to the institutional, economic and cultural environment of their country of origin? How will their presence in Western Europe and North America affect the locational advantages of these regions and the competitive advantages of indigenous firms? How do policy variables in general, and the European single market program in particular, affect the investment decisions of Japanese multinationals, and what is their impact, if any, on the locational advantage of the United States and the competitive advantages of its firms? Finally, what are the implications of increasing Japanese fdi for competition in regional markets where, in the not-too-distant future, non-national champions will be in a position to determine the overall success or failure of a nation's industries?

2. A Theoretical Digression

The theoretical underpinning of this paper is the developmental version of the eclectic paradigm of international production. The structure of this paradigm has been set out in detail in several other writings of one of the authors (*Dunning 1988, 1989, 1990*) and will be only briefly summarized here.

At any given moment of time (time "t") the propensity of one country's firms to engage in value added activities outside their national boundaries rests on three main factors. These are, first, their ability to serve particular foreign or domestic markets relative to that of their competitors of other nationalities. These competitive or ownership-specific (O) advantages are of two kinds. The first arise from the privileged possession of income generating assets (e.g. a patent, a superior production technique, exclusive access to raw materials or markets, etc.). The second type of O advantages are those which stem from the superior ability of firms to take advantage of the economies of common governance of separate but related activities which might otherwise have been coordinated through external markets. Such advantages include economies of scale and synergy, the spreading of geographical risk and the opportunities for cross-border arbitraging.

The second factor influencing international production is the extent to which firms wish to create or acquire these advantages, or add value to them from a foreign versus a domestic production facility. These we shall refer to as the locational (L) advantages of countries. They depend on such variables as production and transport costs, the extent to which a product needs to be adapted for particular markets and the costs of organizing cross-border, compared with domestic multi-product activities.

Thirdly, overseas production will depend upon the extent to which firms choose to organize their O advantages from a foreign or domestic location by making use of the external market, or whether the net production and transaction costs of doing so are lower when undertaken within internal hierarchies (within the firm). These advantages are called internalization (or I) advantages. They essentially reflect the degree to which markets fail to operate in a perfectly competitive way. Of the variables which are likely to cause firms to internalize markets, the likelihood and costs of a contractual default[1] and the inability of a contractor to capture the external economies of any transaction are perhaps the two most important.

Other things being equal, the greater the ownership advantages of firms of a particular country, the more it pays those firms to create, acquire or add value to those advantages from a foreign location, and the greater the incentive to internalize the markets for those advantages or the value added arising from them, the higher will be the propensity to engage in outward direct investment.

One country's outward investment is another country's inward investment and so, to explain the propensity of a country to attract investment, its location-bound resources or markets must be relatively attractive to foreign MNEs. Furthermore, foreign MNEs must be able to service the foreign markets at least as effectively, if not more effectively, than firms which are indigenous to those markets. Finally, there must be some degree of failure in intermediate product markets to make it more attractive for foreign firms to own and control production in the host economy rather than in another country.

Given the configuration of OLI advantages of firms from different countries, and assuming no change in either the value of these variables or of the strategy of the investing firms, and assuming no change in the response of other economic agents or of Governments to the foreign production generated by these advantages, it is possible to determine the amount and distribution of MNE activity over some future period of time.

In fact, however, it is not as simple as that. For when a firm of one nationality invests in another country, it may affect the O advantages of indigenous firms and by influencing, for example, the productivity of the local labor force, the technological competence of suppliers or Government policy towards inward investment, the host country's L advantages may be influenced as well. Moreover, in addition to being affected by the extent and pattern of inter-firm transaction costs, these, in turn, may be influenced by the changing location advantages of countries. Finally, the efficiency with which a firm internalizes cross-border markets, e.g. through acquisitions and mergers, may, itself, affect its own O advantages, as the ability to efficiently organize transactions by hierarchical governance is a competitive advantage in its own right.

Over and above the dynamic interdependence between the OLI variables, there is the question of how individual firms and/or Governments may respond to an existing OLI configuration. The fact that there is every evidence that firms pursue different economic strategies when faced with the same configuration of variables suggests that the determinants of alternative strategy must be incorporated into one paradigm.[2]

Let us now see how far the OLI paradigm can help to explain the level and structure of Japanese investment in US and European manufacturing industries, and the changes which may have occurred over the last decade or so. In particular, we might consider three sets of hypotheses. The first is that as

(i) the O advantages of Japanese firms have increased
(ii) the advantages of producing from a European or US base (relative from a Japanese base) have become more pronounced, and
(iii) Japanese firms perceive that they can better organize the creation or acquisition of the O advantages or add value to them within their existing hierarchies, Japanese participation in European and US industry will increase.

The second hypothesis is that since the OLI configuration facing Japanese firms which invest in the US is likely to be different from the one which confronts Japanese firms in Europe, both the level and the structure of their investments in the two regions will differ. The third hypothesis stems from the differences between, on the one hand, the OLI advantages enjoyed by Japanese firms which have invested in Europe and/or the US and, on the other hand, the OLI advantages of domestic firms in those regions. Because of these differences between Japanese and local firms, it is expected that there will also be differences in terms of the dynamic or developmental impact of cross-border transactions on the future OLI configurations of Japanese and US firms located in the US on the one hand, and Japanese and European firms located in Europe on the other. Indeed, the dynamic impact on the location-bound advantages of the US and Europe are likely to be different.

Much has already been written about the changing nature of the O-advantages of Japanese firms (*Dunning and Cantwell, 1989*), (*Porter, 1990*); and of the increasing L advantages of Europe due to the single market program (*Baldwin, 1989*). The purpose of this contribution is first to describe some recent changes in the composition and structure of Japanese fdi, and second to analyze the extent to which such data uphold the proposition that Japanese subsidiaries in those regions are now exporting the competitive advantages of their parent companies, which were originally specific to their country of origin, and which, in many cases, afforded them their initial trade successes.

We would suggest that exporting these advantages is likely to have two impacts: first the competitive-advantages of Japanese MNEs might, themselves, change as the firms are faced with a different set of locational endowments with which to combine their O advantages. Second, the direct presence of Japanese multinationals will affect the competitive behavior of local rivals, thus undermining or enhancing their own O-advantages.

The outcome of the shifting distribution of O-advantages among Japanese and home country firms will depend on a number of factors - including those described by Michael Porter in his most recent book (*Porter, 1990*). We shall also see, in the present context, that the trade and fdi policies adopted by the Japanese authorities has been of critical importance. Such policies have substantially influenced the pattern of Japanese multinational activity in terms of *where* and *in which* sectors the investment is made, *how* (through joint ventures, wholly-owned subsidiaries, or M&A), *in what measure* (degree of value-added performed by the foreign operation) and *when* they invest abroad.

Thus, investments by Japanese MNEs in the United States and Europe will not just have an impact upon competition between Japanese and host-country multinationals, but, through the channels of host-country policies (L advantages), shifting patterns of competition in their domestic industries (O advantages) and the relative benefits of organizing those advantages through the market or through internal hierarchies may also impact upon the nature of competition between multinationals from Europe and the United States for global positions, not only in each other's markets but also, increasingly, in that of Japan.

3. The Role of Foreign Direct Investment by Japan Prior to the 1980s: a Brief Overview

It is important to note that Japanese outward foreign direct investment (fdi) in manufacturing has traditionally been a response to, rather than a factor determining, Japanese economic progress. At the risk of oversimplifying, Japanese economic strategy up to the early 1980s might be summarized as one in which output for which Japan has a comparative advantage is exported to hard-currency markets in order to pay for a strategic restructuring of economic activity towards sectors in which Japan is developing a comparative advantage, i.e., sectors which represent (or are perceived to represent) the high-growth (income elastic) opportunities which will power future industrial development (*Ozawa, 1989b*).

A buoyant export sector is essential to such a strategy, as is the proper set of macro-economic conditions in which industries may shift into ever-higher value-, knowledge- and capital-intensive sectors. In this process of systematic upgrading, outward fdi has served as an outlet to relieve the pressures which, inevitably, build up in such a system: rising wages and labor shortages;[3] an appreciating currency which undermines the cost position of domestic exporters; the maturation of industries and technologies; and trade frictions with leading partners whose own goods, if let in freely as imports, would cause serious disruptions to the system. Given these circumstances, Japanese fdi policy was expressly guided by the Government's (MITI's) overall strategic goals for domestic industrial restructuring (*Ozawa, 1989a*).

In the late 1960s and early 1970s, for instance, outward fdi was encouraged in light manufacturing sectors (textiles, toys) - former export "stars" which were rendered uncompetitive by the increasing predominance of heavy industries (steel, chemicals, shipbuilding). Most of this labor-intensive fdi was made by small and medium sized Japanese companies and was directed to developing countries in Asia, which are now export power-houses in their own right (*Ozawa, 1989b*)! Subsequently, outward fdi was aimed at securing access to natural resources (oil, minerals) necessary to support the growth of heavy industry at home. Finally, the continuation of the upgrading process (and failure to attain sustainable O advantages in materials- and energy-intensive industries) demanded a shift up the value added chain into higher knowledge and technology intensive activities.

It was at this stage, which occurred in the late 1970s and early 1980s, that Japanese MNE activity was guided to developed host countries (first to the US and later to Europe) to secure access for the exports of firms whose O advantages had by then reached rough parity with their Western counterparts (*Ozawa, 1989c*). In other words, because of changing location advantages in Europe and the United States and much improved O advantages of Japanese firms, the latter showed a preference in the late 1980s to exploit those advantages by foreign production rather than by exports. This was particularly true for Japan's burgeoning automobile and consumer electronics industries, whose highly competitive products (low-cost, high quality and market-oriented) had almost appeared to come out of nowhere in the 1970s and 1980s, to capture alarmingly high market shares in the United States and Europe.

In other words, rationalization and efficiency improvements mainly took place in Japan, with outward manufacturing fdi geared towards maintaining or advancing markets for Japanese exports (in developed countries) and relocating uncompetitive activities (in developing countries). But, relative to the United States and parts of Europe, Japan still possessed relatively weak O advantages in the innovation of many new technologies. This meant that industrial upgrading in Japan required a continual inflow of technology from abroad. Given this, a second important function of fdi (both outward and inward) was to act as a channel to absorb technologies developed in the West (*Ozawa, 1989b*). However, unlike West Germany, Japan preferred to acquire such technology through means other than direct investment (e.g.

licensing, reverse engineering, etc.). Once fed back to the parent, such technologies could be adapted and applied to products which were then exported to - and often came to dominate - the very markets which gave them their technological inception in the first place, e.g. consumer electronics, semiconuuctors, steel, and precision machinery.

Thus, until the mid 1980s at least, manufacturing direct investment into and out of Japan was an important adjunct to, rather than a central facet of, Japanese industrial development. That trade was still the mechanism driving the machine is illustrated by the fact that as late as 1985 Japanese owned firms exported ten times the value of goods to Europe and the United States than their subsidiaries produced in those regions. What follows is a closer look at how these patterns have changed, and current indications that a fundamental shift in the role of outward Japanese fdi is now occurring, such that the very system of exporting -- > domestic upgrading -- > exporting which it has long supported is likely to be profoundly altered and, possibly, disrupted altogether.

4. Key FDI Strategies in Europe and the United States: Comparisons and Contrasts
4.1 1980 - 1984: Defending Current and Future Export Markets

The above overview suggests that, up to and including the early 1980s, the fdi strategies of Japanese companies in the United States and Europe could be broadly classified as falling into two categories: - viz. defensive market oriented and offensive supply oriented.

1. Defensive market-seeking investment
The primary purpose of these investments was to establish operations in Europe and the US to protect pre-existing share in export markets, either in response to actual or potential trade barriers, or to counter the moves of competitors which threatened to disrupt domestic operations.

Since a defensive export-substituting fdi strategy is aimed at maintaining pre-existing market share previously attained via exports, these investments are likely to be concentrated in sectors where Japanese firms already have strong O advantages, sustained and supported by strong L advantages to production in Japan. In the early 1980s, such firms were to be found mainly in the automobile and electrical and electronic equipment industries. The typical mode of this kind of foreign investment was the establishment of greenfield plants which performed relatively low levels of value added activities. Since the O advantages already existed and were located in Japan, there was little incentive to enter into joint ventures and even less to acquire existing assets. At worst these operations were "screwdriver" factories; at best, they were branch plants which replicated the production of the parent company, dependent on the latter for management decision-making and control, inputs, and full product and process specifications.

2. Offensive, supply oriented investment

The second type of MNE strategy is essentially targeted at gaining access to the information and technology needed to upgrade and rationalize domestic operations, and help advance a global competition strategy. Such foreign production differs from the traditional conception of rationalized investment, in which multinationals relocate discrete value-adding activities to maximize operational efficiency by reaping the benefits of common governance over linked, but geographically dispersed, activities. In the Japanese case of offensive strategic fdi, some form of international rationalization is taking place, but the high value activities, e.g. design, research and product development, organization, sourcing and marketing strategy, and financial control are generally retained in Japan. The role of the foreign affiliate, often a joint venture with a local partner, is to aid in the continual upgrading and rationalization of the parent company's operations by feeding it new information about markets, products and technologies. Such investments differ from the first type in that they are aimed at acquiring new O advantages rather than exploiting existing ones, and so will often be in sectors in which firms in the countries receiving the fdi possess O advantages which are superior those possessed by the investing firm.

The evidence suggests that the majority of Japanese fdi in the United States and Europe in the early 1980s were of the first type, viz. defensive market-seeking investment. When Japanese MNEs were asked to rank their motives for investments in Europe and the United States, the most frequently cited answer was access to markets with technology acquisition and/or information sharing as the second most important reason, though given far less weight than the first (*MITI, 1990*). Furthermore, it is likely that a majority of market-seeking investments were of the defensive type, undertaken to avoid restrictions to Japan's exports. Such frictions, beginning in the 1970s, set off a wave of Japanese investments in its major export markets in the early 1980s. *Figure 1* gives some illustrations of the direct relationship between the instigation of protective measures against Japanese exports to Europe and subsequent Japanese direct investments in Europe.

Table 1 shows the remarkable increase in the absolute level of manufacturing fdi in this period, along with the stronger L-advantages of the United States compared to Europe: cumulative flows increased by 88 percent in the United States and by 9 percent in Europe above the cumulated flows of *the previous 30 years combined*. The share of the United States

Figure 1: EC Surveys to Investigate Dumping Charges and Establishment of Japanese Factories in Europe, 1972 - 1987

(Numbers in Bars Show Factories Established That Year)

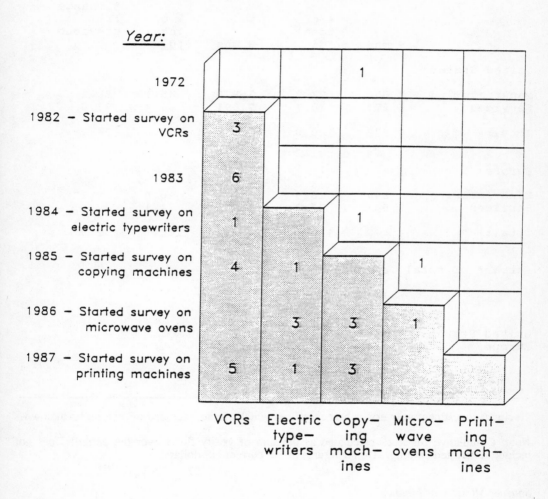

Source: Japan Broadcasting Company (NHK) in Japanese Finance and Industry, Industrial Bank of Japan Quarterly Survey, No. 80 (1989 IV).

Table 1: Cumulative Japanese FDI Stock in the United States and Europe
1951-1980 versus 1981-1984

	1951 - 1980		1981 - 1984		
	$ mns	% of total fdi	$ mns	% of total fdi	% change from previous period
United States:					
Manufacturing	2,056	23.2	3,870	35.1	88.2
Services	6,273	70.7	7,091	64.4	13.0
Total:*	8,878	100.0	11,015	100.0	24.1
Europe:					
Manufacturing	844	18.9	921	20.0	9.1
Services	3,501	78.3	3,412	74.1	(2.6)
Total:*	4,472	100.0	4,601	100.0	2.9

Percent of total Japanese fdi:

	1951-1980	1981-1984
United States	24.3	31.5
Europe	12.3	13.2

*Includes investment in overseas branch offices which are not included in sectoral breakdown.

Note: Cumulative fdi stock calculated as the sum of yearly flows over the period. Does not include reinvested earning. Dollar figures are in current US dollars.

Source: Ministry of Finance

Table 2: Sectoral Composition of Japanese FDI Stock in Manufacturing
and Selected Services in the United States and Europe
1951-1980 to 1981-84
($ mn and %)

	United States 1951-80	1981-84	% change	Europe 1951-80	1981-84	% change
Elec. machinery	653	1073	64.4	128	224	75.0
% of manuf. fdi	31.7	27.7		15.2	24.3	
Transport equip.	87	880	906.0	61	240	293.4
% of manuf. fdi	4.3	22.7		7.2	26.1	
Steel and metals	304	507	66.8	157	68	(56.7)
% of manuf. fdi	14.8	13.1		18.6	7.4	
Chemicals	241	349	45.1	104	97	(6.7)
% of manuf. fdi	11.7	9.0		12.3	10.5	
General machinery	210	310	47.7	119	70	(41.2)
% of manuf. fdi	10.2	8.0		14.1	7.6	
Food, bev,tobacco	184	250	35.7	42	19	(54.8)
% of manuf. fdi	8.9	6.4		5.0	2.1	
Other*	378	503	32.9	233	203	(12.9)
% of manuf. fdi	18.4	13.0		27.6	22.0	
Total manufact.	2057	3870	88.2	844	921	9.1
% of total fdi	23.2	35.1		18.9	20.0	
Distributive trade	3325	3082	(7.3)	817	1260	54.2
% of total fdi	37.5	28.0		18.3	27.4	
Finance and insur.	931	1664	78.6	822	1920	133.6
% of total fdi	10.5	15.1		18.4	41.7	
Total services	6274	7091	13.0	3501	3410	(2.6)
% of total fdi	70.7	64.4		78.3	74.1	
Total	8878	11,015	24.1	4472	4601	2.9

*Other manufacturing includes: textiles, lumber and wood pulp, precision machinery, rubber, glass, other. Other services includes: agriculture/forestry, fishery, mining, construction, hotels and entertainment, transportation services, real estate businesses, other.

Source: Ministry of Finance

in total Japanese fdi rose from one quarter in the 1951-1980 period to nearly one third in 1981-1984.

Table 2 shows the rapidly changing sectoral composition of Japanese manufacturing fdi in the United States and Europe in 1981-1984, and reveals the strong Japanese O advantages in automobiles and electric/electronic machinery prevailing at the time. In the United States, the Japanese investment stake in the motor vehicle industry grew to nearly a quarter of all manufacturing investment by the early 1980s; that of electric/electronic equipment - where a substantial amount of investment was already in place by 1981 - maintained its position as the dominant sector, accounting for about a third of all manufacturing. In Europe, the share of both sectors increased rapidly, such that by 1984 the structure, if not the overall level, of Japanese manufacturing fdi closely resembled that in the United States. In particular, electrical and electronic machinery was the only sector in Europe in which the growth of inward fdi flows outstripped that in the United States. The result was that, by 1981-1984, the electrical and electronics sectors accounted for about the same share of manufacturing fdi in both locations (one quarter) whereas in the earlier period the shares had differed by a factor of two (32 percent in the US; 15 percent in Europe). It would appear that Japanese multinationals in this sector were primarily concerned with shoring up their market positions in Europe, but exhibited less urgency in the United States, where they had already established a substantial investment base.

It is also worth noting from *Table 2* that in the United States, the level of fdi in wholesale and retail trade (essentially import ducts for Japanese products) fell in both absolute and relative terms in 1981-1984 from the preceding period, while in Europe, such investments increased, both in absolute terms and as a percentage share of total fdi. This would seem to suggest that Europe was, in the beginning of the 1980s, at an earlier stage of absorbing Japanese fdi than was the United States. Protecting existing export markets was clearly a concern, but direct investment in European production facilities was not the primary response, as it was in the United States. Instead, new Japanese fdi in Europe mainly took the form of export distribution outlets. It is our contention that the reasons behind this difference lie in the different L advantages of the United States and Europe at that time, which are explored in some detail in Section 4.2.

The data point to signs that the United States, as an industrialized host country to Japanese fdi, has played the role of the "leader" with Europe following behind, such that the level and structure of the former, e.g. with respect to motives and modes of organization, would later be replicated, albeit on a smaller scale, in the latter. In other words, not only were there a series of stages of internationalization which Japan as a home country of fdi passed through (rationalized, resource-seeking, market-seeking, information-seeking) but that, at the same time, developed host countries were mirroring this process by passing through a series of their own "stages" related to inward fdi. If this is so, then the key difference between Japanese fdi in the United States and Europe was not so much one of structure, strategy or even of amount, but merely of the timing with which the investments were made.

4.2 Location Advantages in the United States and Europe

Before comparing the L advantages of the United States and Europe in the period up to 1984, it is important to note that, while the two economic regions differed from one another, from a global perspective they shared many similarities. Both were Japan's major export markets, and both had started to clamp down on Japanese imports in the mid-1970s. Hence, the underlying motives for Japanese investments in the two locations were fundamentally the same, viz. primarily market-seeking, export-substituting fdi, with little or no rationalized (efficiency-seeking and/or cost-reducing) investments, the latter being concentrated in low-cost Asian countries.

From a demand perspective, the two markets, while admittedly different in terms of size and growth, were also structurally comparable. Indeed, it was mainly in the area of production economics where the greatest variances were to be found, although even these were not structural, qualitative differences, but rather reflected different regulatory environments, which made for more marked distortions in Europe.

Looked at from a viewpoint of the Japanese investors seeking to evolve a transnational strategy, then, the two regions were very similar. The United States and Europe represented overseas concentrations of wealth and technology which were the necessary "pull" factors in the upgrading process of domestic Japanese industry.

Having said this, however, the data clearly indicate that the United States did have a far stronger attraction for Japanese fdi than did Western Europe up to and during the early 1980s. For example, the ratio of the cumulative Japanese direct investment flows directed in the United States to that in Europe (including non-EC Europe) rose from 2.4 to 4.2 in manufacturing and 1.9 to 2.4 for all sectors between 1951 - 1980 and 1981 - 1984. The reasons are derived mainly from the larger size and growth of the market for products in which Japanese companies had O-specific advantages in the United States, coupled with the combination of lax inward investment and tight trade-protectionist policies. This policy configuration, reversed in Europe, helped tip the balance of the choice facing Japanese MNEs to engage in fdi versus trade towards the former in the United States and the latter in Europe (*Dunning and Cantwell, 1989*). Put another way, the absence of restrictions on foreign-owned production - both in manufacturing and in services (banking, finance, insurance and trade-related activities) - meant that Japanese firms could internalize the markets for their O advantages more easily in the United States, while arms-length transactions remained the norm in Europe.

More importantly, Europe at that period was a collection of fragmented, relatively protected national markets whose size and growth did not come close to that of the United States. The fragmentation of the European economy meant that not only were economies of scale difficult to achieve along all stages of the value chain (from production to final distribution), but that economies of scope were not feasible in a marketplace which was a patchwork of differing technical, safety and fiscal standards. These production constraints were compounded by prohibitively high cross-border transaction costs, due in part to administrative delays at customs borders (*Cecchini, 1988*). Finally, real wages in most European countries were uncompetitive with those in the United States, a crucial consideration for Japanese companies whose O advantages depended on maintaining lower price/quality ratios than their local competitors. These factors, coupled with the much larger sunk investment already in the United States, made that country a more attractive location for Japanese market-seeking investment in the 1981 - 1984 period.

Additionally, though less important at this stage, Europe's L advantages in innovatory activities, though strong, were nonetheless inferior to those of the United States, particularly in the industries which Japan hoped to foster. The United States thus possessed stronger L advantages for information- and technology-seeking fdi from Japan. Finally, a lower cost of entry favored the United States over Europe for all types of fdi, given cumulated experience gained through previous investments and a more relaxed policy environment towards inward fdi and towards the acquisition of corporate assets through take-overs.

4.3 Summary and Conclusions: Why the Trade-Sustaining Investments of the Early 1980s Were Unsustainable after 1985

The early 1980s, then, was a period in which the principal aim of Japanese MNE activity in the United States and Europe was to protect the existing O advantages for Japanese made goods. This was particularly true in what were then Japan's premier export sectors, viz. automobiles and electronic goods. That more investment was directed to the United States than to Europe was a reflection of the former's more pronounced L advantages, and the fact that because of differing regulatory environments, Japanese firms could internalize the market for their O advantages more easily in the United States than they could in Europe.

While this picture of Japanese foreign production was appropriate in the early 1980s, by the end of the decade this was no longer the case. The change was triggered by a series of developments which occurred roughly between 1985 and 1987, and forced a different fdi strategy by Japan's leading multinationals, away from its trade-replacing function and towards a new phase of advancing global competitive strength. Instead of defensive strategies, Japanese firms had to adopt offensive strategies in their ever-expanding foreign markets. Moreover, overseas affiliates would have to attain a higher level of independence from the parent. Such a strategy was essentially driven by the need for Japanese firms to transform themselves from exporters to "insiders" in the major markets of the world, and to keep in touch with the latest technological and organizational developments, while benefiting from economies of cross-border arbitraging and the gathering and disseminating of information.

The shift from defensive to offensive investment strategies, over time, implies a fundamental change in the traditional post-war system of exporting -- > domestic upgrading -- > exporting practiced in Japan: in the move to become successful insiders, Japanese multinationals had to internationalize the upgrading process, with the ultimate result that foreign direct investment would gradually replace trade as the mechanism driving the machine.

5. 1985 - 1988: Transferring Existing O Advantages to Foreign Territories
5.1 Variables Triggering the Change

Several factors contributed to the demise of a defensive market-seeking fdi strategy in Europe and the United States. Among the first and most important occurred in 1985, when the Plaza Agreement revalued the yen against the dollar. This effectively undermined Japan's ability to export low-cost manufactured products. In an effort to retain their export markets, Japanese producers moved into higher-value market sectors which, at this stage in Japan's industrial development, were mainly in technology- and knowledge- intensive sectors. In many of these sectors, which included pharmaceuticals and specialty chemicals, advanced micro-chips, software and next-generation computers, US firms still maintained comparative O advantages over their Japanese counterparts. Mirroring the rise in price in Japanese exports was the fact that US assets could now be bought inexpensively by Japanese investors. Together, these factors combined to raise the attractiveness of the L advantages of the United States, particularly in knowledge intensive sectors.

In other words, the strong yen encouraged Japanese firms to create, or acquire, new O advantages, as there was now a rapidly expiring time limit on how long firms could defend and exploit existing ones. This was compounded by the fact that Western competitors, particularly in the US, were beginning to emulate some of the O advantages of Japanese MNEs, e.g. their consistency of product quality and flexible production methods. The implication was that offensive information-seeking fdi became a more attractive strategy than it had been in previous years. At a firm level, that meant internationalizing innovatory activities and entering into alliances with partners offering synergistic cutting-edge technologies to feed the current wave of upgrading. At the same time, upgrading existing overseas investments became a more important strategic goal. If more value-added in production had to be located abroad due to the rising yen, then those activities had to be supported and sustained with more coordinating and control functions, including marketing, product development, and forward and backward linkages in the local economy.

Such an approach as this was a novel one for Japanese multinationals, which hadn't previously upgraded their overseas affiliates. Moreover, by the late 1980s, local rivals, particularly in the United States, had adopted cost and product strategies to meet the Japanese challenge, such that increasing competition was forcing a more pro-active local presence. In a survey taken in the late 1980s, 75% of the Japanese automobile affiliates in the US ranked "increasing competition" as the main problem they expected to encounter; the corresponding percentage for a similar group of firms in the EC was 86% (*MITI, 1990*). The appreciation of the yen, then, necessitated a radical reappraisal of the goals and structure of Japanese multinational activity of the home country's strong international market position, won through trade in the late 1970s and defensive foreign production in the 1980s, if it was to be sustained or advanced in the 1990s.

Not only the goals, but also the mode of international involvement had to change, as there began to be high risks to building greenfield facilities. In the world automobile industry and related industries (rubber tires), there was serious threat of overproduction by the late 1980s, caused in part by new Japanese outward investment. The 1986 - 1987 recession in the computer industry and the buildup of worldwide capacity in semiconductors were also reasons why adding to the current stock of productive assets was not a wise choice. In contrast to the preceding years, acquisitions, joint ventures, strategic alliances, and increasing value-added in existing operations were becoming more desirable options than greenfield investments. Indeed, a 1988 survey by the Yamaichi Securities Company found that Japanese take-overs of foreign firms quintupled from 44 in 1984 to 228 in 1987, with 33 and 120 of those involving US companies (*Tokyo Business Today, January 1989*). In the fiscal year 1988 - 1989 no less that

40% of the value of new Japanese direct investment in the EC were by way of acquisition or merger (*Kirkland, 1990*).

Another important factor which undermined the strategies of the past was the decision to create a single, barrier-free market in the European Community by 1992. The boost that this gave to Europe's L advantages was substantial, and inward fdi from all countries has increased markedly in each year following the announcement of the program in 1985. The profit opportunities in Europe were too important to ignore; not only were EC-based firms offered a once-and-for-all cut in costs through the removal of non-tariff barriers; they would also be given a larger market to operate in, in which income growth was estimated to rise by up to 20% (*Baldwin, 1989*). The dynamic gains from the push of industrial rationalization and the pull of growing demand suggested that European industry was poised for a period of rapidly escalating profitability, with the winners being those with O advantages which could best take advantage of the new configuration of L and I advantages being shaped in the region.

At the same time, firms located outside the EC were in danger of being locked out of this pot of gold. Japanese companies, in particular, were viewed as threats to the success of the European single market project. Indeed, one of the central aims of Europe 1992 is to help European multinationals break out of the "sclerosis" which had plagued them in preceding decades, so that they might compete against Japanese firms in sectors such as telecommunications and office equipment. Intra-regional conflicts over local content and rules of origin, the most bitter of which were waged over Japanese products (copiers, automobiles), portended future import barriers. The high degree of uncertainty facing Japanese firms over the future of the EC's trade stance with the rest of the world, coupled with the enormous potential rewards of market unification, meant that Japanese MNEs had to shift gears and switch their mode of supplying the EC market from exports to local production; and that they had to do so with some speed.

5.2 The Nature of the Changes: Same Sectors, Different Structures

Table 3, which builds on the data in Table 2, suggests that in the 1985 - 1988 period, sectors in which Japanese fdi was concentrated in the United States were different from those in the preceding four years. Automobiles and the category "other manufactured products" traded places, with the former shrinking from 23% of total new investment in manufacturing in 1981-1984 to just 10% in 1985-1988, and the latter shooting up from 7% to 25% by 1985-1988.

Table 3: Sectoral Composition of Japanese FDI Stock in Manufacturing and Selected Services in the United States and Europe, 1985-1988

($ mn and %)

	United States	% increase from 1981-84	Europe	% increase from 1981-84
Elec. machinery	4141	286.0	909	305.8
% of manuf. fdi	25.0		29.4	
Transport equip.	1725	96.0	612	155.0
% of manuf. fdi	10.4		19.8	
Steel and metals	1637	222.9	103	51.5
% of manuf. fdi	9.9		3.3	
Chemicals	1715	390.7	393	305.2
% of manuf. fdi	10.4		12.7	
General machinery	2069	567.7	437	524.3
% of manuf. fdi	12.5		14.1	
Food, bev, tob	466	86.9	110	478.9
% of manuf. fdi	2.8		3.6	
Other	4802	855.5	528	160.1
% of manuf. fdi	29.0		17.1	
Total manufact.	16,555	327.8	3092	235.7
% of total fdi	31.9		14.7	
Distributive trade	4942	60.3	1878	49.0
% of total fdi	9.5		8.9	
Finance and insur.	9358	462.4	12,111	530.8
% of total fdi	18.0		57.4	
Total services	34,831	391.2	17,187	404.0
% of total fdi	67.0		81.5	
Total	51,965	371.8	21,091	358.4

Source: Ministry of Finance

There was also an accumulation of new investment in the general machinery industry. This latter trend repeated itself in Europe, where there was also growth in the share of new investment going to the electrical and electronic sector. Transport equipment maintained its relative position, but towards the end of the period began to increase sharply. Also noteworthy in Europe was the plunge in the share accounted for by the wholesale and retail trading sector, mirroring the decline in the United States of the preceding period.

If, at first glance, it appears that Japanese firms were abandoning, in a relative sense, the automobile sector in the United States, upon closer examination of the data it appears that the contrary was occurring. Rather than moving out of this sector, it seems that the Japanese owned segment of the United States automobile industry had, by this stage, reached the point where clusters of supporting firms - which are at the heart of Japanese O advantages in manufacturing - were springing up to support original Japanese investments by big manufacturers. In other words, there were signs that the Japanese automobile industry was beginning to "export" its O advantages (if not its cars) to the United States in response to the rising yen and increasing competition.

5.3 Japanese O Advantages in Automobiles: A Brief Case Study

Before examining the data in more detail, it is worth digressing briefly to explore the specific nature of this key facet of Japanese O advantages in manufacturing, the relationships between firms and their suppliers. Innovations in the organization of work and production, such as just-in-time inventory systems and multi-skilled, multi-task labor, are more important factors behind the Japanese competitive edge in producing high-quality goods at low cost than technical prowess or access to low-cost labor. By perfecting the art of flexible specialization, where clusters of firms specialize in activities which can be re-grouped and re-configured to respond to rapid market changes at minimum cost, Japanese car manufacturers created a powerful O advantage with which to attack the American giants. At the time of the Japanese export onslaught in the 1970s, the latter were locked into mass-production methods that made market-induced changes, such as a shift to smaller cars, prohibitively expensive. Rigid divisions of labor and Fordist labor relations also denied them the productivity gains of Japanese work practices such as job rotation and worker-teams.

At the heart of the Japanese system is the relationship between the motor car manufacturer and the cluster of its suppliers. Not only does the former generally own a portion of the latter's firm, but the component suppliers and subcontractors are put under enormous pressure to reach ever-higher levels of quality within stringent cost constraints. This very considerable bargaining power of manufacturers means that suppliers have little choice but to meet the required specifications, and to reach the desired levels of efficiency. Suppliers are also expected to participate in design and development functions, and deliver whole systems, not just individual components. The relationship is a close - even a filial - one. It is based on cooperation, trust, coercion and a constant interchange of information. In this respect, it is very different from supplier-manufacturer relationships found in the United States and Europe, where manufacturers generally minimize the price of their components through competitive bidding. Without this relationship, and its emphasis on total quality at low cost, it is doubtful that the Japanese car manufacturers could have achieved the astonishing export successes of the late 1970s and early 1980s.

The implication of the above analysis is that - unlike many American multinationals which have O advantages in strong brand names (Coca-Cola) or the common governance of a range of related activities (American Express) or superior technology (IBM) - the O advantages of Japanese firms are not easily internalized in an overseas location; they are, in this sense, more location-bound. Part of the reason for this is that it is initially more difficult to transfer any intra- or inter-firm organizational structures than it is to transfer production or marketing techniques across national boundaries (*Kogut and Parkinson 1990*). And, as Porter points out (*Porter, 1990*), nowhere are the elements underlying the comparative advantages of a country, which help to create and sustain the competitive advantages of its firms (factor conditions, demand conditions, related and supporting industries, and domestic competition) more closely linked to one another than in Japan, where they function as an organic system.

While such a situation is ideal for a country building up its competitive advantage through exports, as Japan had done until recently, difficulties may arise when such a country's firms are compelled to replicate their successes internationally (or internalize the markets for their O advantages through fdi) in different national cultures. In this scenario, the main challenge is to move the entire system to the target market. The risks inherent in such a move are high, since the firm's original O advantages and the conditions which make for their internal use, i.e. the I advantages, are bound to change once transplanted to foreign soil, as indeed are the O advantages of the host country's firms which are now given an opportunity to compete - and cooperate - with their overseas rivals on familiar territory.

5.4 Moving Japanese O and I Advantages to the Foreign Marketplace

The data over the 1985 - 1988 period suggest that this internationalization of Japan's O and I advantages was beginning to happen in the automobile industry in the United States; Japanese fdi strategy was no longer defensive, but offensive, and more importantly, rationalized. Efficiency improvements would no longer be kept to the domain of the home territory. Increasing attention would now be directed to creating a global competitive advantage by ensuring that all value added operations, both at home and abroad, were geared to this end. In some cases, this meant that the Japanese system of organizing production had to be transferred. One indication of the increasing internalization of the market for Japanese O-advantages overseas is given by data on licensing and royalty fees between Japan on the one hand and the United States and the United Kingdom on the other. By measuring the ratio of fees paid by overseas affiliated firms to those paid by overseas non-affiliated firms, an estimate is given as to the importance of fdi versus arms-length licensing transactions: the higher the proportion of fees received by affiliated firms, the greater the emphasis on foreign direct investment. Over the 1980s, the proportion of affiliated to non-affiliated royalty and license fees that were paid from the United States back to Japan rose from 0.4 in 1980 to 2.9 in 1989. In the UK, the ratio also rose, although it remained significantly lower than in the United States, reaching 0.44 in 1987, up from 0.22 in 1981 (Business Monitor).

This indicates that internalizing the market for their O-advantages through fdi had become more important to Japanese MNEs than the licensing of technology to unrelated firms, at least in the United States. In other words, knowledge transferred to overseas locations was increasingly flowing within the firm, from the parent in Japan to the overseas affiliate, instead of to overseas independent (local) firms. One possible explanation is that Japanese MNEs were increasingly investing in sectors where it was strategically important for the owners of O-advantages to control the *use* of those advantages. Such is the case in high-technology sectors or those in which the way value-adding activities are organized is itself a source of O-advantages. As firms move into such sectors, the propensity to internalize O-advantages through fdi will rise. Furthermore, as companies pursue more global strategies - implying that overseas activities are to be integrated and coordinated with the firm's overall strategy - the need to control, or internalize, those activities rises, hence the rise in the importance of fdi. The evidence presented below indicates that this indeed was the prevailing trend concerning Japanese investments in the United States, with signs that a similar trend was beginning in Europe as well.

The growing internalization of the market for Japanese O-advantages in the United States appears to have mainly taken place in the automobile sector, in which, as discussed above, O-advantages are often based on close inter-firm relationships and a highly coordinated organization of production among a network of firms. There are several indications that these O-advantages were transferred by Japanese MNEs to the United States in the late 1980s. One of the most compelling is the fact that, in the 1984 - 1988 period, the average size of a

Japanese direct investment in the automobile sector *fell by 28%* (from $17 million to $12 million) while, as shown in Table 3, the amount invested in this sector rose by nearly 100%. These data suggest that Japanese owned components and parts suppliers were investing in the United States to supply Japanese car manufacturers: indeed, it estimated that about 300 such plants had been set up in the United States by the late 1980s (*Financial Times, 1990*).

A further indication of the localization of Japanese automobile fdi in the United States is the fact that investment in related industries grew rapidly over the period; much of the jump in the "other manufacturing" category was due to the acquisition of Firestone Tire and Rubber by Bridgestone in 1988 for Yen 333.7 bn. The other industry which recorded a strong gain - general machinery - also contains many sectors which are directly linked to car manufacturing. Two other large industries, steel and electrical/electronic equipment, are also related to automobile production, the former directly as an upstream supplier, the latter indirectly through products and innovations which are adapted into automobile subsystems.

As for the necessity to shift overseas the Japanese system of organizing production, surveys indicate that, in response to policy pressures to increase local content, Japanese manufacturers appear to prefer to locate and foster locally-based subcontractors (as opposed to building more internal capacity) (*JETRO, 1988*). This reaction is entirely consistent with the need of such companies to protect one of the main O advantages, e.g. those to do with the flexible specialization of production. It is interesting to note the form that this development is taking; it appears that Japanese companies are not just utilizing more locally-based suppliers and subcontractors, but are replicating the close inter-firm relationships which had been, up to this point, unique to Japan.

Table 4 shows the breakdown of inputs and revenues of Japanese affiliates in the United States and the European Community, for all manufacturing affiliates and for those in the motor vehicles and electrical and electronic equipment industries. It reveals that the local content (percent of inputs locally procured) varies considerably between the sectors identified, though, generally, more stringent local content policies tend to be followed. But, despite the fact that in 1987 more than half of inputs were still being imported from Japan, overseas affiliates had begun to establish backward linkages in the local economy. Furthermore, of their total local procurement in manufacturing, between a third and forty percent were sourced *from other affiliates of the same parent* in the United States and the EC, respectively. Thus, as backward linkages were established, they were also internalized, in order to protect the parent firm's O-advantages in technology and in organizing production.

Table 4: Structure of Japanese Manufacturing and Automobile Subsidiaries, United States and Europe (1987)

	All manufacturing		Transport equipment		Electric/ electronic equipment	
	US	EC	US	EC	US	EC
Percent of total inputs from: (a)						
Local sources	32	46	35	61	17	31
of which:						
Intra-group (b)	(30)	(43)	(68)	(0)	(92)	(79)
Japanese imports	62	51	35	37	79	55
of which:						
Intra-group	(71)	(87)	(74)	(56)	(71)	(89)
3rd-country imports (c)	5	3	30	1	5	14
of which:						
Intra-group	(43)	(33)	0	(52)	(84)	(26)
Total inputs:	100	100	100	100	100	100
of which:						
Intra-group	(56)	(65)	(49)	(21)	(75)	(77)
Local intra-group	(10)	(20)	(24)	(0)	(15)	(25)
Percent of total revenues from:						
Local sales	93	96	82	81	98	90
of which:						
Intra-group	(3)	0	(49)	(0)	(1)	(29)
Sales to Japan	3	1	11	0.1	1	2
of which:						
Intra-group	(78)	0	(97)	(100)	(97)	(100)
3rd-country exports	4	3	8	19	1	9
of which:						
Intra-group	(21)	0	(100)	(10)	(67)	(53)
Total revenues:	100	100	100	100	100	100
of which:						
Intra-group	(6)	0	(58)	(2)	(21)	(33)
Local intra-group	(3)	0	(40)	0	(1)	(26)

(a) All percents calculated from yen values.
(b) Intra-group transactions are between different affiliates, not necessarily majority-owned, of the same parent. Numbers in parentheses are the percent of intra-group transactions within that category of inputs (or revenues).
(c) Third countries in Europe include other European countries.

Source: MITI

By contrast, the forward linkages of Japanese subsidiaries in their overseas locations are generally much smaller.[4] Partly at least, this is a reflection of the fact that in assembly-based production (i.e. trade-supporting branch plants) outputs are finished goods shipped directly to distributors, which are not generally owned by the manufacturer.

The comparative degree of vertical integration of Japanese investments in two key sectors is revealing; Japanese companies in the automobile industry appear to have established backwards and forwards linkages in their United States operations, but none in the EC, while in the electrical and electronic equipment industry, backward linkages have been established in both locations while forward linkages are much stronger in the EC.

One possible explanation for the difference in the comparative structure in the Japanese electrical and electronics sector in the US and the EC is that Japanese companies in the latter have made further inroads into acquiring the assets of downstream companies - computer and peripherals manufacturers - than they have in the United States. This appears likely, given the Japanese manufacturers enjoy relatively stronger O advantages vis-à-vis European computer firms than they do vis-à-vis United States firms, which still lead the world in the industry's most important market segments. The extent of backward linkages of Japanese subsidiaries in the EC, on the other hand, lags somewhat behind the United States, perhaps reflecting the fact that fewer Japanese components subcontractors had invested in the EC than in the US at this time. This possibility is reinforced by the fact that in this industry, 54% of firms polled in the EC in 1987 listed "procurement of local components" as the key manufacturing constraint, versus a response rate to this question of 32% for all manufacturers (*JETRO, 1988*).

In automobiles, the strong backward and forward linkages in the United States and their complete absence in the EC points to the more mature phase of Japanese fdi in the former location. By 1987, it would appear that Japanese companies in the United States automobile sector were well on their way to replicating the networks of inter-firm linkages that are at the heart of their O advantages in Japan.

If the patterns of the past continue, then Europe should follow the lead set by the United States. This would imply that Europe should witness a further build-up of Japanese clusters of supporting subcontractors (and service firms) around already established Japanese car manufacturers, particularly as the latter respond to political pressures to increase local content levels.

One recent example of this likely trend is the acquisition of a UK radiator manufacturer by a leading supplier to Toyota in Japan (Nippondenso) to supply Toyota's nearby production plant

(*Kirkland, 1990*). This kind of development is likely to increase competitive pressure on European owned car firms, already in a vulnerable position due to low productivity levels relative to Japanese manufacturers. And it is likely that similar patterns will emerge in other sectors where the Japanese have strong production O advantages once the major Japanese players have firmly established themselves on European soil. Ironically, by forcing Japan to lessen its dependence on exports because of undue competitive pressures on local industry, European and US producers are likely to face a new wave of competitive pressures, this time within their own borders, from locally-based, highly productive networks of Japanese-owned manufacturers, suppliers and service providers.

6. 1989 and Beyond: Creating New O Advantages as Regional Insiders
6.1 1988 - 1989: Europe Takes the Lead

Data about Japanese fdi in 1989 point to the astonishingly rapid growth of Europe's L advantages as a production base, for both manufacturing and service industry. Indeed, an increasing number of Japanese multinationals now regard the EC as offering more investment opportunities than the United States. In a survey taken in September 1987, only 3.2% of the firms polled listed the EC as the most important location for foreign value added activities; by September 1989, 12.1% cited it as their most important region. At the same time, the number of firms citing North America as the most important region for their investment dropped from 53.4% to 43.1% over the same period (*Industrial Bank of Japan, 1989*)

The data in *Table 5* dramatically illustrate this trend. Between 1988 and 1989, the value of Japanese manufacturing fdi flows into the United States increased by only 1%; in Europe they doubled.

On the level of corporate buy-outs as well, European firms are becoming more important targets for Japanese investors. A recent survey found that in the first half of 1990, Europe accounted for one quarter of all Japanese acquisitions, up from 13% in 1986, while the share of acquisitions made in the United States fell from 62% to 54% over the same period. It seems likely that the numbers, if not the total value, of acquisitions in the two locations will converge in the near future (*Japan Economic Journal, 1990*). At the level of the firm, 1989 was the first year in which Sony's sales of consumer electronics were higher in Europe than they were in the United States (*Kirkland, 1990*).

Table 5: Composition of Japanese FDI in the US and Europe, 1950 - 1989

	$ mns:	Percent of total fdi:				Percent increase:		
United States:	1989	1950-1980	1981-1984	1985-1988	1989	50-80 to 81-84	81-84 to 85-88	1988 to 1989
Manufac.	8959	23.2	35.1	31.9	27.4	88.2	327.8	1.4
Services	23,377	70.7	64.4	67.0	71.5	13.0	391.2	82.4
Total:*	32,657					24.1	371.8	50.5
Europe:								
Manufac.	3090	18.9	20.0	14.7	20.9	9.1	235.7	99.6
Services	11,438	78.3	74.1	81.5	77.4	(2.6)	404.0	56.6
Total:*	14,777					2.9	358.4	62.1
Percent of worldwide fdi:								
United States		24.3	31.5	45.2	48.2			
Europe		12.2	13.2	18.3	21.9			

*Includes branch offices which are not shown in sectoral breakdown.

Source: Ministry of Finance

The 1992 program of the European Community is, to a large extent, responsible for the new wave of Japanese investment into Europe. The single market presents both opportunities (new and larger markets, buoyant demand) and threats (barriers to the import of non-EC goods) to firms from non-EC countries, making fdi in the region a strategic imperative to assure market access. Japanese investors are responding to the new L advantages being created in Europe with fresh capital in knowledge and technology intensive sectors. To the extent that European industry is strong enough to withstand this new competition, as well as the degree to which Japanese firms transfer high value (i.e. innovatory) activities to their foreign subsidiaries, this trend will contribute to the current restructuring and upgrading of European industry, and the resulting emergence of new world-class technology centers in the region (*Dunning and Cantwell, 1989*). And by contributing to the increased rate of technological progress and stimulating local competition in Europe, Japanese investment may not only improve the L advantages of that region, but will, in turn, contribute to the gradual slippage in the competitiveness of the United States in what had traditionally been the former's unchallenged domain, viz. technology intensive manufacturing capability.

6.2 Exploiting the L Advantages of Regional Markets

In addition to the shift towards Europe, and the EC in particular, as the key strategic location for Japanese multinationals, another facet of Japanese fdi that is likely to change in the 1990s is the organization of their cross-border production operations. Increasingly, such organization is likely to reflect the character and needs of regional, rather than national, markets with integrated production and distribution systems.

The data already point to a trend towards the regional organization of Japanese industry in North America and Europe. Japanese investment flows into Canada more than doubled following passage of the US-Canada Free Trade Agreement. In Europe, the rapid increase of Japanese investment flows into Spain ($501 million in 1989, up 211% from the year before) and West Germany ($1,083 million in 1989, a 165% increase from 1988) also testify to changing geographical patterns of Japanese fdi in response to the new configuration of L advantages in the region. In the United Kingdom, historically the largest recipient of Japanese fdi, new investment increased by only 35% in the 1988-1989 period.

A 1987 survey of 709 Japanese manufacturers in Europe reveals that the most frequently quoted response (164) to the unification of the EC was to "Europeanize" operations through increasing local procurement and the localization of management. A large number (126) plan to grant more autonomy and responsibility to their EC operations, saying that they intended to "establish an executive office to supervise our business operations in Europe including, but not limited to, manufacturing, production, financing and R&D" (*JETRO, 1990*). And while Japanese multinationals have been reluctant to venture into the unknown territories in Eastern Europe, it is likely that joint ventures between large Japanese multinationals (Matsushita, Mitsubishi) with West German firms (Siemens, Daimler Benz) will allow several of them to ride into the Eastern European market on the backs of their more experienced partners.

Such moves all point to the increased L and I advantages brought about by the newly integrated European markets. These derive from new opportunities for fresh economies of scale and scope; the efficiency-enhancing effects of organizing cross-border activities so as to exploit the different L advantages of member countries in the region; and the increasing rate of technical innovation which is expected to follow from regional integration, derived from the dynamic impact of income growth and the static impact of a larger market against which a firm can amortize its technology investments. Japanese multinationals are rapidly increasing their overseas investments, particularly in Europe, in order to exploit these new opportunities. Not only do they possess strong O advantages in key industries, they are also making the investments with the latecomer's advantage of being able to integrate regional operations from the outset, without the costs associated with the reorganization of pre-existing assets (costs which many US MNEs, long-established in the EC, must face). An important source of the new O advantages of Japanese firms in the 1990s will, thus, be integrated production structures which, in turn, are likely to further enhance the L advantages of host countries within the regional markets.

6.3 Exploiting the O Advantages of Local Firms

It has been shown that Japanese firms exhibit a propensity to internalize the market for their O advantages in their overseas subsidiaries as they increase local content levels in the United States and Europe by extending to those locations the inter-firm networks which had formerly been specific to the home country (Japan). Other measures also point to the rising strategic importance of Japanese fdi in both the United States and Europe. These include the rising levels of R&D performed by subsidiaries;[5] the setting up of overseas design facilities that help shift responsibility for product development from the parent to the affiliate; the increased numbers of Europeans and Americans in key managerial positions; and an overall rise in the management autonomy of overseas affiliates (*JETRO, 1988 and 1990*).

In other words, the organizational structure of Japanese affiliates in the late 1970s and early 1980s is being abandoned as their parent companies evolve a transnational strategy towards their European and US operations.[6] Partnerships and acquisitions of local firms in both the United States and Europe has become a key element of the change. Through strategic acquisitions, Japanese MNEs are gaining access to firms that capture L advantages which are unique to the target country, and in so doing create new O advantages which would be otherwise unattainable through trade or even greenfield fdi.

By acquiring Columbia Pictures, for instance, Sony now has access to a broad spectrum of cultural-specific distribution channels for its manufactured goods; Fujitsu's newly-won control of ICL in the United Kingdom put it in a position to participate in the European R&D consortia, e.g. Esprit, Eureka, which had been off-limits to Japanese companies and are, indeed, intended to develop technologies that will help the Europeans compete against Japanese multinationals.

Japanese investments in luxury branded items in Europe (cognac, high-fashion brand names) provide an opportunity to enter specialty niches which are intimately bound to the local culture. They are increasing investments - mainly via mergers and acquisitions - in industries where Japanese O advantages are inferior to local ones (processed foods, pharmaceuticals, and chemicals in Europe, and household product, biotechnology, computers in the United States). In summary, Japanese multinationals are strategically positioning themselves to acquire or create the *new* O advantages which will complement their existing competitive strengths and power their future growth. Offensive moves such as these are likely to increase, as part of the strategic imperative to become "insiders" in the major markets of the Triad. By adopting pluralistic modes of sustaining or advancing competitive advantages, Japanese firms have been able to exploit differences in cross-border market failure both in the intermediate and final goods markets. It would seem that these new forms of international involvement by Japanese firms have, in part at least, replaced *domestic* upgrading as the primary weapon with which to prepare for future competitive bids in global markets.

7. Conclusions - After 1990: Rising O Advantages of Japanese Multinationals, Falling L Advantages of Japan?

The story of Japanese fdi in the United States and Europe is one of remarkable strategic dexterity in response to the rapidly changing OLI configuration facing Japanese firms in the 1980s. In moving swiftly from exporting to defensive fdi strategies in both the United States and Europe in the early 1980s, Japanese multinationals are managing to maintain their O advantages in increasingly competitive markets.

The question that begs to be answered at this point is whether, and for how long, the evolution of Japanese fdi from defensive to offensive strategies can continue. Can Japan continue to upgrade its industrial infrastructure if many of the necessary instruments of that upgrading (specialized R&D assets, technical and managerial personnel, inter-firm supplier networks) are geographically dispersed outside of Japan?

Moreover, are the economic and cultural conditions and institutional framework which helped Japan build up its O advantage in the last 30 years, likely to continue in the future?[7] To what extent, too, is it likely that Japanese MNEs will be able to sustain their traditional O advantages in organizing production in countries where the social, political and legal structures differ radically from those in Japan? Will the transaction costs associated with transferring these advantages to the US and European environments be too great? How long will it be before the moves of host country rivals to "copy" Japanese production methods succeed in eroding key Japanese O advantages? All these questions lead ultimately to the issue of the degree to which Japan can maintain its extraordinary economic performance, if and when foreign direct investment replaces trade as the engine of industrial upgrading.

Numerous factors will determine the outcome to these questions. Among the most important are the trade policies adopted by the newly-integrated regional markets in Europe and North America (the latter of which is likely to eventually include Mexico) and the gradual opening up of the Japanese economy to inward direct investment. Throughout most of the 1980s, Europe lagged behind the United States in terms of the structure and organization of Japanese inward investment, but current trends indicate that in the post-1992 era, Europe could surpass the United States in terms of its strategic importance to Japanese MNCs. What is clear is that there has been a radical change in the nature of the "Japanese challenge"; through the mechanism of fdi in Europe and the United States, the challenge has intensified, while at the same time it has become less Japanese.

Endnotes

* The authors are grateful to Mr. Andrew Barnes for his translation of Japanese-language materials.

[1] E.g. through the failure of subcontractors to keep to delivery dates or to supply agreed product quality; and the inability or unwillingness of industrial customers or distributors to maintain the reputation of the contracting firm.

[2] For example, depending upon their firm-specific characteristics, the leading US motor vehicle firms may pursue different foreign investment strategies, as may the leading Japanese CTV firms or the leading UK pharmaceutical companies.

[3] Real wages tripled in Japan between 1950 and 1970, evidence that productivity gains were not fast enough to keep up with the desired rate of upgrading (*Dunning and Narula, 1990*).

[4] Exceptions are the quite high ratios of intra-group local sales of Japanese affiliates in the US auto industry and in the EC electrical and electronic industry.

[5] In the US, at least, 100 Japanese affiliates had R&D facilities in 1988 (*Research Management, 1990*).

[6] For a recent examination of the alternative organizational strategies which MNEs might pursue, see *Bartlett and Ghoshal, 1990*. According to the authors, a transitional strategy is one in which there is a regular interchange of knowledge and ideas between the different parts of the organization, which better enable decisions to be taken for the benefit of the system as a whole.

[7] Examples include the high savings ratios, a dedicated work ethic and highly personalized transactional relationships.

References

BALDWIN, R. (1989) The Growth Effects of 1992, Economic Policy, 9 November.

BARTLETT, C. and S. GHOSHAL (1990) Managing Across National Boundaries: The Transnational Solution, Harvard: Harvard University Press.

CECCINI, P. (1988) The European Challenge: 1992, Aldershot, England: Wildwood House.

DUNNING, J. H. (1988) Explaining International Production, London: Unwin Hyman.

DUNNING, J. H. (1989) The Theory of International Production, in FATEMI, K. (ed) The Theory of International Trade, New York: Taylor and Francis.

DUNNING, J. H. (1990) The Globalization of Firms and the Competitiveness of Countries, University of Lund, Crafoord Lectures 1989.

DUNNING, J. H.; CANTWELL, J. A. (1989) Japanese Manufacturing Direct Investment in the EEC, Post 1992: Some Alternative Scenarios, University of Reading Discussion Paper in International Investment and Business Studies No. 132, September.

DUNNING, J. H.; NARULA, R. (1990) Transpacific Foreign Direct Investment and the Investment Development Path: The Record Assessed, mimeo, Rutgers University, July.

FINANCIAL TIMES OF LONDON (1990) World Industrial Review (Special Survey) 8 January, 4.

JAPANESE EXTERNAL TRADE ORGANIZATION (JETRO) (1988 and 1990) Current Situation of Business Operations of Japanese-Manufacturing Enterprises in Europe, Fourth and Sixth Survey Reports, March.

INDUSTRIAL BANK OF JAPAN (1989) Factors Behind Japanese Direct Investment Abroad, Quarterly Survey of Japanese Finance and Industry, No. 80 IV, 13-24.

JAPAN ECONOMIC JOURNAL (1990) M & A Activity Shifting to Europe, July 28, 1.

KIRKLAND, R. I. (1990) The Big Japanese Push into Europe, Fortune, 2 July, 94-98.

KOGUT, B. and D. PARKINSON (1990) The Defusion of American Organizing Principles to Europe, Paper prepared at workshop on The Organization of Work and Technology: Implications for Country Competitiveness, Brussels, May-June 1990.

MINISTRY OF INTERNATIONAL TRADE AND INDUSTRY (MITI) (1990) 1987 Survey of Overseas Activities of Japanese Enterprises, March.

OZAWA, T. (1989a) Japan's "Strategic" Policy Toward Outward Direct Investments, mimeo, University of Colorado, July.

OZAWA, T.(1989b) Japan's Strategic Investment Policy Toward the Developing Countries: from the Ad Hoc to a New Comprehensive Approach, mimeo, University of Colorado, October.

OZAWA, T.(1989c) The EC and Japan as Investment Partners: A case Study, mimeo, University of Colorado, July.

PORTER, M. E. (1990) The Competitive Advantages of Nations, New York: The Free Press.

RESEARCH MANAGEMENT (1990) R&D by Japanese Manufacturing Subsidiaries in the US, 1989, Research Management.

TOKYO BUSINESS TODAY (1989) Rapid Increase in Japanese Overseas M & A, January, 20-24.

UNITED KINGDOM CENTRAL STATISTICAL OFFICE (annual) Business Monitor MA4.

UNITED NATIONS CENTRE ON TRANSNATIONAL CORPORATIONS (1989) The Process of Transnationalization and Transnational Mergers, UNCTC Current Studies Series A No. 8, United Nations.

UNITED STATES DEPARTMENT OF COMMERCE (1990) U.S. International Sales and Purchases of Services, Survey of Current Business, 70, 37-73.

COMMENTS ON: JAPANESE MULTINATIONALS IN EUROPE AND THE UNITED STATES: SOME COMPARISONS AND CONTRASTS

Terutomo Ozawa

The theme of the Dunning/Gittelman paper can be summarized as follows: The competitive advantages of Japanese corporations (O-advantages) in the global market have been built largely within the confines of their national environment (L-advantages at home). Their overseas investments so far have been either of the resource-seeking or of the market-seeking type, all intended to support the continuous upgrading of their export industries. In other words, their competitive base has long been confined to their own economy; exporting has been the main vehicle of exploiting their O-advantages. Yet the very success of Japan's economic development and the sharp appreciation of the yen are now changing Japan's industrial landscape. To protect existing share in their export markets, particularly, in the United States and Europe where trade friction is frequent, Japan's star export industries, notably automobiles, electronics goods, and machinery, are forced to transplant their manufacturing systems overseas.

In order to make these manufacturing outposts competitive and profitable vis-à-vis local competitors, moreover, these Japanese firms cannot help but to "export" or "externalize" their O-advantages to the local communities and simultaneously become dependent on the L-advantages of the United States and Europe. In other words, Japanese manufacturing ventures have been turning from the defensive to the offensive type, engaging in a variety of strategic alliances that are intended to share their O-advantages with local partners and to develop new advantages in the overseas environment. Thus the competitive base of Japanese industry itself is being globalized -- that is to say, it has begun to be detached from its secure anchor in the national environment. In this new approach, Japanese multinationals may end up assisting local industries in improving their O-advantages.

The upshot of this new phase of Japan's multinationalism, then, is that such multinational activities no longer contribute to the upgrading of their domestic industry as much as before, and that the "Japanese challenge" is becoming "less Japanese." Hence, whether Japan can continue its extraordinary economic performance is in doubt. Thus Dunning and Gittelman raise a critical question about the compatibility of the current outward advance of Japanese corporations (multinationalism) and the future growth of the Japanese economy whose admirable expansion up until now has been the product of home-production-based exporting activity.

My comment is directed at this interesting question raised by Gittelman and Dunning rather than at their analysis of Japanese multinationals' investment patterns in the United States and Europe, an analysis which is carefully presented in a revealing manner as the core of their paper and with which I have no quarrel.

It is clear that Japan's mode of external commercial relations is rapidly changing from trade (exporting of comparatively advantaged goods) to foreign direct investment (FDI) (local production of such goods). Trade-oriented production is necessarily home-based, while FDI-led production and marketing encompass cross-border and intra-host-economy involvements. This ineluctably creates a number of conflicts with national interests, including a possible loss of the home government's power to control (and guide) national economic activities and a potential hollowing-out of domestic industrial base.

We must, however, be a bit cautious about making a clear-cut distinction between trade and FDI, and especially about treating them as if they were always substitutes for one another. The implicit assumption in the Gittelman/Dunning paper is that FDI is becoming anti-trade (i.e., trade-replacing) for Japanese industry as a whole, while it has been pro-trade up to now. It is true that Japanese industry has become more and more FDI- or local-production-oriented than ever before, and that its "screwdriver" manufacturing outposts in automobiles and electronics products are being localized with the stepped-up procurement of locally produced parts and components in the host economies. But what has lately been happening to Japan's trade is a shift from the mainly home-based type to the multinational operation-based one, from the inter-industry type to the intra-industry type, with the rather unexpectedly surprising result of a rise--not a fall--in Japanese manufactured exports. Indeed, exports of capital goods and intermediate products are expanding rapidly. FDI thus still remains pro-trade.

In this connection, so far, two types of intra-industry--and often intra-company--division of labor have come into existence. One involves an international division of labor in intermediate goods; production of fairly standardized (hence relatively low value-added) parts and components or those that can be economically procured locally has been transferred to the U.S. and European markets. But the establishment of these operations has been accompanied by the rising exports from Japan of plant machinery, equipment, and other capital goods. In addition, more and more sophisticated components are produced at home and shipped out to the overseas manufacturing outposts. This development, therefore, is resulting in a vertical division of labor under which Japanese industry endeavors to retain --and further develop-- higher value-added, critical components at home.

Here we can discern a more refined, more sharply delineated, and specialized form of trade within an industry (that is, intra-industry trade) and even within a company (that is, intra-company trade). Thus FDI of this type is a vehicle for a new form of trade, a complement and not a substitute for trade. FDI is a medium through which a continuous qualitative upgrading of Japan's export activities is facilitated.

A second type of a newly emerging division of labor is seen in the transfer to overseas of standardized, low-end models of a product which Japanese industry used to mass-produce at home for export. This constitutes a horizontal pattern of specialization. For example, standardized models (mostly subcompact and small cars) of Japanese automobiles are being shifted to overseas manufacturing. Honda is transferring the production of the Civic and the Accord models to the United States and Europe, while at home it is concentrating on the Prelude and the Acura models (the latter including the latest $60,000 sports car, NSX). So are Toyota and Nissan, who are retaining the production of luxury models such as Lexus and Infiniti only in Japan. True, Japanese car makers' efforts to operate its U.S. factories successfully may contribute to the revitalization of the American auto industry. Hence it may be said that Japan is giving back to the United States a comparative advantage in the auto industry--but only in standardized compact models and certainly not in upscale, higher value-added ones.

Moreover, by introducing a series of new models, one after another, on the high end of the market at a pace faster than their overseas competitors, they are capturing economies of scope as a new competitive source--in addition to the economies of scale. This reinforces price competitiveness which long characterized their trade competitiveness for subcompact and small cars in the past. In very recent years, indeed, Japan's auto industry has become a faster model changer by offering a much wider variety than its American and European counterparts who once set the pace in model changes.

All in all, then, Japan is not exporting its entire structure of comparative advantages in autos and electronics but, on the contrary, is effectively refining its pattern of comparative advantages through FDI by discarding only low value-added products or models and capturing higher value-added ones. In other words, I can modify the title of the Gittelman/Dunning paper to "Japanese Multinationals in Europe and the United States: Refining the Pattern of Comparative Advantages in Cars and Computers through Foreign Direct Investment."

Concomitant with these types of division of labor across borders is thus a sharp rise in Japan's intra-industry and intra-company trade in intermediate goods (which are shipped simultaneously out of and to Japan) as well as in finished goods (which are increasingly imported from the overseas subsidiaries and affiliates of Japanese corporations). The current deepening involvement of Japanese corporations as multinationals in autos and electronics is thus pushing Japan into a new phase of trade, that is, FDI-carried trade both in intermediate goods and in finished goods. This phase of direct overseas engagement thus still serves as a powerful catalyst in upgrading Japan's industrial structure as its previous phases have done.

Besides, it should be kept in mind that Japan's economic development is now in a new phase of industrial restructuring (as I elsewhere emphasized in terms of the "restructuring" theory of FDI) in which assembly-based, scale-economies-exploiting goods such as medium-range-price, standardized car models and electronics goods are destined to be shed away from the Japanese economy (*Ozawa, 1990*).

So far, since the end of World War II, Japan has gone through three major phases of industrialization and is currently on the threshold of another new phase of industrial metamorphosis; Japan went through (1) labor-intensive industrialization centered on the manufacturing of low value-added light industry goods, (2) heavy and chemical industrialization with emphasis on steel, shipbuilding, and petrochemicals and related goods, and (3) assembly-based industrialization with the major focus on scale-economies goods such as small cars and relatively simple consumer electronics.

Japan is now entering a new fourth stage, the stage of small-lot, flexible manufacturing with "mechatronics" to produce multi-variety, upmarket goods to satisfy the ever-diversifying needs and tastes of the increasingly affluent consumers at home. In this new stage, the development of brand-new growth products such as high definition (HD) TVs, digital audio tape (DAT) products, new materials, biotechnology, optoelectronics, and mechatronics (computer-linked robotics) is targeted and pursued vigorously at home. The current investment boom in new productive facilities in Japan harbingers the arrival of the next phase of industrial expansion. Overseas transplantation of standardized product lines in autos and electronics analyzed in the Gittelman/Dunning paper is merely another "industrial shedding" no different from the previous phenomenon of yesterdays in textiles and sundries. Indeed, another paper, "Japanese Multinationals in Asia: Exporting Textiles and Sundries and Comparative Advantage through Foreign Direct Investment," could be presented as a companion paper to describe Japan's bygone stage of FDI, an earlier stage that actually promoted industrial upgrading at home.

In connection with the current phase of Japan's overseas investment, Gittelman and Dunning also make the interesting observation: "the United States, a host country to Japanese FDI, played the role of 'leader' with Europe following behind, such that patterns established in the former (sectors, motives, and modes of organization) would later be replicated, albeit on a smaller scale, in the latter." This "lag" pattern is a natural outcome, since in the assembly-based manufacturing phase of Japan's industrialization and overseas investment the United States provided the most appropriate mass market where Japanese industry could transplant the very efficient mass-manufacturing system it had perfected to produce standardized scale-economies goods. It is only in conjunction with its 1992 program that Europe is about to duplicate itself as a unified market in the image of the United States.

Yet, as Japan moves to the new phase of industrialization and overseas investment in which diversity and heterogeneity replace standardization and homogeneity as the dominant characteristics of product development, it is likely to be Europe rather than the United States that will serve as the model market for Japanese multinationals. It would be no surprise, then, to see this role reversal occur. After all, European cultural diversities and idiosyncrasies will be the wellspring of ideas and inspirations for product development in the new era of manufacturing and consumerism. Japan's nouveaux riches consumers are already finding European manufactures far more attractive than their American counterparts. The European cultural diversity might have been "a burden" during the American era of mass production but will likely be a blessing for the coming new age of diversified consumerism and flexible manufacturing.

As mentioned earlier, a loss of Japan's comparative advantage in standardized autos and electronics goods may be occurring in the wake of its active FDI in these fields. It is, however, not clear that the local producers in the United States and Europe are really able to significantly benefit from the presence of Japanese FDI. One can easily understand this weak spill-over effect by looking at the U.S. automobile industry; U.S. car makers' sales have been plummeting while Japan's transplant factories have been gaining market share rapidly and continuously. True, under the pressure of local content rules Japan's major transplants are all eagerly fostering local suppliers by providing technical, financial, and organizational assistance. Many of these newly created suppliers are the subsidiaries or affiliates of Japanese parts manufacturers who produce highly differentiated, specification-based components for their group-affiliated customers. When pure local suppliers are involved, they are guided, again, to produce specifically designed parts which are in most cases not readily usable by the local competitors. I wonder, therefore, how much Ford, for example, is actually benefiting in its production of, say, Taurus, from the existence of Honda's local parts suppliers for Civic and Accord.

Moreover, although Japanese auto and electronics industries are "externalizing" their comparative advantages by way of FDI, their multinationals are busily "internalizing" their close-knit interfirm relationships overseas. I would argue that this type of strongly group-focused investment is likely to minimize, if not eliminate, the likelihood of the technological and business spill-over effect to local competitors.

To paraphrase D.H. Robertson's classic distinction between market and organization, Europe is becoming more like "an ocean of unconscious co-operation" in the wake of 1992 trade liberalization and deregulation; there will be many more giant Japanese armadas, each led by a flag ship with its own flotilla of supporting vessels. Some strategic alliances may occur between the Japanese armadas and their Western counterparts, but fierce battles are a more likely outcome.

References

OZAWA, TERUTOMO (1990), Europe 1992 and Japanese Multinationals: Transplanting a Subcontracting System in the Expanded Market, in Burgenmeier, B.; Mucchielli, J.L., Eds., Multinationals and Europe 1992, London: Routledge.

INDEX

Printing: Druckhaus Beltz, Hemsbach
Binding: Buchbinderei Kränkl, Heppenheim

New Books on Economic Dynamics

P. J. J. Welfens (Ed.)

European Monetary Integration

From German Dominance to an EC Central Bank?

1991. XII, 260 pp. 8 figs. 7 tabs. Hardcover
ISBN 3-540-53790-2

Monetary integration in the EC will continue
with the desired hardening of the European
Monetary System that is expected to lead to
an EC central bank in the 1990s. Why has the
European Monetary System been so successful and what role has the Deutsche Bundesbank played in monetary policy and the EMS
in Europe?
This book gives an assessment of the EMS
developments and its stability record,
analyzes the impact of German monetary
unification and shows how financial market
liberalization as well as the EC 1992 project
affect the process of Economic and Monetary
Union.

N. Nakićenović, A. Grübler (Eds.)

Diffusion of Technologies and Social Behavior

1991. XXV, 605 pp. 107 figs. 56 tabs.
Hardcover ISBN 3-540-53846-1

The diffusion of innovations is at the core of
the dynamic processes that underlie social,
economic, and technological change. The
book illustrates the progress that has been
made in understanding the nature of diffusion processes and their underlying driving
forces, both theoretically and empirically.
The contributions by leading scholars provide
a novel interdisciplinary perspective and span
a wide range of modeling and empirical
research backgrounds.

P. Hackl, A. H. Westlund (Eds.)

Economic Structural Change

Analysis and Forecasting

1991. X, 385 pp. 101 figs. 56 tabs. Hardcover
ISBN 3-540-53839-9

In modern economic model building, structural change is a key concept. Under the auspices of the International Institute for
Systems Analysis (IIASA) a very active
community of statisticians and econometrici-
ans has made a very influential contribution
to the development of methods for identification of structural change. The purpose of this
volume is to document these activities, to
present new methods and developments in
this area, and to demonstrate applications.
Particular weight is given to nonparametric
and robust methods for identification of and
modeling under structural change, a Bayesian
approach to forecast combination, and time-
varying parameter cointegration.

T. Puu

Nonlinear Economic Dynamics

2nd rev. and enl. ed. 1991. X, 151 pp. 64 figs.
Hardcover ISBN 3-540-53351-6

This book studies nonlinear economic
dynamics. Formation of spatial patterns,
population dynamics in space and time, and
spatial waves of business cycles are discussed.
The main part dwells on business cycle
theory, using a multiplier-accelerator
model in a spatial setting
with interregional
trade. The
model is capa-
ble of producing
frequency
locking, quasi-
periodic
motion, and
chaos. The tools
of analysis are
classical pertur-
bation methods
(Poincaré-
Lindstedt).

Springer-Verlag
Berlin
Heidelberg
New York
London
Paris
Tokyo
Hong Kong
Barcelona
Budapest